What Counts as Credible Evidence in APPLIED RESEARCH and EVALUATION PRACTICE?

*To those engaged in the struggle to help create a better future,
including those whose efforts involve the use of applied research
and evaluation*

What Counts as Credible Evidence in APPLIED RESEARCH and EVALUATION PRACTICE?

Stewart I. Donaldson
Claremont Graduate University

Christina A. Christie
Claremont Graduate University

Melvin M. Mark
The Pennsylvania State University

Editors

Los Angeles • London • New Delhi • Singapore

For information:

SAGE Publications, Inc.
2455 Teller Road
Thousand Oaks,
   California 91320
E-mail: order@sagepub.com

SAGE Publications Ltd.
1 Oliver's Yard
55 City Road
London EC1Y 1SP
United Kingdom

SAGE Publications India Pvt. Ltd.
B 1/I 1 Mohan Cooperative
   Industrial Area
Mathura Road, New Delhi 110 044
India

SAGE Publications
   Asia-Pacific Pte. Ltd.
33 Pekin Street #02-01
Far East Square
Singapore 048763

Printed in the United States of America

Library of Congress Cataloging-in-Publication Data

What counts as credible evidence in applied research and evaluation practice? /
Stewart I. Donaldson, Christina A. Christie, [and] Melvin M. Mark, editors.
   p. cm.
Includes bibliographical references and index.
ISBN 978-1-4129-5707-6 (pbk.: acid-free paper)
   1. Research—Evaluation. 2. Research—Social aspects. 3. Social sciences—Methodology. 4. Evaluation research (Social action programs) 5. Educational accountability. I. Donaldson, Stewart I. (Stewart Ian) II. Christie, Christina A. III. Mark, Melvin M.

Q180.55.E9W53 2009
001.4'2—dc22   2008017667

This book is printed on acid-free paper.

10 11 12 10 9 8 7 6 5 4 3 2

Acquisitions Editor:	Vicki Knight
Editorial Assistant:	Lauren Habib
Production Editor:	Catherine M. Chilton
Copy Editor:	Teresa Herlinger
Typesetter:	C&M Digitals (P) Ltd.
Proofreader:	Annette R. Van Deusen
Indexer:	Kathleen Paparchontis
Cover Designer:	Candice Harman
Marketing Manager:	Stephanie Adams

Contents

Preface

This volume addresses one of the most important and contentious issues challenging applied research and evaluation practice today: what constitutes credible evidence. We fear that history has been repeating itself of late, with the earlier quantitative–qualitative paradigm war appearing again in varied guises. These include public debates and serious professional arguments about federal research and evaluation design priorities, as well as statements from several professional associations regarding the role of randomized controlled trials (RCTs) and the existence of "gold standards" for evidence. Much human capital and more than one friendship have been lost in heated disagreements about what counts as credible and actionable evidence. Lost too, we fear, have been potentially productive conversations about the varied ways in which applied research and evaluation can contribute to action and understandings that can assist in addressing important social needs.

One goal of this book was to address these thorny issues in a more positive and productive manner. We hope that collectively the chapters in this book provide more light than heat regarding the fundamental challenge of providing credible evidence, a challenge that faces contemporary applied researchers and evaluators in professional practice on a day-to-day basis.

In an effort to accomplish this goal, a diverse and internationally renowned cast of applied researchers and evaluators were invited to participate in the Claremont Graduate University Stauffer Symposium focused on the question of "What Counts as Credible Evidence in Applied Research and Evaluation Practice?" This illuminating and action-packed day in Claremont was experienced by more than 200 participants from a wide variety of backgrounds—evaluators, researchers, private consultants, students, faculty, and professionals from many fields. The presenters all shared their latest thinking about how to answer the question, and later each prepared a more detailed chapter to help illuminate from their vantage point the key challenges about the nature of evidence in applied research and evaluation practice.

The result of these efforts is this volume. It explores a broad array of issues that address the fundamental challenges of designing and executing high-quality applied research and evaluation projects. Few works have attempted to sort out these issues in a way that directly informs contemporary applied research, evaluation, and evidence-based practice. We hope that readers will garner a new and clear understanding of the philosophical, theoretical, methodological, political, ethical, and pragmatic dimensions of gathering credible and actionable evidence to answer fundamental research and evaluation questions across diverse disciplinary boundaries and real-world contexts. Among the key features of this volume are that it

> Offers authoritative statements about what counts as credible evidence in applied research and evaluation, provided by leading scholars across such fields as education, psychology, health and human services, public policy, and public administration

> Covers experimental and nonexperimental methods, with experts in their use critically appraising the credibility of evidence from these varied approaches

> Provides summaries of strengths and weaknesses across the varied approaches to gathering credible evidence

> Contains diverse definitions of evidence, so that students and other readers can better understand and evaluate the landscape of this highly debated topic

> Includes a full chapter on the practical implications of the discussions about how best to gather credible evidence in modern applied research, evaluation, and evidence-based practice

In sum, then, we hope this volume will become a valuable resource for practicing evaluators; applied researchers; students preparing for applied research and evaluation careers; scholars and teachers of evaluation and applied research methods; and other professionals interested in how best to study and evaluate programs, policies, organizations, and other initiatives designed to improve some aspect of the human condition and societal well-being.

Acknowledgments

The editors of this volume would like to express their deep gratitude to our editorial assistant, Shabnam Ozlati, for her wonderful dedication and excellent work on the production of this manuscript. Special thanks to the coordinator of the Claremont Graduate University Stauffer Symposium, Paul Thomas, and his fantastic group of graduate student volunteers for making the Stauffer Symposium a smashing success. We are very thankful to the chapter authors for sharing with us their best thinking and advice about what counts as credible evidence, and for going the extra mile to make their chapters engaging and widely accessible. We sincerely appreciate the helpful reviews and suggestions for improvement provided by the reviewers, Larry A. Braskamp, Loyola University, Chicago; John C. Ory, University of Illinois, Melvin Hall, Northern Arizona University; Michael Schooley, Centers for Disease Control and Prevention; and the Sage editorial staff: Vicki Knight, Senior Acquisitions Editor; Sean Connelly, Associate Editor; Lauren Habib, Editorial Assistant; Stephanie Adams, Marketing Manager; Catherine Chilton, Production Editor; Teresa Herlinger, Copy Editor.

Finally, this project would not have been possible without the generous gift provided by the John Stauffer Charitable Trust to the School of Behavioral and Organizational Sciences, Claremont Graduate University. We are abundantly grateful for this essential financial support.

Stewart I. Donaldson
Christina A. Christie
Claremont, CA

Melvin M. Mark
State College, PA

About the Editors

Stewart I. Donaldson is Professor and Chair of Psychology, Director of the Institute of Organizational and Program Evaluation Research, and Dean of the School of Behavioral and Organizational Sciences at Claremont Graduate University. Dr. Donaldson continues to develop and lead one of the most extensive and rigorous graduate programs specializing in applied psychological and evaluation science. He has taught numerous university courses and professional development workshops, and has mentored and coached more than 100 graduate students and working professionals during the past two decades. Dr. Donaldson has also provided organizational consulting, applied research, or program evaluation services to more than 100 different organizations. He has been Principal Investigator on more than 30 grants and contracts to support research, evaluations, scholarship, and graduate students at Claremont Graduate University. Dr. Donaldson serves on the editorial boards of the *American Journal of Evaluation, New Directions for Evaluation,* and the *Journal of Multidisciplinary Evaluation*; is cofounder and leads the Southern California Evaluation Association; and served as Cochair of the *Theory-Driven Evaluation and Program Theory* Topical Interest Group of the American Evaluation Association for 8 years. He has authored or coauthored more than 200 evaluation reports, scientific journal articles, and chapters. In addition to this edited volume, his recent books include *Evaluating Social Programs and Problems: Visions for the New Millennium* (2003; with Michael Scriven), *Applied Psychology: New Frontiers and Rewarding Careers* (2006; with Dale E. Berger and Kathy Pezdek), *Program Theory–Driven Evaluation Science: Strategies and Applications* (2007), and *Social Psychology and Program/ Policy Evaluation* (forthcoming; with Melvin Mark and Bernadette Campbell). Dr. Donaldson has been honored with Early Career Achievement Awards from the Western Psychological Association and the American Evaluation Association.

Christina A. Christie is an Associate Professor and Associate Director of the Institute of Organizational and Program Evaluation Research in the School of Behavioral and Organizational Sciences at Claremont Graduate University. Dr. Christie has received funding from a variety of sources to evaluate social, education, and health behavior programs targeting high-risk and underrepresented populations, including the Haynes Foundation, National Science Foundation, the U.S. Department of Education, First 5 Los Angeles, the Hewlett Foundation, and the Irvine Foundation. She cofounded the Southern California Evaluation Association, a local affiliate of the American Evaluation Association, and is the former Chair of the Theories of Evaluation Division and current Chair of the Research on Evaluation Division of the American Evaluation Association. In 2004, Dr. Christie received the American Evaluation Association's Marcia Guttentag Early Career Achievement Award. Christie is a section editor of the *American Journal of Evaluation* and is on the editorial board of *New Directions in Evaluation*. She is also the editor of the upcoming book *Exemplars of Evaluation Practice* (with Jody Fitzpatrick and Melvin Mark; Sage).

Melvin M. Mark is Professor and Head of Psychology at Pennsylvania State University. A past President of the American Evaluation Association, he has also served as Editor of the *American Journal of Evaluation* where he is now Editor Emeritus. Dr. Mark's interests include the theory, methodology, practice, and profession of program and policy evaluation. He has been involved in evaluations in a number of areas, including prevention programs, federal personnel policies, and various educational interventions including STEM program evaluation. Among his books are *Evaluation: An Integrated Framework for Understanding, Guiding, and Improving Policies and Programs* (2000; with Gary Henry and George Julnes) and the recent *SAGE Handbook of Evaluation* (2006; edited with Ian Shaw and Jennifer Greene), as well as forthcoming books *Evaluation in Action: Interviews With Expert Evaluators* (with Jody Fitzpatrick and Christina Christie; Sage) and *Social Psychology and Program/Policy Evaluation* (with Stewart Donaldson and Bernadette Campbell).

About the Contributors

Leonard Bickman is Professor of Psychology, Psychiatry, and Public Policy at Vanderbilt University, where he also directs the Center for Evaluation and Program Improvement and serves as Associate Dean for Research at Peabody College. He is Coeditor of two handbooks on social research methods and the *Applied Social Research Methods* series for Sage Publications. He is Editor of *Administration and Policy in Mental Health and Mental Health Services Research*. Dr. Bickman is among an elite group of grantees who rank above the 95th percentile in the distribution of extramural National Institutes of Health (NIH) grants over the past 25 years. He is currently the Principal Investigator on grants from NIH, the Institute of Education Sciences, and the U.S. Department of Defense. He has received several national awards recognizing the contributions of his research including the U.S. Health & Human Services Secretary's Award for Distinguished Service, the American Psychological Association's Public Interest Award for Distinguished Contribution to Research in Public Policy, the Education and Training in Psychology Award for Distinguished Contributions, the American Evaluation Association Outstanding Evaluation Award, and Vanderbilt University's Earl Sutherland Prize for Achievement in Research. He is a past President of the American Evaluation Association and the Society for the Psychological Study of Social Issues. Dr. Bickman has extensive experience in developing and successfully conducting major randomized field experiments in several substantive areas including education, health, mental health, and criminal justice.

Dreolin Fleischer received her B.A. from Mount Holyoke College (2001). For the next 4 years she worked as a Research Assistant at Goodman Research Group, Inc. (GRG), evaluating mostly educational programs, materials, and services. In 2005, she began the Evaluation and Applied Research Methods Ph.D. program in the School of Behavioral and Organizational Sciences at Claremont Graduate University (CGU). In 2007, she received her M.A. in psychology. For her master's thesis, she surveyed U.S. members of the American Evaluation Association on the topic of evaluation use. Currently a student at CGU, she continues to work in the field of evaluation on a variety of projects.

Russell Gersten is Executive Director of the RG Research Group, an educational research institute, as well as Professor Emeritus of Special Education in the College of Education at the University of Oregon. Dr. Gersten is nationally renowned for his knowledge, design, and implementation of research studies using experimental and quasi-experimental designs. He is particularly sought to help translate research into classroom practice. In 2002, Dr. Gersten received the Distinguished Special Education Researcher Award from the American Educational Research Association's Special Education Research Division. Dr. Gersten has conducted numerous randomized trials, many of which have been published in major journals in the field of education. He has either directed or codirected 42 applied research grants addressing a wide array of issues in education, and has been a recipient of many federal and nonfederal grants (totaling more than $12 million). He has substantial expertise in field research on instructional innovations for reading, mathematics, and special education, and the measurement of program implementation. He is currently the Principal Investigator for three large Institute of Education Sciences (IES) Projects Involving randomized trials. He is the Director of the Math Strand for the Center on Instruction, the Director of Research for the Regional Educational Laboratory—Southwest, and the Principal Investigator for several What Works Clearinghouse projects. He has over 150 publications and serves on the editorial boards of many prestigious journals in the field. Dr. Gersten was recently appointed to the National Mathematics Panel, a Presidential Committee to develop research-based policy in mathematics for U.S. schools.

Jennifer C. Greene is Professor of Educational Psychology at the University of Illinois, Urbana-Champaign. She has been an evaluation scholar-practitioner for 30 years. Her work focuses on the intersection of social science methodology and social policy and aspires to be both methodologically innovative and socially responsible. Greene's conceptual work in evaluation has concentrated on advancing the methodology of qualitative and mixed methods approaches to social and educational program evaluation, as well as participatory-democratic commitments in evaluation practice. Her evaluation practice has spanned the multiple domains of formal and informal education, and community-based support programs for families and youth. Greene has held leadership positions in the American Evaluation Association and the American Educational Research Association. She has also provided considerable editorial service to both communities, including a 6-year position as Coeditor-in-Chief of *New Directions for Evaluation*. Her own publication record is extensive and includes a coeditorship of the recent *SAGE Handbook of Evaluation* (2006) and authorship of *Mixed Methods in Social Inquiry* (2007).

Gary T. Henry holds the Duncan MacRae 2009 and Rebecca Kyle MacRae Professorship of Public Policy in the Department of Public Policy and directs the Carolina Institute for Public Policy at the University of North Carolina (UNC) at Chapel Hill. Also at UNC, he holds the appointment as Senior Statistician in the Frank Porter Graham Institute for Child Development. Formerly, he held the William Neil Reynolds Distinguished University Visiting Professorship at UNC. He has served as Professor in the Andrew Young School of Policy Studies, Department of Political Science, and Department of Education Policy Studies at Georgia State University and the Department of Public Policy at Georgia Institute of Technology. He previously served as the Director of Evaluation and Learning Services for the David and Lucile Packard Foundation. Dr. Henry has evaluated a variety of policies and programs, including North Carolina's Disadvantaged Student Supplemental Fund, Georgia's Universal Pre-K, public information campaigns, and the HOPE Scholarship, as well as school reforms and accountability systems. The author of *Practical Sampling* (1990, Sage) and *Graphing Data* (1995, Sage) and coauthor of *Evaluation: An Integrated Framework for Understanding, Guiding, and Improving Policies and Programs* (2000), Dr. Henry has published extensively in the fields of evaluation and education policy. He received the Outstanding Evaluation of the Year Award from the American Evaluation Association in 1998 for his work with the Georgia Council for School Performance, and the Joseph S. Wholey Distinguished Scholarship Award in 2001 from the American Society for Public Administration and the Center for Accountability and Performance, along with Steve Harkreader. Dr. Henry currently serves on the Standing Committee for Systemic Reform, Institute of Education Sciences, U.S. Department of Education. Recently, he completed service on a National Research Council/National Academies of Sciences committee assessing the effects of "green schools" on the health and productivity of teachers and students, and he coauthored the committee report.

John Hitchcock is an Assistant Professor in the College of Education at Ohio University. He holds a Ph.D. in educational psychology, with a concentration in research methods, from the University at Albany, State University of New York. He is also a provisionally certified school psychologist. His professional interests lie in developing and evaluating educational and psychological interventions in the United States and in international settings. He is currently serving as a Coprincipal Investigator of two federally funded, randomized controlled trials and is affiliated with two smaller studies dealing with Response-to-Intervention practices. His other work has focused on evaluating studies for the What Works Clearinghouse, providing technical assistance in areas such as student progress monitoring and technology-enriched curricula, and developing culturally specific interventions and assessments through the use of mixed method research designs. In all of these areas, he has produced scholarly works presented in peer-reviewed journal articles and at national conferences.

George Julnes, Associate Professor of Psychology at Utah State University, received his Ph.D. in clinical/community psychology, working with Roland Tharp within the neo-Vygotskiian framework that emphasizes *assisted performance* as the way to promote human and social development. Subsequent graduate work with Larry Mohr (program evaluation) and Karl Weick (organizational sensemaking) led to the formulation of *evaluation as assisted sensemaking*. His recent work involves consulting with federal agencies on random assignment experimental designs and running a random assignment policy experiment for the U.S. Social Security Administration.

Sandra Mathison is Professor of Education at the University of British Columbia. Her research is in educational evaluation, and her work has focused especially on the potential and limits of evaluation to support democratic ideals and promote justice. She has conducted small- and national-scale evaluation of curriculum reforms, teacher professional development, and informal education programs. Her current research focuses on the narrowing conception of evaluation of education as manifested in the standards-based and outcomes-based accountability systems. With funding from the National Science Foundation, she is studying the effects of state-mandated testing on teaching, learning, school structure, and the practice of evaluation in public education. She is Editor of the *Encyclopedia of Evaluation*, Coeditor (with E. Wayne Ross) of *Defending Public Schools: The Nature and Limits of Standards-Based Reform and Assessment*, and coauthor (with Melissa Freeman) of the soon-to-be-published *Researching Children's Experience*. She is Editor-in-Chief of the journal *New Directions for Evaluation*. She can be found on the Web at http://web.mac.com/sandra.mathison.

Sharon F. Rallis is the Dwight W. Allen Distinguished Professor of Educational Policy and Reform in the School of Education at the University of Massachusetts Amherst where she teaches courses in inquiry, program evaluation, qualitative methodology, and organizational theory. Her doctorate is from the Harvard Graduate School of Education. A former President of the American Evaluation Association, Rallis has been involved with education and evaluation for over three decades. She has been a teacher, counselor, principal, researcher, program evaluator, and director of a major federal school reform initiative. Rallis's research expertise lies in qualitative research. Her *Learning in the Field: An Introduction to Qualitative Research* (written with Gretchen Rossman; Sage), is in its second edition. She has published extensively in evaluation books and journals, including a chapter in *Evaluation Ethics for Best Practices* (edited by Michael Morris) and an article, "Trustworthiness in Evaluation Practice: An Emphasis on the Relational," in *Evaluation and Program Planning*. Her chapter, "Mixed Methods in Evaluation Contexts: A Pragmatic Framework," appears in the *Handbook of Mixed Methods in the Social and Behavioral Sciences* (edited by Tashakkori and Teddlie; 2001, Sage). Her most recent book is *Leading Dynamic Schools: How to Create and Implement Ethical Policies* (2007, Corwin Press), which she coauthored with Rossman, Cobb, Reagan, and Kuntz.

Stephanie M. Reich, Ph.D., is an Assistant Professor of Education at the University of California, Irvine. Trained as a community psychologist with a focus on child development and program evaluation, Dr. Reich's research interests focus on social interventions for children and families, applied and theoretical models of program evaluation, definitions and applications of community theory, and historical underpinnings to social inequality. She has worked on a variety of evaluations of family-based, school-based, and medically focused interventions and has been an active member of the American Evaluation Association, especially the quantitative topical interest group. Dr. Reich is the recipient of the Newbrough Award for academic writing, a NIMH fellowship in children's mental health services research, and the Julius Seeman Award for academic and professional excellence.

Debra Rog is Vice President of the Rockville Institute. Before joining the organization, Dr. Rog was Director of the Washington office of Vanderbilt University's Center for Evaluation and Program Improvement, where she managed a number of multisite research and evaluation projects in the areas of poverty, homelessness, housing for vulnerable populations, mental health, and applied research methodology. She recently led a series of evaluability assessments of childhood obesity prevention projects for the Robert Wood Johnson Foundation. Dr. Rog has provided project management and subject matter expertise for research funded by clients such as the Robert Wood Johnson Foundation, the Ford Foundation, Pew Charitable Trusts, the Center for Mental Health Services, the National Institute of Mental Health, the Substance Abuse and Mental Health Services Administration, the National

Mental Health Association, and the Bill and Melinda Gates Foundation, among others. Between 1987 and 1989, she was Associate Director of the Office of Programs for the Homeless Mentally Ill, National Institute of Mental Health. Dr. Rog has published and presented widely on mental health treatment issues, program evaluation, and methodological topics, and is a recognized expert in evaluation methodology, homelessness, and mental health. She is an editor of numerous books, series, and journals.

Thomas A. Schwandt is Professor and Chair, Department of Educational Psychology, at the University of Illinois at Urbana-Champaign where he also holds appointments in the Department of Educational Policy Studies and the Unit for Criticism and Interpretive Theory. Schwandt's scholarship is primarily focused on the intersection of social research and practical philosophy. His work is heavily influenced by the tradition of philosophical hermeneutics and the insights that can be drawn from that body of work for the way we think about the practices of evaluation and research. He is the author of *Evaluation Practice Reconsidered* (2004); *Evaluating Holistic Rehabilitation Practice* (2004); the *Dictionary of Qualitative Inquiry* (1997, 2001, 2007; Sage); and, with Edward Halpern, *Linking Auditing and Meta-Evaluation* (1988, Sage). With his Norwegian colleague Peder Haug, he has coedited *Evaluating Educational Reforms: Scandinavian Perspectives* (2003); with Katherine Ryan, *Exploring Evaluator Role and Identity* (2002); and with Bridget Somekh, *Knowledge Production: Research Work in Interesting Times* (2007). In addition, he has authored more than 60 papers and chapters on issues in theory of evaluation and interpretive methodologies that have appeared in a variety of books and journals. He has also given numerous keynote speeches to evaluation associations and societies in the United States and Europe. In 2002, he received the Paul F. Lazarsfeld Award from the American Evaluation Association for his contributions to evaluation theory. He is currently a member of the Standing Committee on Social Science Evidence for Use, National Academy of Sciences, Division of Behavioral and Social Sciences and Education.

Michael Scriven took two degrees in mathematics (University of Melbourne) and a doctorate in philosophy (Oxford University), and has held positions in departments of mathematics, philosophy, psychology, history and philosophy of science, and education, in Australia, New Zealand, and the United States, including 12 years at UC Berkeley; he is currently at Claremont Graduate University. He has also held research positions at the Center for Advanced Study in the Behavioral Sciences at Stanford, at Harvard, and at the National Science Foundation. His 400+ publications and 40 editorial board positions have been in 11 fields: about 90 are in evaluation, where he founded and coedits an online journal and a monograph series for the

American Evaluation Association (AEA). He has been President of the American Educational Research Association (AERA) and AEA and Director of the autonomous doctoral program in evaluation at Western Michigan University. Less conventional milestones include the following: in 1957–1958, he was elected a member of the Frisbee Hall of Fame, and in 2007 he traveled 70,000 miles on evaluation missions to seven countries.

PART I

Introduction

- Chapter 1: In Search of the Blueprint for an Evidence-Based Global Society
- Chapter 2: Social Inquiry Paradigms as a Frame for the Debate on Credible Evidence

1

In Search of the Blueprint for an Evidence-Based Global Society

Stewart I. Donaldson

As we near the end of the first decade of the 21st century, approximately 1.5 billion members of our vast global community live in pain and misery, and another 2.5 billion are also shut out of the "good life"—just simply getting by, day by day (a total of 4 billion people; Gallup, 2007). On a brighter note, there are now approximately 2 billion people on planet earth, or 33% of the world's population, who have a favorable standard of living and report high levels of health and well-being on a regular basis (Gallup, 2007). This picture is obviously not good enough for those of us who devote our lives and careers to conducting applied research and evaluation, in efforts to prevent and ameliorate human misery and suffering, and to promote social justice and human betterment.

Basic research is typically driven by scientists' personal interests and curiosity, and its purpose is to advance knowledge. In contrast, the purpose of applied research is to understand how to prevent or solve practical problems that affect "real" people, organizations, communities, and societies across the globe. Some applied research is descriptive and helps advance our understanding of practical problems and their potential solutions, while other efforts are evaluative and improve or determine the effectiveness of actions (e.g., programs and policies) to prevent and solve practical problems. Donaldson and Christie (2006) described some of the major differences between basic research and applied research and evaluation, such as the origin of the study questions, the purposes for which study information is gathered, and the settings in which the work is conducted. For the purposes of this volume, we are going to focus on what counts as credible evidence in applied research and evaluation. That is, most of the scientific work we will be discussing is problem based or solution oriented, and conducted in "real world" settings as opposed to highly controlled, traditional scientific laboratories.

The Rise and Fall of the Experimenting Society

In 1969, one of the legendary figures in the history of applied research and evaluation, Donald T. Campbell, gave us great hope and set what we now call the "applied research and evaluation community" on a course for discovering a utopia he called the "Experimenting Society" (Campbell, 1991). His vision for this utopia involved rational decision making by politicians based on hard-headed tests of bold social programs designed to improve society. The hard-headed tests he envisioned were called randomized experiments and were focused on maximizing bias control in an effort to provide unambiguous causal inferences about the effects of social reforms. This ideal society would broadly implement social reforms demonstrated to be highly effective by experimental research and evaluation, with the goal of moving at least more, if not most, of the population toward the "good life."

Some of the most important methodological breakthroughs in the history of applied research and evaluation seemed to occur during this movement toward the Experimenting Society (e.g., Campbell, 1991; Campbell & Stanley, 1963; Cook & Campbell, 1979). For example, detailed understanding of threats to validity, multiple types of validity, bias control, and the implementation of rigorous experimental and quasi-experimental designs in "real world" or field settings were advanced during this era.

However, the progress and momentum of the movement were not sustained. By the early 1980s, it was clear that Campbell's vision would be crushed by the realities of programs, initiatives, and societal reforms. Shadish, Cook, and Leviton (1991) reported that information or evidence judged to be poor by experimental scientific standards, was often considered acceptable by key decision makers including managers, politicians, and policy makers. Further, they argued that rigorous experimental evaluations did not yield credible evidence in a timely and useful manner, thus inspiring the field to develop new tools, methods, and evaluation approaches. The practice of applied research and evaluation today has moved way beyond the sole reliance on experimentation and traditional social science research methods (Donaldson, 2007; Donaldson & Lipsey, 2006; Donaldson & Scriven, 2003).

An Evidence-Based Global Society

Shades of Campbell's great hopes for evidence-based decision making can be seen in much of the applied research and evaluation discourse today. However, while the modern discussion remains focused on the importance of the production and use of credible evidence, it is not limited to evidence derived from experimentation. The new vision for a utopia seems to require broadening Campbell's vision from an "experimenting" to an "evidence-based society." This ideal society would certainly include evidence from experimentation under its purview, but would also include a wide range of evidence derived from other applied research and evaluation designs and approaches. Many of these newer approaches have been developed in the past two decades and no longer rely primarily on the traditional social science experimental paradigm (see Alkin, 2004; Donaldson & Scriven, 2003).

The momentum for developing an evidence-based global society seems to be at an all-time peak. No longer is applied research and evaluation primarily concentrated in Washington, D.C., or federal governments more broadly. Rather, organizations of all types, shapes, and sizes are commissioning applied research and professional evaluations in pursuit of evidence-based decision making at an accelerating rate.

One striking indicator of the demand for evidence and the growth of applied research and evaluation is the popularity of professional societies across the globe. For example, in 1980 there were only three national and regional evaluation societies. This number almost doubled (five) by 1990. Just one decade later (by 2000), there were more than 50 professional evaluation societies, and today there are more than 75 with a formal international cooperation network to build evaluation capacity across the globe (Donaldson, 2007; Donaldson & Christie, 2006). Members of most of these societies meet regularly to learn and discuss how best to conduct applied research and evaluation in order to yield credible evidence for promoting human betterment.

Another window into the promise of an evidence-based society and the accelerating demand for credible evidence, is the recent proliferation of evidence-based discussions and applications. For example, these discussions and applications are now prevalent throughout the fields of health care and medicine (Sackett, 2000; Sackett, Rosenberg, Gray, & Haynes, 1996), mental health (Norcross, Beutler, & Levant, 2005), management (Pfeffer &

Sutton, 2006), executive coaching (Stober & Grant, 2006), career development (Preskill & Donaldson, 2008), public policy (Pawson, 2006), and education (Chapter 5, this volume) just to name a few. In fact, a cursory search on Google yields many more applications of evidence-based practice. A sample of the results of a recent search illustrates these diverse applications:

- Evidence-based medicine
- Evidence-based mental health
- Evidence-based management
- Evidence-based decision making
- Evidence-based education
- Evidence-based coaching
- Evidence-based social services
- Evidence-based policing
- Evidence-based conservation
- Evidence-based dentistry
- Evidence-based policy
- Evidence-based thinking about health care
- Evidence-based occupational therapy
- Evidence-based prevention science
- Evidence-based dermatology
- Evidence-based gambling treatment
- Evidence-based sex education
- Evidence-based needle exchange programs
- Evidence-based prices
- Evidence-based education help desk

One might even consider this interesting new phenomenon across the disciplines to be expressed in the following formula:

Mom + The Flag + Warm Apple Pie = Evidence-Based Practice

Or it might be expressed as

In God We Trust—*All Others Must Have Credible Evidence*

The main point here is the movement toward evidence-based decision making now appears highly valued across the globe, multidisciplinary in scope, and supported by an ever-increasing number of practical applications.

But wait—while there appears to be strong consensus that evidence is our "magic bullet" and a highly valued commodity in the fight against social problems, there ironically appears to be much less agreement, even heated disagreements, about what counts as evidence. Unfortunately, seeking truth or agreement about what constitutes credible evidence does not seem to be an easy matter in many fields. Even in periods of relative calm and consensus in the development of a discipline, innovations occur and worldviews change in ways that destabilize. We may be living in such a destabilizing period now in the profession and discipline of applied research and evaluation. That is, despite unprecedented growth and success on many fronts, the field is in considerable turmoil over its very foundation—what counts as credible evidence. Furthermore, contemporary applied research and evaluation practice rests firmly on the foundation of providing credible evidence. If that foundation is shaky, or built on sand, studies wobble, sway in the wind, and ultimately provide little value, and can even mislead or harm.

Recent Debates About Evidence

Before exploring this potentially destructive strife and dilemma in more detail, let's briefly look at the recent history of debates about applied research and evaluation. The great quantitative-qualitative debate captured and occupied the field throughout the late 1970s and 1980s (see Reichhardt & Rallis, 1994). This rather lengthy battle also become known as the "Paradigm Wars," which seemed to quiet down a bit by the turn of the century (Mark, 2003).

In 2001, Donaldson and Scriven (2003) invited a diverse group of applied researchers and evaluators to provide their visions for a desired future. The heat generated at this symposium suggested that whatever truce or peace had been achieved remained an uneasy one (Mark, 2003). For example, Yvonna Lincoln and Donna Mertons envisioned a desirable future based on constructivist philosophy, and Mertons seemed to suggest that the traditional quantitative social science paradigm, specifically randomized experiments, were an immoral methodology (Mark, 2003). Thomas Cook responded with a description of applied research and evaluation in his world, which primarily involved randomized and quasi-experimental designs, as normative and highly valued by scientists, funders, stakeholders, and policy makers alike. Two illustrative observations by Mark (2003) highlighting differences expressed in the discussion were (1) "I have heard some quantitatively oriented evaluators disparage participatory and empowerment approaches as technically wanting and as less than evaluation," and (2) "It can, however, seem more ironic when evaluators who espouse inclusion, empowerment, and participation would like to exclude, disempower, and see no participation by evaluators who hold different views." While the symposium concluded with some productive discussions about embracing diversity and integration as ways to move forward, it was clear there were lingering differences and concerns about what constitutes quality applied research, evaluation, and credible evidence.

Donaldson and Christie (2005) noted that the uneasy peace seemed to revert back to overt conflict in late 2003. The trigger event occurred when the U.S. Department of Education's Institute of Education Sciences declared a rather wholesale commitment to privileging experimental and some types of quasi-experimental designs over other methods in applied research and evaluation funding competitions. At the 2003 Annual Meeting of the American Evaluation Association (AEA), prominent applied researchers and evaluators discussed this event as a move back to the "Dark Ages" (Donaldson & Christie, 2005). The leadership of the American Evaluation Association developed a policy statement opposing these efforts to privilege randomized controlled trials in education evaluation funding competitions:

AEA Statement:

American Evaluation Association Response
to U. S. Department of Education

Notice of Proposed Priority, Federal Register
RIN 1890-ZA00, November 4, 2003

"Scientifically Based Evaluation Methods"

The American Evaluation Association applauds the effort to promote high quality in the U.S. Secretary of Education's proposed priority for evaluating educational programs using scientifically based methods. We, too, have worked to encourage competent practice through our Guiding Principles for Evaluators (1994), Standards for Program Evaluation (1994), professional training, and annual conferences. However, we believe the proposed priority manifests fundamental misunderstandings about (1) the types of studies capable of determining causality, (2) the methods capable of achieving scientific rigor, and (3) the types of studies that support policy and program decisions. We would like to help avoid the political, ethical, and financial disaster that could well attend implementation of the proposed priority.

(1) Studies capable of determining causality. Randomized controlled group trials (RCTs) are not the only studies capable of generating understandings of causality. In medicine, causality has been conclusively shown in

(Continued)

(Continued)

some instances without RCTs, for example, in linking smoking to lung cancer and infested rats to bubonic plague. The secretary's proposal would elevate experimental over quasi-experimental, observational, single-subject, and other designs which are sometimes more feasible and equally valid.

RCTs are not always best for determining causality and can be misleading. RCTs examine a limited number of isolated factors that are neither limited nor isolated in natural settings. The complex nature of causality and the multitude of actual influences on outcomes render RCTs less capable of discovering causality than designs sensitive to local culture and conditions and open to unanticipated causal factors.

RCTs should sometimes be ruled out for reasons of ethics. For example, assigning experimental subjects to educationally inferior or medically unproven treatments, or denying control group subjects access to important instructional opportunities or critical medical intervention, is not ethically acceptable even when RCT results might be enlightening. Such studies would not be approved by Institutional Review Boards overseeing the protection of human subjects in accordance with federal statute.

In some cases, data sources are insufficient for RCTs. Pilot, experimental, and exploratory education, health, and social programs are often small enough in scale to preclude use of RCTs as an evaluation methodology, however important it may be to examine causality prior to wider implementation.

(2) Methods capable of demonstrating scientific rigor. For at least a decade, evaluators publicly debated whether newer inquiry methods were sufficiently rigorous. This issue was settled long ago. Actual practice and many published examples demonstrate that alternative and mixed methods are rigorous and scientific. To discourage a repertoire of methods would force evaluators backward. We strongly disagree that the methodological "benefits of the proposed priority justify the costs."

(3) Studies capable of supporting appropriate policy and program decisions. We also strongly disagree that "this regulatory action does not unduly interfere with State, local, and tribal governments in the exercise of their governmental functions." As provision and support of programs are governmental functions so, too, is determining program effectiveness. Sound policy decisions benefit from data illustrating not only causality but also conditionality. Fettering evaluators with unnecessary and unreasonable constraints would deny information needed by policy-makers.

> While we agree with the intent of ensuring that federally sponsored programs be "evaluated using scientifically based research ... to determine the effectiveness of a project intervention," we do not agree that "evaluation methods using an experimental design are best for determining project effectiveness." We believe that the constraints in the proposed priority would deny use of other needed, proven, and scientifically credible evaluation methods, resulting in fruitless expenditures on some large contracts while leaving other public programs unevaluated entirely.

Donaldson and Christie (2005) documented an important response to the AEA Statement from an influential group of senior members. This group opposed the AEA Statement, and did not feel they were appropriately consulted as active, long-term members of the association. There response became known as "The Not AEA Statement."

The Not AEA Statement:

(Posted on EvalTalk, December 3, 2003; available at http://bama.ua.edu/archives/evaltalk.html)

AEA members:

The statement below has been sent to the Department of Education in response to its proposal that "scientifically based evaluation methods" for assessing the effectiveness of educational interventions be defined as randomized experiments when they are feasible and as quasi-experimental or single-subject designs when they are not.

This statement is intended to support the Department's definition and associated preference for the use of such designs for outcome evaluation when they are applicable. It is also intended to provide a counterpoint to the statement submitted by the AEA leadership as the Association's position on this matter. The generalized opposition to use of experimental and quasi-experimental methods evinced in the AEA statement is unjustified, speciously argued, and represents neither the methodological norms in the evaluation field nor the views of the large segment of the AEA membership with significant experience conducting experimental and quasi-experimental evaluations of program effects.

We encourage all AEA members to communicate their views on this matter to the Department of Education and invite you to endorse the statement below

(Continued)

(Continued)

in that communication if it is more representative of your views than the official AEA statement. Comments can be sent to the Dept of Ed through Dec. 4 at comments@ed.gov with "Evaluation" in the subject line of the message.

This statement is in response to the Secretary's request for comment on the proposed priority on Scientifically Based Evaluation Methods. We offer the following observations in support of this priority.

The proposed priority identifies random assignment experimental designs as the methodological standard for what constitutes scientifically based evaluation methods for determining whether an intervention produces meaningful effects on students, teachers, parents, and others. The priority also recognizes that there are cases when random assignment is not feasible and, in such cases, identifies quasi-experimental designs and single-subject designs as alternatives that may be justified by the circumstances of particular evaluations.

This interpretation of what constitutes scientifically based evaluation strategies for assessing program effects is consistent with the presentations in the major textbooks in evaluation and with widely recognized methodological standards in the social and medical sciences. Randomized controlled trials have been essential to understanding what works, what does not work, and what is harmful among interventions in many other areas of public policy including health and medicine, mental health, criminal justice, employment, and welfare. Furthermore, attempts to draw conclusions about intervention effects based on nonrandomized trials have often led to misleading results in these fields and there is no reason to expect this to be untrue in the social and education fields. This is demonstrated, for example, by the results of randomized trials of facilitated communication for autistic children and prison visits for juvenile offenders, which reversed the conclusions of nonexperimental studies of these interventions.

Randomized trials in the social sector are more frequent and feasible than many critics acknowledge and their number is increasing. The Campbell Collaboration of Social, Psychological, Educational, and Criminological Trials Register includes nearly 13,000 such trials, and the development of this register is still in its youth.

At the same time, we recognize that randomized trials are not feasible or ethical at times. In such circumstances, quasi-experimental or other designs may be appropriate alternatives, as the proposed priority allows. However, it has been possible to configure practical and ethical experimental designs in such complex and sensitive areas of study as pregnancy prevention programs, police handling of domestic violence, and prevention of substance abuse. It is similarly possible to design randomized trials or strong quasi-experiments to be ethical and feasible for many educational programs. In such cases, we believe the Secretary's proposed priority gives proper guidance for attaining high methodological standards and we believe the nation's children deserve to have educational programs of demonstrated effectiveness as determined by the most scientifically credible methods available.

The individuals who have signed below in support of this statement are current or former members of the American Evaluation Association (AEA). Included among us are individuals who have been closely associated with that organization since its inception and who have served as AEA presidents, Board members, and journal editors. We wish to make clear that the statement submitted by AEA in response to this proposed priority does not represent our views and we regret that a statement representing the organization was proffered without prior review and comment by its members. We believe that the proposed priority will dramatically increase the amount of valid information for guiding the improvement of education throughout the nation. We appreciate the opportunity to comment on a matter of this importance and support the Department's initiative.

The subsequent exchanges about these statements on the AEA's electronic bulletin board, EvalTalk, seemed to generate much more heat than light and begged for more elaboration on the issues. As a result, Claremont Graduate University hosted and webcasted a debate for the applied research and evaluation community in 2004. The debate was between Mark Lipsey and Michael Scriven, and it attempted to sort out the issues at stake and to search for a common ground.

Donaldson and Christie (2005) concluded

> somewhat surprisingly, that Lipsey and Scriven agreed that randomized control trials (RCTs) are the best method currently available for assessing program impact (causal effects of a program), and that determining program impact is a main requirement of contemporary program evaluation. However, Scriven argued that there are very few situations where RCTs can be successfully implemented in educational program evaluation, and that there are now good alternative designs for determining program effects. Lipsey disagreed and remained very skeptical of Scriven's claim that sound alternative methods exist for determining program effects, and challenged Scriven to provide specific examples. (p. 77)

What Counts as Credible Evidence?

In 2006, the debate about whether randomized controlled trials (RCTs) should be considered the gold standard for producing credible evidence in applied research and evaluation remained front and center across the applied research landscape. At the same time, the zeitgeist of accountability and evidence-based practice was now widespread across the globe. Organizations of all types and sizes were being asked to evaluate their practices, programs, and policies at an increasing rate. While there seemed to be much support for the notion of using evidence to continually improve efficiency and effectiveness, there appeared to be growing disagreement and confusion about what constitutes sound evidence for decision making. These heated disagreements among leading lights in the field had potentially far-reaching implications for evaluation and applied research practice, for the future of the profession (e.g., there was visible disengagement, public criticisms, and resignations from the main professional associations), for funding competitions, as well as for how best to conduct and use evaluation and applied research to promote human betterment.

So in light of this state of affairs, an illustrious group of experts working in various areas of evaluation and applied research were invited to Claremont Graduate University to share their diverse perspectives on the question of "What Counts as Credible Evidence?" The ultimate goal of this symposium was to shed more light on these issues, and to attempt to build bridges so that prominent leaders on both sides of the debate would stay together in a united front against the social and human ills of the 21st century. In other words, a full vetting of best ways to produce credible evidence from both an experimental and nonexperimental perspective was facilitated in the hope that the results would move us closer to a shared blueprint for an evidence-based global society.

This illuminating and action-packed day in Claremont, California, included over 200 attendees from a variety of backgrounds—academics, researchers, private consultants, students, and professionals from many fields—who enjoyed a day of stimulating presentations, intense discussion, and a display of diverse perspectives on this central issue facing the field (see webcast at www.cgu.edu/sbos). Each presenter was asked to follow up his or her presentation with a more detailed chapter for this book. In addition, George Julnes and Debra Rog were invited to contribute a chapter based on their findings from a recent project focused on informing federal policies on evaluation methodology (Julnes & Rog, 2007).

Our search for a deeper and more complete understanding of what counts as credible evidence begins with an analysis of the passion, paradigms, and assumptions that underlie many of the arguments and perspectives expressed throughout this book. In Chapter 2, Christina Christie and Dreolin Fleischer provide us with a rich context for understanding the nature and importance of this debate. Ontological, epistemological, and methodological assumptions that anchor views about the nature of credible evidence are explored. This context is used to preview the positions expressed about credible evidence in the subsequent sections of the book.

Experimental Routes to Credible Evidence

Part II contains four chapters that discuss the importance of experimental and quasi-experimental approaches for producing credible and actionable evidence in applied research and evaluation. In Chapter 3, Gary Henry sketches out an underlying justification for the U.S. Department of Education's priority for randomized experiments and high quality quasi-experiments over nonexperimental designs "when getting it right matters." His argument has deep roots in democratic theory, and stresses the importance of scientifically based evaluations for influencing the adoption of government policies and programs. He argues that high-quality, experimental evaluations are the only way to eliminate selection bias when assessing policy and program impact, and that malfeasance may occur when random assignment evaluations are not conducted. Henry urges his readers to consider his arguments in favor of the proposed priority in an open-minded, reflective, and deliberative way to do the greatest good in society.

In Chapter 4, Leonard Bickman and Stephanie Reich explore in great detail why RCTs are commonly considered the "gold standard" for producing credible evidence in applied research and evaluation. They clearly articulate why RCTs are superior to other evaluation designs for determining causation and impact, and alert us to the high cost of making a wrong decision about causality. They specify numerous threats to validity that must be considered in applied research and evaluation, and provide a thorough analysis of both the strengths and limitations of RCTs. In the end, they conclude that, "For determining causality, in many but not all circumstances, the randomized design is the worst form of design except all the others that have been tried."

One popular approach for determining if evidence from applied research and evaluation is credible for decision making has been to establish what might be thought of as "supreme courts" of credible evidence. These groups establish evidence standards and identify studies that provide the strongest evidence for decision and policy making. For example, the Cochrane Collaboration is known as the reliable source for evidence on the effects of health care interventions, and it aims to improve health care decision making globally (www.cochrane.org). The Campbell Collaboration strives to provide decision makers with evidence-based information to empower them to make well-informed decisions about the effects of interventions in the social, behavioral, and educational arenas (www.campbellcollaboration.org). In Chapter 5, Russell Gersten and John Hitchcock describe the role of the What Works Clearinghouse (WWC) in informing decision makers and being the "trusted source of scientific evidence in education" (http://ies.ed.gov/ncee/wwc). They discuss in some detail how the Clearinghouse defines and determines credible evidence for the effectiveness of a wide range of educational programs and interventions. It is important to note that well-implemented RCTs are typically required to meet the highest standards in most of these evidence collaborations and clearinghouses, and applied research and evaluations that do not use RCTs or strong quasi-experimental designs do not make it through the evidence screens or meet credible evidence standards.

George Julnes and Debra Rog discuss their new work on informing method choice in applied research and evaluation in Chapter 6. Their pragmatic approach suggests that for evidence to be useful, it not only needs to be credible but "actionable" as well, deemed both adequate and appropriate for guiding actions in targeted real-world contexts. They argue that evidence can be credible in the context studied but of questionable relevance for guiding actions in other contexts. They provide a framework to address the controversy over method choice and review areas where there is at least some consensus, in particular with regard to the key factors that make one method more or less suitable than others for particular situations. The contexts and contingencies under which RCTs and quasi-experimental designs are most likely to thrive in providing credible and actionable evidence are described. They conclude by suggesting that their approach to the debate about evidence, focusing on the specific application of methods and designs in applied research and evaluation, promises to develop a "fairer" playing field in the debate about credible evidence than one that is based solely on ideological instead of pragmatic grounds.

Nonexperimental Approaches

Part III includes five chapters that explore nonexperimental approaches for building credible evidence in applied research and evaluation. Michael Scriven (Chapter 7) first takes a strong stand against the "current mythology . . . that scientific claims of causation or good evidence . . . require evidence from . . . RCTs." He asserts, "to insist that we use an experimental approach is simply bigotry . . . not pragmatic, and not logical. In short, it is a dogmatic approach that is an affront to scientific method. Moreover, to wave banners proclaiming that anything less will mean unreliable results or unscientific practice is simply absurd." Next, he provides a detailed analysis of alternative ways to determine causation in applied research and evaluation, and discusses several alternative methods for determining policy and program impact including the general elimination methodology or algorithm (GEM). He ends with a proposal for marriage of warring parties, complete with a prenuptial agreement, that he believes would provide a win-win solution to the "causal wars," with major positive side effects for those in need around the world.

In Chapter 8, Jennifer Greene outlines the political, organizational, and sociocultural assumptions and stances that comprise the current context for the demand for credible evidence. She quotes Stronach, Piper, and Piper (2004), "The positivists can't believe their luck, they've lost all the arguments of the last 30 years and they've still won the war," to illuminate that the worldview underlying the current demand for credible evidence is a form of conservative post-positivism, or in many ways like a kind of neo-positivism. She laments that "many of us thought that we'd seen the last of this obsolete way of thinking about the causes and meaning of human activity, as it was a consensual casualty of the great quantitative-qualitative debate." She goes on to describe the ambitions and politics behind priorities and approaches privileging methods and designs like RCTs, and the problems with efforts to promote one master epistemology and the interests of the elite, which she concludes is radically undemocratic. Greene offers us an alternative view on credible evidence that meaningfully honors complexity, and modestly views evidence as "inkling" in contrast to "proof." She describes how credible evidence can provide us a window into the messy complexity of human experience; needs to account for history, culture, and context; respects differences in perspective and values; and opens the potential for democratic inclusion and the legitimization of multiple voices.

Sharon Rallis describes qualitative pathways for building credible evidence in Chapter 9. She emphasizes throughout her chapter that probity, goodness or absolute moral correctness, is as important as rigor in determining what counts as credible evidence in applied research and evaluation. It is also important to her that scientific knowledge be recognized as a social construct, and that credible evidence is what the relevant communities of discourse and practice accept as valid, reliable, and trustworthy. A wide range of examples focused on reported experiences rather than outcomes are provided, and offered as a form of credible evidence to help improve policy and programming and to better serve the people involved. Rallis argues that these qualitative experiences provide credible evidence that is the real basis of scientific inquiry.

In Chapter 10, Sandra Mathison explores the credibility of image-based applied research and evaluation. She asserts that the credibility of evidence is contingent on experience, perception, and social convention. Mathison introduces the notion of an anarchist epistemology, the notion that every idea, however new or absurd, may improve knowledge of the social world. She asserts that credible evidence is not the province of only certain methods (e.g., RCTs), and can't be expressed in only one way (e.g., statistical averages). Qualities of good evidence include relevance, coherence, verisimilitude, justifiability, and contextuality. She concludes by pointing out that it is too simplistic to assert that "seeing is believing," but the fact that our eyes sometimes deceive does not obviate credible knowing from doing and viewing image-based research and evaluation.

Thomas Schwandt provides the final chapter of Part III. He claims that evaluating the merit, worth, and significance of our judgments, actions, policies, and programs requires a variety of evidence generated via both experimental and nonexperimental methods. He asserts in Chapter 11 that RCTs are not always the best choice of study design, and in some situations do not provide more credible evidence than nonrandomized study designs. That is, observational studies often provide credible evidence as well. Schwandt believes that careful thinking about the credibility, relevance, and probative value of evidence in applied research and evaluation will not be advanced in the future by continuing to argue and debate the merits of hierarchies of evidence as a basis for decision making. Rather, he suspects that the field of applied research and evaluation would be better served by working more diligently on developing a practical theory of evidence, one that addressed matters such as the nature of evidence as well as the context and ethics of its use in decision making.

Conclusions

In Chapter 12, the final chapter, Melvin Mark reviews some of the central themes about credible evidence presented throughout the book, and underscores that at this time in our history this is a topic where we do not have consensus. For example, some authors firmly believe that RCTs are needed to have credible and actionable evidence about program effects, while others assume that nonexperimental methods will suffice for that purpose, and yet other authors argue that the question of overall program effects is too complex to answer in a world in which context greatly matters. In an effort to move the field forward in a productive and inclusive manner, Mark provides us with an integrative review of the critical issues raised in the debate, and identifies a few underlying factors that account for much of the diversity in the views about what counts as credible evidence. He concludes by giving us a roadmap for changing the terms of a debate that he believes will help us dramatically improve our understanding of what counts as credible evidence in applied research and evaluation.

The Epilogue by Donaldson supports and expands this roadmap and begins to flesh out a possible blueprint for an evidence-based global society.

Together, Mark and Donaldson provide us with hope that the result of this volume will be to inspire new efforts to improve our understanding of deeply entrenched disagreements about evidence, move us toward a common ground where such can be found, enhance the capacity of evaluation practitioners and stakeholders to make sensible decisions rather than draw allegiances to a side of the debate based on superficial considerations, and ultimately provide applied researchers and evaluators with a useful framework for gathering and using credible evidence to improve the plight of humankind across the globe as we move further into the 21st century.

References

Alkin, M. C. (2004). *Evaluation roots: Tracing theorists' views and influences.* Thousand Oaks, CA: Sage Publications.

Campbell, D. T. (1991). Methods for the experimenting society. *American Journal of Evaluation, 12*(3), 223–260.

Campbell, D. T., & Stanley, J. C. (1963). *Experimental and quasi-experimental design for research.* Chicago: Rand McNally.

Campbell Collaboration website: www.campbellcollaboration.org.

Cochrane Collaboration website: www.cochrane.org.

Cook, T. D., & Campbell, D. T. (1979). *Quasi-experimentation: Design and analysis issues for field settings.* Chicago: Rand McNally.

Donaldson, S. I. (2007). *Program theory–driven evaluation science: Strategies and applications.* Mahwah, NJ: Erlbaum.

Donaldson, S. I., & Christie, C. A. (2005). The 2004 Claremont Debate: Lipsey versus Scriven. Determining causality in program evaluation and applied research: Should experimental evidence be the gold standard? *Journal of Multidisciplinary Evaluation, 3,* 60–77.

Donaldson, S. I., & Christie, C. A. (2006). Emerging career opportunities in the transdiscipline of evaluation science. In S. I. Donaldson, D. E. Berger, & K. Pezdek (Eds.), *Applied psychology: New frontiers and rewarding careers* (pp. 243–259). Mahwah, NJ: Erlbaum.

Donaldson, S. I., & Lipsey, M. W. (2006). Roles for theory in contemporary evaluation practice: Developing practical knowledge. In I. Shaw, J. C. Greene, & M. M. Mark (Eds.), *The handbook of evaluation: Policies, programs, and practices* (pp. 56–75). London: Sage Publications.

Donaldson, S. I., & Scriven, M. (2003). *Evaluating social programs and problems: Visions for the new millennium.* Mahwah, NJ: Erlbaum.

Gallup. (2007). *The state of global well-being 2007.* New York: Gallup Press.

Joint Committee on Standards for Education Evaluation (1994). *The program evaluation standards: How to assess evaluations of educational programs.* Newbury Park, CA: Sage Publications.

Julnes, G., & Rog, D. J. (Eds.). (2007). *Informing federal policies on evaluation methodology: Building the evidence base for method choice in government-sponsored evaluations* [Entire issue]. (Vol. 113 of *New Directions for Evaluation* series). San Francisco: Jossey-Bass.

Mark, M. M. (2003). Toward an integrative view of the theory and practice of program and policy evaluation. In S. I. Donaldson & M. Scriven (Eds.), *Evaluating social programs and problems: Visions for the new millennium* (pp. 109–141). Mahwah, NJ: Erlbaum.

Norcross, J. C., Beutler, L. E., & Levant, R. F. (2005). *Evidence-based practices in mental health: Debate and dialogue on the fundamental questions.* Washington, DC: American Psychological Association.

Pawson, R. (2006). *Evidence-based policy: A realist perspective.* London: Sage Publications.

Pfeffer, J., & Sutton, R. I. (2006). *Hard facts, dangerous truths, and total nonsense: Profiting from evidence-based management.* Boston: Harvard Business School Press.

Preskill, H., & Donaldson, S. I. (2008). Improving the evidence base for career development programs: Making use of the evaluation profession and positive psychology movement. *Advances in Developing Human Resources, 10*(1), 104–121.

Reichhardt, C. S., & Rallis, S. F. (1994). *The qualitative–quantitative debate: New perspectives* [Entire issue]. (Vol. 61 in *New Directions for Program Evaluation* series). San Francisco: Jossey-Bass.

Sackett, D. L. (2000). *Evidence-based medicine: How to practice and teach EBM.* Edinburgh/New York: Churchill Livingstone.

Sackett, D. L., Rosenberg, W. M. C., Gray, J. A. M., & Haynes, R. B. (1996). Evidence-based medicine: What it is and what it isn't. *British Medical Journal, 312,* 71–72.

Shadish, W. R., Cook, T. D., & Leviton, L. C. (1991). *Foundations of program evaluation: Theories of practice.* Newbury Park, CA: Sage Publications.

Stober, D. R., & Grant, A. M. (2006). *Evidence-based coaching handbook: Putting best practice to work for your clients.* Hoboken, NJ: Wiley.

Stronach, I., Piper, H., & Piper, J. (2004). Re-performing crises of representation. In H. Piper & I. Stronach (Eds.), *Educational research, difference and diversity* (pp. 129–154). Aldershot, UK: Ashgate.

What Works Clearinghouse website: http://ies.ed.gov/ncee/wwc.

2

Social Inquiry Paradigms as a Frame for the Debate on Credible Evidence

Christina A. Christie

Dreolin Fleischer

This book deals with the question, "What constitutes credible evidence in evaluation and applied research?" Specifically, we are concerned with evidence used to support claims about the impact of a practice, program, or policy. In the previous chapter, Donaldson described the context for the resurgence of this debate, namely current federal policies that identify the randomized controlled trial (RCT)[1] as the "gold standard" design for generating credible "scientific" evidence of program effectiveness. The identification of a particular research design as *the* design from which decisions are made about what should and should not be considered an "evidence-based" practice, program, or policy has frustrated many in the field of evaluation (as well as other social science fields) and has reignited a heated debate among respected colleagues and friends, some of whom have been driven to "agree to disagree" over this issue.

This debate is not a new one, however. The current credibility-of-evidence debate is preceded by a reoccurring yet persistent one in social science and evaluation research over how to best study social phenomena. This debate is rooted in philosophical differences about the nature of reality and epistemological differences about what constitutes knowledge and how it is created (Patton, 2002). Thus, theories of knowledge and paradigms of social inquiry have been commonly used as a frame for describing the debate—for example, positivism versus constructivism or, as it relates to methods, quantitative versus qualitative. This describes the "paradigm wars" of the past 20 years, on which the literature is extensive (e.g., Lincoln & Guba, 1985; Reichardt & Cook, 1979; Tashakkori & Teddlie, 1998).

Why has the question of credible evidence ignited such a long-standing and passionate debate among scholars? Kuhn (1970) observed that scientists preferred quantitative over qualitative data when making predictions, and that hierarchy in data existed where "hard" numeric data were valued over "soft" qualitative data (Patton, 2002). Thus, by extension, identifying a type of quantitative study design as "strong" and "scientific" suggests that all others are "weaker" (if not weak) and "unscientific" and, to be sure, this is troubling to some. It is argued that the distinction drawn between scientific (hard) and unscientific (soft) evidence based solely on the methods used to gather information is a false one, and is ill-conceived. On the other side, it is argued that when questions of effectiveness call for rigorous investigation, it is necessary for researchers and evaluators to offer the most reliable evidence possible, and the best method we have available to us to answer this question is the RCT. For all other questions, quasi-experimental[2] and nonexperimental designs are legitimate choices.

Mixed method designs for studying programs have been offered as design choices that integrate the merits of experimental and nonexperimental designs. Presumably, few would argue against this more general point. However, when asked to identify the feature of a mixed methods study design that is intended to get at program impact, we find ourselves returning to the same issue of which design will offer the most credible evidence to answer the question, "Did this program work?" In this context, those who support the use of RCTs argue that without some measure of causality, a reliable measure of impact cannot be obtained, while those on the other side of the RCT debate tend to de-emphasize causality as the central factor in determining program impact. Thus, the credible evidence debate may be less about design and methods than how each "side" conceptualizes "impact."

It is fair to say that all applied researchers and evaluators would agree that there will always be limitations to evidence, in other words, that no study design is flawless. Where they disagree is on whether we can and how we should control for or intervene in an attempt to strengthen our evidence. Disagreements about whether conditions in applied studies can or should be controlled stem from and are informed by notions about truth and whether and how one can observe truth. Thus, arguments about evidence, and more specifically credible evidence, call into question our basic notions of truth and science and the ways in which we perceive the world around us.

Notions of truth, and thus by extension the arguments centered on credible evidence, can be better understood when some key notions about knowledge put forth by philosophers of science are introduced. In line with how the credibility-of-evidence debate has been discussed historically, we offer a brief overview of the philosophical issues germane to a discussion about generating credible evidence in applied research and evaluation as a frame for the arguments presented by the authors in subsequent chapters of this book. The intention is not to offer comprehensive descriptions of theories of knowledge or social inquiry paradigms. This has been done well elsewhere (see, for example, Tashakkori & Teddlie, 1998). Instead, our aim is to make this and upcoming chapters more accessible for those who may be unfamiliar with some of the philosophical issues related to knowledge by introducing these topics more generally.

Framing the Credible Evidence Debate: Social Inquiry and the Paradigms

Evaluation and applied research are grounded in and are forms of social inquiry.[3] Described most generally, social inquiry is the systemic study of the behavior of groups of individuals in various kinds of social settings, using a variety of methods. It begins with the recognition that there is a unique social dimension to human action, and the central focus of concern is, "Why do people in social groups act as they do?" In the Western world, inquiry along these lines has its origins in 17th- and 18th-century figures such as Hobbes, Montesquieu, and Rousseau. While these theorists systematically studied and commented on social groups, their descriptions and theories were more a product of contemplation rather than empirical investigations. Not until the mid- to late 19th century were society and social groups studied empirically through the collection and analysis of empirical data.

A subject of ongoing debate is what methods are appropriate for the study of society, social groups, and social life and whether the methodologies of the physical sciences, broadly defined, are applicable to social phenomena. Philosophers of science and social science continue to disagree on what constitutes the methods of the sciences and their potential applicability to the study of social life (Popper, 1963; Kuhn, 1970). Cutting across social science disciplines are broad philosophical and methodological questions that continue to be debated in contemporary social inquiry. Important questions include the following: What is the relationship between theory and observation? Should social scientists have a moral stance toward the individuals and groups that they study? Is this stance appropriate and would it compromise the researcher's objectivity? These and other questions form part of the theory and practice of social inquiry.

The classical social scientists made extensive use of statistics, among other data, in coming to form particular judgments regarding social life. The influence of the discipline of psychology introduced into the social realm the experimental method, where the overriding question is whether a treatment is effective in bringing about desired effects. Discussions regarding the feasibility and desirability of this methodology for the study of the social world continue to this day, prompting heated debates related to and reflective of the more general question of the applicability of the methods of the sciences to the social sciences.

Alternatively, the discipline of anthropology has given rise to ethnographies and more broadly qualitative studies of the social world. The distinction between these methods and the ones just mentioned above is sometimes couched in terms of the distinction between explanation and prediction on the one hand, and interpretation and understanding on the other. Geertz's classical essay "Thick Description: Toward an Interpretive Theory of Culture" in *The Interpretation of Cultures* (1973) epitomizes the latter approach and in part has come to define interpretive social science where the emphasis is placed not on prediction but on meaning.

The influence of these social inquiry debates is infused in the chapters to follow. Specifically, the impacts of psychology and social experimentation are central to the arguments presented in support of the RCT. Anthropological influences such as "thick description" and observation are evidenced in the chapters in the second section, where authors argue for a more expanded view of evidence.

Informing the arguments around social inquiry is the philosophy of science, which is concerned with the assumptions, foundations, and implications of science, including the formal sciences, natural sciences, and social sciences. When examining this vast body of philosophical literature, we find scholars discussing the various ways one can think about the world around us, or the nature of reality, and the assumptions about social inquiry in terms of paradigms. The *Encyclopedia of Evaluation* (Mathison, 2005) offers the following description of a paradigm:

Paradigm is a term used to capture a worldview or perspective that, in the case of research and evaluation, includes conceptions of methodology, purposes, assumptions, and values. . . . [A] paradigm typically consists of an ontology (the nature of reality), an epistemology (what is knowable and who can know it), and a methodology (how one can obtain knowledge). (p. 289)

Another way to think of a paradigm is as a theory of knowledge. Shadish, Cook, and Leviton (1991), in their well-known evaluation textbook, explain that ontological, epistemological, and methodological assumptions make up theories of knowledge (i.e., paradigms). These authors define ontology as an assumption about the nature of reality, epistemology as an assumption about justifications for knowledge claims, and methodology as an assumption about constructing knowledge. Tashakkori and Teddlie (1998) describe these three assumptions, as well as several others—for example, assumptions about the values in inquiry (axiology), logic (i.e., either deductive or inductive), generalizability, and causality.

Those who engage in the debate about credible evidence typically are referred to as belonging to one of two "camps": post-positivism or constructivism (and related thinking), and thus, we will focus this description primarily on these paradigms. Logical positivism will be described first as a precursor to the aforementioned paradigms, and at the end of this section pragmatism will be briefly described as one particular alternative to either the post-positivist or constructivist paradigms. Before moving into a discussion about the paradigms, we acknowledge that this kind of description as it is being offered for this book can be polarizing. Our reasons for this type of categorization are threefold. First, in order to be accessible to a wide range of readers, this introduction to the philosophy of science needs to be as straightforward and clear as possible. Second, the polarizing categorization does indeed mirror the polarizing effects of the debate on "what constitutes credible evidence." Third, these paradigms provide background and are closely related to the much publicized quantitative/qualitative debate that transpired previously within the evaluation field. We would be remiss if we did not make it clear that the present debate concerning credible evidence encapsulates many of the issues of the quantitative/qualitative, but it is not the same debate. We acknowledge that contributors to this book do not necessarily fall plainly into either of the paradigms we are suggesting; nonetheless we believe that it is a useful frame for better understanding the origins of each argument.

Logical Positivism. Logical positivism is linked to Comte, a 19th-century French philosopher. It wasn't until the end of World War II that the logical positivist paradigm began to lose its following. At that point, the post-positivist paradigm thinking developed and grew in popularity, particularly among the social scientists of the 1950s and 1960s. In almost a reactionary fashion, those who saw themselves as different from both positivists and post-positivists began writing about notions of relativism and constructivism. As constructivist thinking gained recognition, contention between the post-positivist and constructivist paradigms led to a fierce and ongoing debate quickly dubbed the "paradigm wars." Some considered the paradigms mutually exclusive and therefore incompatible. Others saw an opportunity for compromise and common ground, from which the pragmatist paradigm was formed.

From an ontological perspective, the logical positivist position is that there is a single reality. In other words, reality is something that can be agreed upon and observed objectively by multiple viewers. This type of realism is referred to as "naive realism." Faith in objectivity characterizes both the axiology (in this case value-free) and the epistemological position of the positivists. Thus, the knower is independent of that which he or she is trying to know. As for how knowledge can best be obtained, positivists consider quantitative methods superior to all else. There are several other axioms that help to define this paradigm, such as a rule of deductive logic. This means moving from theory or a priori hypotheses to a narrow conclusion, with the generalizability of this conclusion being of the utmost importance. Finally, causes are linked to effects and this causal relationship is observable. Both post-positivism and constructivism grew from the positivist paradigm; however, post-positivism retained more of the positivist notions than constructivism did.

Post-Positivism. Post-positivism has notable similarities to positivism. For instance, post-positivists, like positivists, believe that there is a single reality that can be studied objectively. However, the difference between the two paradigms on this point is critical, for post-positivists believe that there is no way to understand reality *in its totality.* Thus, full understanding of truth can be approached, but never reached. This type of realism is referred to as "critical realism." Beyond ontology, there are other commonalities between the positivist and post-positivist paradigms. For example, post-positivists have a strong preference for quantitative methods and deductive reasoning. However, in alignment with the notion of "approaching" truth rather than "capturing" it, post-positivists would not argue that quantitative methods or deductive reasoning should be used exclusively, just predominantly. The "approaching" truth ideal extends to views on causality as well. It is believed that causation is observable and that over time predictors can be established, but always some degree of doubt remains associated with the conclusion.

As for axiology, values and biases are noted and accounted for, yet the belief is that they can be controlled within the context of scientific inquiry.

Constructivism (and Related Thinking). The constructivist ontological position argues that there are multiple realities. These multiple realities are subjective and change according to the "knower," who constructs his or her own reality using past experiences and individual contexts to perceive what is "known." This is referred to as "ontological relativism." In the constructivist paradigm the "knower" and the "known" are interrelated, unlike positivist epistemology where they are considered independent. Inductive logic is the rule, which means particular instances are used to infer broader, more general laws. Of notable distinction, inquiry is considered value-bound, rather than value-free. It is the constructivists' position that it is better to acknowledge and consider bias than to attempt to ignore or control it. Qualitative methods are used most frequently within the constructivist paradigm because they are thought to be better suited to investigate the subjective layers of reality. Generalizability is not nearly as important as local relevance. Cause and effect are thought impossible to distinguish because relationships are bidirectional, and thus everything is impacting everything else at one time.

Related to constructivism is social constructivism, a sociological theory of knowledge that considers how social phenomena are not independent from the society they exist within. In other words, social phenomena cannot be divorced from their societal and cultural contexts, because the definition and meaning attributed to those phenomena are constructed by that society. To investigate social phenomena through a social constructivist lens is to consider the phenomena as others perceive them.

Also juxtaposed to post-positivism is relativism. Relativism, simply put, consists of a collection of viewpoints, all of which suggest that social phenomena are relative to other social phenomena and vice versa. One form of relativism is "truth relativism"; that is, there are no absolute truths. This means that truth is relative to its societal, cultural, and historical contexts. This is of course similar to notions of truth put forth by constructivists. Taken together, constructivist, social constructivist, and relativist thinking, which we have described under constructivism, serve to inform the arguments of those opposed to relying only on RCTs as the method for observing program impact.

Pragmatism. Pragmatism is not typically cited in the "paradigm wars" and is often misinterpreted to be the compromise between the two more popularly debated paradigms. True, pragmatists embrace objectivity and subjectivity as two positions on a continuum, which appears to be a truce of some kind between post-positivist and constructivist thinking. After all, there is now room for both subjectivity and objectivity to be useful at different points within an evaluation or applied research study. Another seemingly agreed-upon point is that both quantitative and qualitative methods are legitimate methods of inquiry. The decision of what method to use is based on the nature of the study question. Pragmatists also argue that deductive and inductive logic should be used in concert. Pragmatists do, however, move away from embracing equally the axioms of the post-positivist and constructivist paradigms. For example, pragmatists are more similar to post-positivists with regard to notions about external reality, with the understanding that there is no absolute "truth" concerning reality. More in line with constructivist thought, however, pragmatists argue that there are multiple explanations of reality, and at any given time there is one explanation that makes the most sense. In other words, at one point in time one explanation of reality may be considered "truer" than another. Pragmatists are again similar to post-positivists in that they believe causes may be linked to effects. However, pragmatists temper this thinking by providing the caveat that absolute certainty of the causation is impossible. In contrast, pragmatists are more similar to constructivists in that they do not believe inquiry is value-free, and they consider their values important to the inquiry process. The pragmatist paradigm should be given attention as a paradigm unto its own.

Post-Positivism and Constructivism: A Ceasefire? While some argue the superiority of either post-positivism or constructivism, others have offered a rationale for a "ceasefire." They reason as follows:

- Both paradigms have, in fact, been used for years.
- Many evaluators and researchers have urged using both paradigms.
- So much has been taught by both paradigms.
- Funding agencies have supported both paradigms.
- Both paradigms have influenced policy. (Tashakkori & Teddlie, 1998, p. 11)

Indeed, these points are by most accounts valid; however, the last two have been called into question in recent years. As Donaldson described in the previous chapter, this is a significant moment in time. The federal government announced the decree, in the form of the 2002 Education Sciences Reform Act, that the randomized controlled trial is the gold standard design for research and evaluation focused on the question of program impact. As a result, it is argued that designs from both paradigms cannot and will not be supported equally by the federal government and thus will not enjoy a balanced position in informing important policy debates and decisions related to social, behavioral, and educational programs and policies.

Chapter Authors: Paradigm Positions

The purpose of this chapter is to elucidate some of the conceptual content of the chapters that follow. Regardless of whether contributors talk directly about social inquiry or the philosophy of science in their particular chapter, it serves as a framework for their conceptual arguments. Each contributor has a history of supporting notions related to either the post-positivist or constructivist paradigm; indeed, authors were asked to contribute to this book in part because of their beliefs about truth and knowledge and social inquiry.

In each chapter, authors offer a contemporary argument about evidence. While each chapter could stand alone, taken together they become a dialogue about what constitutes credible evidence in evaluation and applied research. The first section of this book includes chapters from contributors who offer insights and arguments about credible evidence that position them most closely with the post-positivist paradigm. A prominent theme running through each chapter in this section is the importance of making causal inferences. Moreover, most of the contributors in this section have long argued, to at least some extent, that randomized controlled trials are the best (available) method for studying causality, and have pushed on many occasions for an increased presence of post-positivist thinking in our methodological discussions and applied work. For example, Bickman (coauthor of Chapter 4) conducted a large-scale RCT of a system of care designed to improve mental health outcomes for children and adolescents who were referred for mental health treatment, which he argues could only be understood well if studied using experimental methods (Fitzpatrick, Christie, & Mark, 2008). This is in line with his years of arguing for the use of RCTs to better understand mental health interventions and practice. Henry's (Chapter 3) position on the use of RCTs has intensified over time, with his more recent work, both theoretical and practical, being more focused on the exclusive use of experiments, when possible, to study educational policies, particularly related to early childhood education (e.g., Henry, Gordon, & Rickman, 2006). Gersten (coauthor of Chapter 5) has been a long-standing proponent of using scientific research to inform classroom practices, specifically in the area of special education and mathematics education (e.g., Gersten, Schiller, & Vaughn, 2000). The authors of Chapter 6, Julnes and Rog, have recently edited a *New Directions for Evaluation* issue (2007) focused on scientific method choice for building an evidence base in federal evaluation studies.

The second section of this book includes chapters from contributors—with the exception of Michael Scriven (Chapter 7)—whose viewpoints position them most closely with the constructivist paradigm. Scriven, a post-positivist by most accounts, critically questions RCTs as the gold standard for providing credible causal evidence, and because of this his chapter is best grouped with the constructivists. All contributors in this section offer an argument for why it is detrimental to consider the randomized controlled trial as the best way to provide credible evidence or to effectively make causal claims. As with the post-positivist authors, the contributors to the "non-RCT" section of the book have extensive histories arguing for alternative methods and thinking about scientific evidence. For example, Greene (Chapter 8) strongly believes that inquirers' assumptions about the social world and our knowledge of it inevitably influence decisions of practice (e.g., Greene & Caracelli, 1997). She has critiqued performance measurements as inadequate measures of social program quality, as inadequate representations of program quality, and as at odds with evaluative processes that advance the ideals of deliberative democracy. Rallis (Chapter 9) has argued specifically for the use of qualitative methods in evaluation and educational research and maintains that qualitative work is not only about precision of method but is also an art (e.g., Rossman & Rallis, 2003). Mathison (Chapter 10) argues for fair and democratic evaluation of educational programs, evaluations that consider local context and values as well as the use of multiple indicators of quality, and that involve diverse and often disenfranchised stakeholders (e.g., Mathison, 2007). Schwandt (Chapter 11) has published widely on constructivist, interpretivist approaches to human inquiry (e.g., Schwandt, 1994). Thus, it is evident from these brief descriptions of their work how the views and beliefs of our authors in each section of this book differ and how they are informed by the scientific paradigms.

Conclusion

For all contributors to this book, the purpose of evaluation is to promote social good. While they share this common purpose, they differ on exactly what philosophical underpinnings should inform the strategies and procedures used to accomplish this. The appropriateness and validity of using randomized controlled trials as a method for pursuing social good is debated under the nuanced topic of what constitutes credible evidence. They bring to bear the methodological arguments surrounding this notion of credible evidence, highlight the implications of these arguments, and offer examples related to and descriptions of contexts where the relevance of the arguments can be seen.

As evident in the chapters to follow, this debate is of great concern to our contributors. The authors offer us insight into the history surrounding credible evidence, as well as the current debate as it has waned and swelled in importance and relevance to the field of evaluation and the practice of applied social research. Most notable, however, is that this debate has yet to fade away. We hope that you find the debate presented here to be both stimulating and illuminating.

Notes

1. Randomized controlled trials require the random assignment of individuals to a treatment group (the group receiving the intervention or program) or a control group (the group not receiving the intervention or program). Random assignment is argued to reduce most threats to internal validity (e.g., selection bias, maturation, history), and the use of a control group provides data to determine the relative performance of the treatment group, helping to answer the "compared to what?" question when measuring program impact (Azzam & Christie, 2007).

2. Quasi-experiments do not require random assignment and often involve the use of a comparison group, as opposed to a control group. The defining feature of an RCT design is the random assignment of participants to a control and an experimental group, where quasi-experiments do not have randomization as a feature of the study design.

3. This description of social inquiry is summarized from Alkin and Christie (2004).

References

Alkin, M. C., & Christie, C. A. (2004). An evaluation theory tree. In M. C. Alkin (Ed.), *Evaluation Roots* (pp. 12–66). Thousand Oaks, CA: Sage Publications.

Azzam, T., & Christie, C. A. (2007). Using public databases to study relative program impact. *Canadian Journal of Program Evaluation, 22*(2), 57–68.

Fitzpatrick, J., Christie, C. A., & Mark, M. (Eds.). (2008). *Evaluation in action: Interviews with expert evaluators.* Thousand Oaks, CA: Sage Publications.

Geertz, C. (1973). *The interpretation of cultures.* New York: Basic Books.

Gersten, R., Schiller E., & Vaughn, S. (Eds.). (2000). *Contemporary special education research: Syntheses of the knowledge.* Mahwah, NJ: Erlbaum.

Greene, J. C., & Caracelli, V. J. (1997). Defining and describing the paradigm issues in mixed-method evaluation. In J. G. Greene & V. J. Caracelli, *Advances in mixed-method evaluation: The challenges and benefits of integrating diverse paradigms* (pp. 5–18). (Vol. 74 in *New Directions for Evaluation series*). San Francisco: Jossey-Bass.

Henry, G. T., Gordon, C. C., & Rickman, D. K. (2006). Early education policy alternatives: Comparing the quality and outcomes of Head Start and state prekindergarten. *Educational Evaluation and Policy Analysis, 28*, 77–99.

Julnes, G., & Rog, D. J. (2007). *Informing federal policies on evaluation methodology: Building the evidence base for method choice in government-sponsored evaluations*. (Vol. 113 in *New Directions for Evaluation* series). San Francisco: Jossey-Bass.

Kuhn, T. (1970). *The structure of scientific revolutions*. Chicago: University of Chicago Press.

Lincoln, Y., & Guba, E. (1985). *Naturalistic Inquiry*. Thousand Oaks, CA: Sage Publications.

Mathison, S. (Ed.). (2005). *Encyclopedia of evaluation*. Thousand Oaks, CA: Sage Publications.

Mathison, S. (2007). The accumulation of disadvantage: The role of educational testing in the school career of minority children. In B. A. Arrighi & D. J. Maume (Eds.), *Child poverty in America today: The promise of education*. New York: Praeger.

Patton, M. Q. (2002). *Qualitative research and evaluation methods*. Thousand Oaks, CA: Sage Publications.

Popper, K. R. (1963). *Conjectures and refutations*. London: Routledge/Kegan Paul.

Reichardt, C. S., & Cook, T. D. (1979). *Qualitative and quantitative methods in evaluation research*. Thousand Oaks, CA: Sage Publications.

Rossman, G., & Rallis, S. F. (2003). *Learning in the field: An introduction to qualitative research* (2nd ed.). Thousand Oaks, CA: Sage Publications.

Schwandt, T. (1994). Constructivist, interpretivist approaches to human inquiry. In N. K. Denzin & Y. S. Lincoln (Eds.), *The landscape of qualitative research: Theories and* issues (pp. 221–259). Thousand Oaks, CA: Sage Publications.

Shadish, W. R., Cook, T. D., & Leviton, L. C. L. (1991). *Foundations of program evaluation*. Newbury Park, CA: Sage Publications.

Tashakkori, A., & Teddlie, C. (1998). *Mixed methodology: Combining qualitative and quantitative approaches*. Thousand Oaks, CA: Sage Publications.

PART II

Experimental Approaches as the Route to Credible Evidence

3

When Getting It Right Matters

The Case for High-Quality Policy and Program Impact Evaluations

Gary T. Henry

In 2003, on a slightly warmer-than-usual November third in Washington, D.C., Rod Paige, the Secretary of Education, asked for comments on a departmental policy that would give randomized controlled trials (random assignment experiments) and high-quality quasi-experiments extra points in the scoring of reviews for proposals to evaluate the effectiveness of educational programs (U.S. Department of Education, 2003). This turned out to be the shot fired over the bow of the evaluation community and became the flashpoint that sparked the ongoing credibility war. A group of American Evaluation Association (AEA) members prepared an official response for the organization that ended, "We believe that the constraints in the proposed priority would deny use of other needed, proven, and scientifically credible evaluation methods, resulting in fruitless expenditures on some large contracts while leaving other public programs unevaluated entirely" (AEA, 2004). A group of eight evaluators, including former AEA presidents, AEA board members, and AEA journal editors, developed their own statement that ended, "We believe that the proposed priority will dramatically increase the amount of valid information for guiding the improvement of education throughout the nation" (Bickman et al., 2003).[1] The credibility war had been joined, and the battles over the use of scientifically based research methods in evaluation are ongoing.

Some might have quickly and, in my opinion, incorrectly viewed the credibility war as a sequel to the paradigm war that pitted quantitative approaches to evaluation against qualitative approaches. Certainly it has characteristics in common with the earlier paradigm war, but after 10 years or more of uneasy and sometimes begrudging acknowledgment of the need for methodological diversity in the field of evaluation, a discussion about credible evidence stands as an opportunity for taking stock and deepening our understanding of the differences between evaluation in the 20th and 21st centuries. To be sure, many of the ensuing debates and comments generated more heat than light, with little meaningful dialogue in the immediate aftermath of the call for comments and the unswerving commitment to the priority (U.S. Department of Education, 2003) by the Institute for Education Sciences (IES), the research arm of the U.S. Department of Education. But sufficient time has passed for us to raise fundamental issues for the field and to consider the possibility that evaluation practice is a contingent endeavor (Mark, Henry, & Julnes, 2000). That is, we need to come to grips with the notion that evaluation practice should look different depending on the circumstances surrounding the evaluation and what attitudes or actions the evaluation may (or should) attempt to influence (Henry & Mark, 2003; Mark & Henry, 2004). Specifically, when evaluations are intended to influence the adoption or reform of government policies or programs, randomized experiments and high-quality quasi-experiments are the preferred approaches for evaluation. In other circumstances, particularly when prior evidence has established that a public policy or program can be effective, other methods including case studies, surveys, and implementation studies may be preferred.

In this chapter, I will sketch out an underlying justification for the priority. The case presented here has deep roots in democratic theory and acknowledges the vast developments in social sciences in the last quarter-century. I will make four main points and support them in this chapter:

1. Assessing the effectiveness of public policies and programs is a significant presenting problem for modern democracies, and addressing this problem requires accurate and highly credible evidence about the consequences of public policies and programs.

2. While often denigrated as an atheoretical and, perhaps, unsophisticated approach to evaluation, the methods-based approach is deeply rooted in the theory of representative democracy and the value that evaluation can bring to society.

3. Incredible developments in social science research methods since most of the original (and still echoed) criticisms of experimental methods were first levied have largely been ignored by those who oppose more widespread use of rigorous and well-conducted experimental, quasi-experimental, and observational studies.

4. Transparency of evaluation process and method is essential to producing influential information in democracies, and conventions have been developed that can improve this aspect of evaluation practice.

In the next four sections, each of these points will be laid out for the intended purpose of creating a deeper understanding of the specific contingencies that affect the type of evaluation that is most likely to be influential in modern democracies. The arguments also provide a coherent justification for the Secretary's priority (U.S. Department of Education, 2003) when effectiveness evaluations are needed.

The Presenting Problem in Modern Democracies

Modern democracies are representative governments that function in an age of unprecedented flow of information. Perhaps the most surprising turn of the late 20th century was the apparent acceptance by many that representative democracy was the most desired form of government and, by virtue of it being desired by the governed, superior to other forms of government. One quest of philosophers and political scientists is to understand why representative democracies are assumed to be superior to all others or, at least, preferred at this historical moment to all others (Henry, 2001). Susan Hurley (1989) has reasoned that modern representative democracies allow for a cognitive function to be performed that sets them apart from the others. Hurley's shorthand for describing this function is that democracies "debunk bad ideas." Certainly, there is no shortage of bad ideas in democracies or any other form of government. Moreover, democracies have no way to prevent these ideas from becoming bad, ineffective, or even deplorable policies. Although we hope that the deliberative and relatively open processes in modern democracies filter out the worst of the bad ideas, a quick scan of recent legislative history in modern democracies would indicate that there are no guarantees preventing the adoption of ineffective or even harmful policies.

The cognitive justification for democracy lies not in prevention of bad policies but in the fact that the bad ideas promulgated in the form of policies and programs can be detected. Moreover, evidence persuading the public and policy makers that the ideas were in fact bad can be collected, and the aspects of the policies that are flawed and ineffective can be brought to light; the need for reform accepted by citizens and their elected representatives; and the policies reformed, dismantled, or replaced. One could argue that a system guaranteeing welfare payments for people as long as they remained poor was a flawed idea. This idea was debunked over a number of years and through a number of studies from a variety of perspectives, and the policies were reformed in the United States. The fact that the consequences of this aspect of the welfare system were exposed and that the idea was debunked does not mean that it was replaced by a perfect policy, but rather that any bad ideas embodied in the last round of welfare reforms will have their chance to be debunked as the process continues to unfold.

The clear implication of the need to debunk bad ideas is that we need evidence about the consequences of public policies. Negative consequences can be used to debunk bad ideas, and evidence of positive consequences may forestall misguided attacks on policies that are effective in the respects that have been assessed. Negative consequences of policies could be failure to meet the original goals or expectations of the policy or negative side effects that have arisen. Positive consequences could be indicated if the expected benefits of the policy have been realized, or if negative consequences that were predicted by opponents to its adoption failed to occur. In order for the cognitive function of democracy to be fulfilled, we need accurate evidence that is both truthful and equally capable of finding good or bad consequences of public policies. In other words, modern democracies need credible assessments of the causal impacts of public policies and the programs developed to carry out the policies to inform voters and policy makers.

Furthermore, the evidence needs to be broadly considered as true and accurate. This is the criteria suggested by credibility. Credibility mandates that the methods be sufficiently sound and sufficiently fair to convincingly indicate that the program is either good or bad. Again, using the welfare reform example, randomized experiments persuaded stakeholders that the welfare system that existed prior to 1996 was less likely to lead to work and independence from welfare than policies based on a "work first" strategy, and that implementation of "work first" reforms was feasible (Greenberg, Mandell, & Onstott, 2000). The accurate assessment of consequences of policies and programs implies the importance of methodologically sound cause-and-effect studies, which are known as impact evaluations.

Certainly, no reasonable person would argue that the only important research questions for evaluation are causal questions, but I maintain that to fulfill their promise, modern democracies must focus significant resources on evaluations that address the effectiveness of public policies. Moreover, the cause-and-effect issues that are raised within these democracies are of a specific nature that has direct implications for the types of methods that can be used to produce accurate and credible findings. Public policies and programs are intentional acts undertaken with the coercive force of government behind them. Authoritative bodies, such as legislatures, make public policy and program choices in most cases. The choices of these bodies are binding on the governed and therefore, to inform citizens' attitudes about which public programs are good or bad and potentially to influence voting decisions, democracies require that the consequences, both intended and unintended, of programs and policies are determined and made widely known in order that "bad ideas" can be debunked.

The stated purpose of public policies and programs is to produce a different pattern of social outcomes than currently exist. Since Pressman and Wildavsky (1973) pointed out the parallel between cause-and-effect relationships in social science and the cause-and-effect theories embedded in social policies, we have understood that causal methods are fundamental to evaluation and that certain approaches to making causal assertions are better than others given the presenting problem. The causal methods required to assess the impacts of intentional interventions must be able to detect the differences in the social outcomes that result from *intentional actions* that represent a change to the social environment. The policy, program, or intervention, in this case, represents an intention to change or reform the current state of affairs *for the better*. The findings must be as conclusive as possible and rule out alternative explanations for the differences detected in the pattern of social outcomes when differences are detected. The most conclusive and widely regarded as compelling means for producing findings that have these attributes are random assignment experiments. Other types of studies that approximate random assignment experiments, such as matching comparison group designs and other quasi-experiments, can detect differences but are not as powerful in eliminating a particular type of alternative explanation. The problematic alternative explanation that cannot be decisively ruled out by quasi-experiments is that the individuals that participated in the program were different from those in the comparison group to begin with, and any observed differences between the participants and nonparticipants after the program was made available are attributable to the initial differences. This is commonly known as *selection bias*.

Assessing the effects of reforms or interventions intentionally undertaken to improve social outcomes is not parallel to establishing causal connections in many other social situations, such as the negative consequences of individual choices or determining the causes of a social problem. To detect the causes of social problems, such as lung cancer, or the harmful consequences of individual actions, such as smoking, the more straightforward path of conducting randomized trials is eliminated from the potential evaluative methods due to ethical restrictions. In this case, the action being investigated is likely to have caused harm and not be intended to improve health or well-being. Using random assignment studies to investigate social problems or harmful action would require exposing individuals to harm, which is clearly immoral and unethical. Thus, other methods are required to study the consequences of harmful behaviors or actions.

Without the most straightforward path, strategies must be combined to establish causal connections. For example, the linkage between smoking and cancer has been well established by a twofold strategy of (1) research indicating that smoking is highly correlated with incidence of lung cancer, which has relied on evidence from quantitative observational studies analyzed through advanced statistical techniques, and (2) studies that have shown the mechanism by which active ingredients in tobacco smoke trigger cancer in animal-based random assignment studies that take place under laboratory conditions. A plethora of expert witness testimony has been given in the suits brought against the tobacco industry, arguing the merits of the evidence drawn from observational studies and the applicability of rat studies to humans.

Random assignment experiments, while limiting in certain respects, can virtually eliminate the most powerful point of contention that arises in these disputes. The contentious point is that those who chose to engage in these behaviors were different from those who did not, prior to the decision to engage in the behavior, and it is these differences, not the behavior, that led to the negative consequences. All other means to establish causal connections are second best in comparison to the random assignment study. Specifically, for the study of the effectiveness of public programs, random assignment experiments are the most conclusive means to debunk bad ideas, and they are available for almost all situations where actions (read: policies and programs) are intended to be beneficial, but where the benefits have not been previously established. This leads to the conclusion that random assignment studies are the most accurate, credible, economical, and straightforward means of establishing causal connections between public actions and social consequences that democracies can bring to bear. While this connection is not often made, the "methods-oriented" approaches to evaluation have these theories of democracy deeply embedded within them.

The Value of Evaluation Findings in Representative Democracies

In the field of evaluation, there are those who have reached the conclusion that approaches that evaluators choose based on their ability to produce highly accurate evidence should be lumped into a category of "methods-oriented" approaches that are not quite evaluations as indicated by the label, "quasi-evaluation" (Stufflebeam, 2001). In this next section, the connection between a theory of representative democracy and the importance of highly accurate methods will be drawn. In addition, I will show that the unifying concept connecting methods-oriented evaluators is not the choice of a single method for all evaluations but the idea that *the value of evaluation to society is directly related to the accuracy and credibility of the information produced.*

By 1956, Robert Dahl had laid out a theory of democracy that connected the information on the consequences of public policies to voters' choices for candidates. In his *A Preface to Democratic Theory,* he spelled out the importance of information on the benefits of public policies and the availability of that information, as well as information on the positions of candidates and political parties, for voters to make informed choices in representative democracies. In essence, this theory of representative democracy, which includes a central role for information concerning the consequences of public policies, provides the point of departure for a theory of evaluation. A theory of evaluation grounded in democratic theory would include the requirement that evaluations be carried out in order to provide information about the consequences of public policies and programs in a manner that is accurate and widely accepted as credible. Credibility may hinge on the methods of the evaluation adhering to the soundness standards that are generally accepted by professionals in the particular field of inquiry, if citizens choose to defer to experts, as many will do in order to take cognitive shortcuts, or it may hinge on citizens' own assessment of the accuracy of the evaluation.

By no means have the potential ramifications of these theories of modern democracies fully been worked out. For example, it is unclear how to set up institutional arrangements for funding evaluations that ensure that evaluation sponsors do not have undue effects on the evaluation questions, designs, and methods, thereby reducing the available and credible evidence about the consequences of public programs. In fact, recent work by evaluation scholars as diverse as Eleanor Chelimsky (2006) and Ernest House (2006) have pointed out the struggle to achieve independence and thereby achieve accuracy. However, the democratic imperative for accurate and credible evidence concerning the consequences of public policies and programs is largely taken for granted by some of those who have lumped together a diverse set of evaluators under the methods-oriented approach.

The theories of representative democracy stress methodological soundness, meeting technical standards for evaluation information, and making evaluation processes and findings transparent. These elements largely correspond to what is often labeled the methods-oriented approaches to evaluation, in that "the methods-oriented approaches emphasize technical quality"

(Stufflebeam, 2001, p. 17). However, Stufflebeam belittles approaches emphasizing technical quality as "quasi-evaluation." In part, the error of this attribution stems from the fact that he subdivides the methods-oriented approaches based on the method that the evaluators prefer. His perception seems to reflect that preferences for a method (random assignment experiments or mixed methods) or type of data (outcome indicators or standardized tests) arose from a tabula rasa for those adopting one of these approaches. That is, he does not seem to consider that the choice of a method or type of data could be grounded in particular circumstances or a particular presenting problem, perhaps the only circumstances in which the "quasi-evaluator" works. Stufflebeam's categorization may marginalize evaluations that place a priority on the technical quality of an evaluation's findings.

Alkin and Christie (2004) and Christie and Alkin (in press) feature methods-oriented evaluators on one of the three branches of their evaluation theory tree, giving the approach an equal standing with evaluation theories rooted in use or values. Furthermore, they offer a rationale for the theorists' beliefs in the importance of methods and meeting high technical standards for accuracy, while indicating that their methods preferences may be different and may be contingent on context of the evaluation. Many methods-oriented evaluators have firm theoretical underpinnings, some of which are explicitly linked to the value that evaluation can bring to society or a theory of representative democracy. Methods-oriented theories of evaluation *should not* be understood as entirely or even mainly the terrain of the methodologically dogmatic. To be sure, many methods-oriented evaluators advocate random assignment experiments. This stance has most often been developed out of the widely held recognition that random assignment experiments produce the most accurate estimates of the effects of public programs, and estimates of the effects of public programs provide the greatest value that evaluation can bring to society. Other methods-oriented evaluation theorists, such as Chatterji (2004), advocate mixed methods, because they believe that multiple sources of data provide a more complete, timely, and accurate picture of the program being evaluated, its intended beneficiaries, and its consequences.

Methods-oriented evaluation theories can be rooted in democratic theory that indicates the need for accurate information about program consequences, if representative democracies are actually able to serve the will of the people. Alternatively, methods-oriented theories can be rooted in other theories detailing how evaluations bring value to society. But the common thread in these approaches is the recognition that accuracy of the information is essential to having evaluation realize its value in society. The importance of accuracy and the importance of credibility are tightly bound together in ways that are well understood by many who fall within the methods-oriented category. The shorthand "methods-oriented" evaluation does not adequately convey the extent to which "high technical quality" is fundamental to the functioning of representative governments. Indeed, the methods-oriented approach to evaluation is integral to well-developed theory of achieving the highest values for which democracies have been established and the means for achieving influence in modern democracies. Values and use (or influence) are the other branches of the Christie and Alkin (in press) theory tree. Methods-oriented evaluators don't omit values or use of their findings, but the unifying idea of these evaluators is that the findings have to be accurate.

Of course, other evaluation approaches may prove more appropriate and valuable when other evaluation circumstances arise. Take democratic, deliberative evaluation as described by House and Howe (1999). This type of evaluation may be the best for assessing a local program, organization, or institution *in situ*. The approach is supportive of democratic values such as self-determination and local control, and the criteria they develop for inclusiveness, dialogue, and deliberation offer clear guidance for conducting an evaluation as well as criteria to judge the adequacy of the evaluation. The so-called methods-oriented approaches to evaluation deal with programs and policies that are on a wider scale (Rossi, 1994) and seek to influence different types of action and attitudes (Henry & Mark, 2003; Weiss, 1979); therefore, the decision to use one approach or the other is conditioned on the circumstances and purpose of the evaluation. Both are viable evaluation theories.

In addition to relegating methods-oriented evaluation to a subordinate category of evaluation, the use of these approaches has been hindered by problems in carrying out these evaluations. When social scientists moved from the laboratories into the field during the initial stage of the modern period of evaluation, the logic of their designs transferred, but the methods were not sufficiently robust to produce conclusive results in all cases. The evaluators, social scientists, and statisticians who clung to the need for accurate assessments of the consequences of public programs have made substantial improvements in the last quarter-century that have addressed many of the biases that undermined the accuracy of the earlier evaluations.

Methodological Developments Aiding Impact Evaluation

Initially, evaluators who sought to take experiments and surveys using probability sampling into the field to assess the consequences of public programs ran into significant problems implementing their elegant study designs. The biases of studies such as the Westinghouse Evaluation of Head Start became the subject of much intense criticism and reanalysis as well as the source of great frustration (Datta, 1982). Other evaluation approaches were developed that took less time, cost less, and provided as much if not more information about the programs. However, many refused to give up on social experiments and continued to work to address the biases in a concentrated and focused manner.

It is important to be clear about the term *bias* in this context. Bias has two distinct but related meanings that are relevant to evaluation and the credibility of evaluation findings. One of the meanings inhibits the progress of the field, while the other provides a challenge that has moved us ever closer to accurate assessments of program effectiveness and conducting evaluations that make a unique and distinctive contribution to social betterment.

The first meaning of bias is the most common, everyday use of the term, which refers to something that is fundamentally flawed or overwhelmed by error. Bias, when used in this way, makes a sweeping statement about an evaluation as a whole or the methods that have been used in the evaluation, and it conveys that the information produced is inaccurate and lacks truthfulness and validity. Invoking the term bias about a specific evaluation creates a perception that the evaluation's findings should not influence either actions or attitudes. Moreover, the charge of fundamental bias attacks the credibility of the findings directly and strongly conveys that the findings should be dismissed by stakeholders and the public.

While still pejorative, there is a second, more technical definition of bias that has been developed and refined in the past quarter-century by social scientists, researchers, statisticians, and evaluators. Bias in this sense is a systematic difference between a true value and the value that has been observed. For measures of program impact, bias means the estimate of the size of the program's effect that has been observed through the evaluation is different from the true estimate of the program's effect. But the development of this definition has not stopped at the gross or aggregate level. It is common practice in the evaluation of the effects of policies and programs to more thoroughly and painstakingly expose bias by systematically breaking down bias into its sources, and to quantify or establish limits on the extent of the bias that is likely from each source. For the most part, threats to validity can be understood as attempts to identify sources of bias. Bias, when viewed from a technical standpoint, is a problem to be confronted, quantified, and—when possible—reduced to practical insignificance.

Perhaps, the most well-known example of bias in applied social research came not from evaluation but from the early days of political polling and is etched in many people's minds as the image of President Truman holding up a newspaper on which bold headlines read, "Dewey Defeats Truman."

Of course, Dewey was not elected, but his election victory was unanimously predicted by the polling firms of that era. These firms used survey methods that allowed human judgments to influence the selection of participants in their surveys. All of them used a form of nonprobability sampling known as quota sampling (Henry, 2007), which sets strict guidelines for interviewers to select survey respondents so that their aggregated demographic characteristics, such as gender, race, and place of residence, precisely match the study population, but allows interviewers to select the specific individuals to be interviewed. Of course, the individuals selected for the survey also had a say in the process, and their decision to participate could have been another source of bias in the selection process. In this case, bias occurred in both the selection of respondents and in their willingness to cooperate with the interviewers, which combined to skew the results. Unfortunately, since we do not have data on failed attempts to interview respondents who were otherwise eligible, it is impossible to determine the amount of bias from each source.

While this well-worn example is not drawn from an evaluation, it is directly relevant to evaluations since in this case, like most evaluations, the researchers collected information from a subset of a group or population and then extrapolated the data to report on the entire group. For example, often in an evaluation, a sample of teachers is interviewed and the findings reported refer to "teachers" or "the teachers," not specifically to the teachers interviewed for this study. In evaluations that use subsets of the population to describe the conditions of the population, bias can occur in the selection process for interviewees, whether the interviews collect qualitative or quantitative data. But when a technical definition of bias is used, then bias can be decomposed into component parts, including both of those listed above,[2] and the extent of the bias rigorously investigated, often initially by collecting and analyzing a little more data about the interviews, such as the number of interviews attempted, number refused, and so forth. Methods can be developed that aim to eliminate or reduce to insignificance particular sources of bias. For example, probability sampling, which removes judgment from the selection of particular interviewees, can remove the most intractable source of bias from the sample selection process. In addition, rather than assuming that the newly developed methods have reduced or eliminated bias, the methods can be tested and, upon showing their effectiveness, put into wide-scale practice.

Many biases that formerly plagued evaluation of program effectiveness have been taken as a challenge, and innovative methods have been developed to reduce the bias and produce more accurate estimates of a program's effectiveness. The bias caused by missing data or differential attrition has been addressed through procedures that have increased social scientists' ability to locate and obtain data from participants in the evaluation (Greenberg & Shroder, 2004), and statistical techniques that impute data to avoid losing the participant from the study and reduce the bias and increase the efficiency of the estimates of program effectiveness (Graham, Hofer, & Piccinin, 1994; King, Honaker, Joseph, & Schieve, 2001; Schafer, 1997; Schafer & Graham, 2002).

Another bias that crept into many evaluation studies is known as cluster effects. This bias arises when the program or intervention is delivered in social settings such as schools or clinics and the observations were taken on individuals. Since the individual observations within a specific school or clinic are not all independent, the standard tests of statistical significance are biased in a way that makes it more likely to find an effect (Hox, 2002). Hierarchical models (Raudenbush & Bryk, 2001), also known as multilevel models (Hox, 2002), have been developed in part to correct for this bias and to accurately test the hypotheses.

The most pernicious form of bias for drawing accurate claims of causal effects is the one mentioned earlier, known as selection bias. This bias occurs when individuals volunteer or are assigned to participate in a program by the staff, say, based on the staff's perception that the individual will benefit from the program. The only way to eliminate this form of bias is by random assignment of individuals to treatment. However, in the past quarter-century, statisticians, economists, and others have worked on methods that can reduce the bias. Propensity score matching (Heckman & Navarro-Lozano, 2004; Ravallion, 2001; Rosenbaum, 2002; Rosenbaum & Rubin, 1983) is one such technique that has been developed. While not able to eliminate the potential for bias in the estimates of effect size, it is a promising technique that may reduce bias to levels of practical insignificance when baseline scores on the outcome variables and the likelihood of participation in the program can be shown to be equivalent between the participants and the comparison group (Rubin, 2001).

While only scratching the surface, this list of recent developments in confronting known biases in earlier evaluations that sought to assess the consequences of public programs should persuade most that significant improvements in the methods used for causal analysis have occurred. Indeed, in many other ways that experiments have been criticized, such as the tendency to shed little light on the way that the program works or fails to work, there have been substantial developments, such as testing hypotheses about how the effects occurred, known as mediator analysis (Donaldson, 2001). However, it is important to note that substantial education, training, and experience are needed to appropriately apply these techniques. Many of those pursuing graduate degrees in evaluation or closely related fields may not have sufficient coursework or practical experience to know about these methods, or when and how to apply them.

One of the issues that is clearly implied by work on identifying and confronting bias in causal analyses is that the findings and methods from evaluations must be transparent and available to all. The need for ensuring that the public has access to findings concerning the consequences of public policies places another imperative on transparency. This is the topic for the fourth section of this chapter.

Need for Complete Transparency of Method and Sponsorship in Evaluations

Much like the realization that we can't prevent some ideas from becoming bad or deplorable policies, we cannot prevent misdirected or careless evaluations from being conducted. At least with bad policies, a diligent and free press and open records requirements can expose the existence of policies that are producing bad consequences. However, evaluations that show that policies have produced negative consequences may never see the light of day. Professional standards are the first line of defense against evaluations of poor quality and allowing evaluation findings to be dropped into a file drawer, never to be seen. The American Evaluation Association's "Guiding Principles for Evaluators" has several principles that have direct implications for transparency and making publicly funded evaluations available to the public. One such principle recognizes that "freedom of information is essential in a democracy" (AEA, 2004). This is fundamentally important. The guidelines go on to indicate that evaluators have the responsibility to actively disseminate the evaluation results to all who have a stake in the policies or programs being evaluated, but that these activities may be reasonably constrained by resources. In addition, the Guiding Principles indicate that evaluators should decline to conduct an evaluation that they determine is likely to produce misleading results, and that they should not mislead anyone about their procedures or methods.

While the Guidelines set the stage for appropriate practice in terms of recognizing an evaluator's responsibility to society, there is need to go further. Three areas may need to be considered for evaluation to progress in terms of adding value to society. First, the guidance to clearly communicate the methods and to avoid misleading others about them doesn't establish firm standards about what procedures and methods should be reported, nor the level of detail. For example, in terms of potential bias in the selection of interviewees, one must know how many potential interviewees were identified, how many refused, and conversely how many cooperated, to get a handle on the likely bias in the responses. Simply reporting that interviews were conducted and the number of individuals interviewed is not sufficient. In fact, the American Association for Public Opinion Research (AAPOR) has developed standards for reporting response rates and cooperation rates for telephone and mail surveys (AAPOR, 2006). These standards could be adapted for qualitative interviews and focus groups and extended to evaluation reports that involve original data collection. It is important to establish that evaluators should not mislead, but it is also important to develop standard definitions and minimum requirements for the amount of information that should be provided in order to avoid omitting information that could cause stakeholders and the public to be misled.

Second, the principles are silent with respect to intellectual property rights for the data collected as a part of the evaluation. If the evaluator does not explicitly have the right to use the data from an evaluation, then sponsors can prohibit distribution of findings that the sponsor finds detrimental to their interests. In these cases, information needed by the public to debunk bad ideas can be censored and the value of evaluation to society undermined. The Guidelines do acknowledge the special responsibility of evaluators who conduct publicly funded evaluations, but stop short of developing directions that would ensure public access to publicly funded evaluation reports. However, the Guidelines do specify that society's interests are "rarely" the same as specific stakeholder groups such as the sponsor and that evaluators have an obligation to society as a whole. This can be used as a basis for the argument that findings should be released, but consideration should be given to requiring that evaluators have intellectual property rights subject only to review provisions and the requirement to protect human subjects.

Finally, through dialogue and careful reasoning and eventually empirical evidence, we need to begin to consider whether there is a point at which a careful, rigorous assessment of the consequences of public policies and programs must be undertaken. It is possible for administrators who also control evaluation funds to focus evaluations on questions of program coverage, studies of variations in implementation, single case studies of a program or organization, descriptive studies of program participants, or subjective assessments of satisfaction. At a given time and in a specific situation, any of these could be the best choice for evaluation funding. But continually and indefinitely postponing addressing the public program effectiveness question cannot be in the interest of society.

There is no compelling answer to overcoming this non-methodological source of bias. Regulations requiring that efficacy tests of policies and programs be conducted prior to full implementation of a policy are not advisable.

Implementation problems may indeed hinder program effectiveness and need to be assessed prior to testing the effectiveness of the program. It may be that alternative institutions are needed to provide funding priorities for evaluations to assess program effectiveness. It may be that the role of agencies such as IES, the National Institute of Justice, and the National Institutes of Health is in part to rebalance existing institutional priorities. While evaluations sponsored and conducted by the agencies administering the programs are likely to be biased toward questions that do not include an assessment of the program's consequences, these quasi-independent institutes can help to ensure that methodologically sound evaluations of the consequences of public policies and programs receive a portion of the funding for evaluation.

Conclusion: So What Counts as Credible Evidence?

The IES proposal, which sparked the credibility war and to some extent this volume, presented an opportunity for evaluation and the development of a contingency-based theory of evaluation. Clearly, there are many approaches to evaluation. These approaches, including monitoring, effectiveness evaluation, implementation evaluation, and deliberative democratic evaluations of schools, have been developed to help make judgments about social policies, programs, and institutions. Rather than suggesting that effectiveness evaluation should drive out all other evaluation approaches, in this chapter I have made the case for the social benefits that can be derived from effectiveness evaluation. Moreover, I have argued that the benefits from sound, accurate, and fair assessments of program impacts are so important that we need to continue to develop institutional arrangements that will support high-quality impact evaluations. In summary, these conclusions have been drawn by making four points:

1. Modern democracies must produce accurate and highly credible information on the consequences of their policies and programs in order to "debunk bad ideas" and motivate reform that could yield greater social benefits.

2. The value to society of producing accurate and highly credible information about the effects of social programs motivates many of the evaluators that have been labeled "methods-based."

3. Many of the issues that were correctly identified in the initial efforts to conduct rigorous and well-run experimental, quasi-experimental, and observational studies have been improved through intense developmental work,

making the critique of evaluations in the 1970s and 1980s largely irrelevant to the debate about the utility or quality of rigorous designs conducted by 21st-century standards.

4. The institutional arrangements for making important findings widely available and ensuring that rigorous and fair impact evaluations receive adequate resources, given the benefits they produce for society, deserve the attention of the field of evaluation and those in the public policy communities.

This being said, another point from the chapter should be firmly and strongly emphasized in this summary. This point is for debate by those who see the importance of evaluation, mainly those in the various communities of evaluators. It is important and appropriate for students, parents, teachers, administrators, and local board members to understand how well a school is doing. These efforts should go beyond a review of average test scores, a cursory walk through the school, or casual conversations with teachers or students. Analogies can be drawn to hospitals, juvenile detention centers, police departments, long-term care facilities, public health offices, foster care agencies, and the list goes on. Society also needs information about how tax dollars are being spent and the extent to which the targeted beneficiaries of services are actually receiving the services. All of these evaluative activities take resources, and no matter how well one type of evaluation is undertaken, it does not substitute for the others. Therefore, we need to develop a contingency theory of evaluation that guides the allocation of limited evaluation resources, and we need to assess how well the fragmented and often financially constrained agencies and foundations that fund evaluation are doing.

In this chapter, I argue that Secretary Paige's priority statement redressed an existing imbalance in the allocation of evaluation funds within the Department of Education. The paucity of available evidence about the effects of different educational strategies, policies, and programs supports that contention. Only time, and a high-quality, rigorous evaluation of the impacts of the evaluations funded since 2003, will tell.

Notes

1. For the sake of full disclosure, it is important for you to know that I helped draft this statement and signed it.

2. It is important to note that probability samples eliminate human judgments about the selection of individuals, but flaws in the listings of the population can cause biases in selection.

References

Alkin, M. C., & Christie, C. A. (2004). An evaluation theory tree. In M. C. Alkin (Ed.), *Evaluation roots: Tracing theorists' views and influences*. Thousand Oaks, CA: Sage Publications.

American Association for Public Opinion Research. (2006). *Standard definitions: Final dispositions of case codes and outcome rates for surveys* (4th ed.). Lenexa, KS: Author.

American Evaluation Association. (2004). *American evaluation association guiding principles for evaluators*. Retrieved September 23, 2007, from http://www.eval .org/Publications/GuidingPrinciples.asp.

Bickman, L., Boruch, R. B., Cook, T. D., Cordray, D. S., Henry, G. T., Lipsey, M. W., et al. (2003). *Response to the Secretary's request for comment on the proposed priority on Scientifically Based Evaluation Methods*. Available online at http://www .eval.org/doestatement.htm.

Chatterji, M. (2004). Evidence on "what works": An argument for extended-term mixed-method (ETMM) evaluation designs. *Educational Researcher, 33*(9), 3–13.

Chelimsky, E. (2006, November). *Consequences of evaluation: A federal perspective*. Presentation at the Annual Meeting of the American Evaluation Association, Portland, OR.

Christie, C. A., & Alkin, M. C. (in press). Evaluation theory tree re-examined. *Evaluation*.

Dahl, R. (1956). *A preface to democratic theory: How does popular sovereignty function in America?* Chicago: University of Chicago Press.

Datta, L-e. (1982). A tale of two studies: The Westinghouse-Ohio evaluation of Project Head Start and the Consortium for Longitudinal Studies report. *Studies in Educational Evaluation, 8*(3).

Donaldson, S. I. (2001). Mediator and moderator analysis in program development. In S. Sussman (Ed.), *Handbook of program development for health behavior research and practice* (pp. 470–496). Newbury Park, CA: Sage Publications.

Graham, J. W., Hofer, S. M., & Piccinin, A. M. (1994). Analysis with missing data in drug prevention research. In L. M. Collins & L. Seitz (Eds.), *Advances in data analysis for prevention intervention research* (pp. 13–62). Washington, DC: National Institute on Drug Abuse.

Greenberg, D. H., Mandell, M. B., & Onstott, M. (2000). Evaluation research and its role in state welfare policy reform. *Journal of Policy Analysis and Management, 19*, 367–382.

Greenberg, D. H., & Shroder, M. (2004). *The digest of social experiments*. Washington, DC: Urban Institute Press.

Heckman, J., & Navarro-Lozano, S. (2004). Using matching, instrumental variables and control functions to estimate economic choice models. *Review of Economics and Statistics, 86*, 30–57.

Henry, G. T. (2001). How modern democracies are shaping evaluation and the emerging challenges. *American Journal of Evaluation, 22*(3), 419–429.

Henry, G. T. (2007). Practical sampling. In L. Bickman & D. Rog (Eds.), *The handbook of social science research methods* (2nd ed.). Thousand Oaks, CA: Sage Publications.

Henry, G. T., & Mark, M. M. (2003). Toward an agenda for research on evaluation. In C. A. Christie (Ed.), The practice–theory relationship in evaluation (pp. 69–80). (Vol. 97 of *New Directions for Evaluation* series). San Francisco: Jossey-Bass.

House, E. R. (2006, November). *Blowback.* Presentation at the Annual Meeting of the American Evaluation Association, Portland, OR.

House, E. R., & Howe, K. R. (1999). *Values in evaluation and social research.* Thousand Oaks, CA: Sage Publications.

Hox, J. J. (2002). *Multilevel analysis: Techniques and applications.* Mahwah, NJ: Lawrence Erlbaum.

Hurley, S. L. (1989). *Natural reasons: Personality and polity.* New York: Oxford University Press.

King, G., Honaker, J., Joseph, A., & Schieve, K. (2001). Analyzing incomplete political science data: An alternative algorithm for multiple imputation. *American Political Science Review, 95*(1), 49–63.

Mark, M. M., & Henry, G. T. (2004). The mechanisms and outcomes of evaluation influence. *Evaluation, 10*(1), 35–57.

Mark, M. M., Henry, G. T., & Julnes, G. (2000). *Evaluation: An integrated framework for understanding, guiding, and improving policies and programs.* San Francisco: Jossey-Bass.

Pressman, J. L., & Wildavsky, A. (1973). *Implementation: How great expectations in Washington are dashed in Oakland; or, Why it's amazing that federal programs work at all.* Berkeley: University of California Press.

Raudenbush, S. W., & Bryk, A. S. (2001). *Hierarchical linear models: Applications and data analysis methods* (2nd ed.). Thousand Oaks, CA: Sage Publications.

Ravallion, M. (2001). The mystery of the vanishing benefits: An introduction on impact evaluation. *The World Bank Economic Review, 15*(1), 115–140.

Rosenbaum, P. R. (2002). Attributing effects to treatment in matched observational studies. *Journal of the American Statistical Association, 97*(457), 183–192.

Rosenbaum, P. R., & Rubin, D. B. (1983). The central role of the propensity score in observational studies for causal effects. *Biometrika, 70,* 41–55.

Rossi, P. (1994). The war between the quals and the quants: Is a lasting peace possible? In C. S. Reichardt & S. F. Rallis (Eds.), *The qualitative-quantitative debate: New perspectives* (pp. 23–36). (Vol. 61 in *New Directions for Evaluation* series). San Francisco: Jossey-Bass.

Rubin, D. B. (2001). Using propensity scores to help design observational studies: Application to the tobacco litigation. *Health Services and Outcomes Research Methodology, 2,* 169–188.

Schafer, J. L. (1997). *Analysis of incomplete multivariate data.* London: Chapman & Hall.

Schafer. J. L., & Graham, J. W. (2002). Missing data: Our view of the state of the art. *Psychological Methods, 7*(2), 147–177.

Stufflebeam, D. (2001). Evaluation models. *New Directions for Evaluation, 89,* 7–98.

U.S. Department of Education. (2003, November 4). Scientifically based evaluation methods. *Federal Register, 68,* 213. RIN 1890-ZA00. Retrieved September 23, 2007, from http://www.eval.org/doestatement.htm.

Weiss, C. H. (1979). The many meanings of research utilization. *Public Administration Review, 39,* 426–431.

4

Randomized Controlled Trials

A Gold Standard With Feet of Clay?

Leonard Bickman

Stephanie M. Reich

Randomized controlled or clinical trials or RCTs[1] have been taking on increasing importance, especially outside of the medical field. The number of RCTs is increasing as well as the number of areas in which they are conducted (Bloom, in press; Boruch, Weisburd, Turner, Karpyn, & Littell, in press). Moreover, these designs are being recommended and favored over other designs by prestigious research organizations (e.g., Shavelson & Towne, 2002). In addition, several U.S. federal agencies deemed the RCT as the gold standard that should be used in considering the funding of research and evaluation but also in initiating and terminating programs (Brass, Nunez-Neto, & Williams, 2006). However, over the last several years, there has been considerable debate about whether RCTs should be the gold standard (Cook & Payne, 2002; Maxwell, 2004).

AUTHORS' NOTE: We are not the first to use metals to describe standards. Both Rossi (1987) and Berk (2005) have used similar terms, but we take full responsibility for the mixed metaphor in the chapter title.

While most would argue that the RCT is a powerful research design, many debate whether it should be labeled as the standard. Dissenters of this design as the model for research cite issues of appropriateness, ethics, feasibility, and cost, arguing that other methods can answer causal questions equally well. Most claim that RCTs are more appropriate for medical and basic science investigations, where such things as blinding are possible, and not for the bulk of behavioral science research. For instance, Michael Scriven (2005) argues that numerous other designs can infer causation for far less money and in less time than the RCT. He lists cross-sectional designs with triangulation of information, regression discontinuity designs, and interrupted time series designs as just a few equally, if not more, credible designs. Others note that some research areas are not amenable to RCTs, such as safe-sex interventions for HIV/AIDS prevention (e.g., Van de Ven & Aggleton, 1999); broad spectrum programs (e.g., Cook & Campbell, 1979); and, comically, the efficacy of parachutes (Smith & Pell, 2003).

The debate over RCTs as the gold standard for research is highly relevant to the evaluation of social and educational programs that are designed to improve the quality of lives of others. At the heart of this dispute is whether RCTs are the only credible design for testing causal relationship. That is, are the findings believable, trustworthy, convincing, and reliable, and do specific designs, like the RCT, truly yield more credible findings? To address these issues, this chapter will first briefly focus on the issue of credibility and its subjective nature. Then we will consider how credible RCTs are for the study of cause-and-effect relationships. We will describe some of the important limitations of RCTs and briefly consider alternative designs.

Credibility

Credibility is a highly subjective term. The quality of evidence cannot be determined without knowing which questions were asked and why, what evidence was gathered to answer these questions, who asked the questions and gathered the evidence, how the evidence was gathered and analyzed, and under which conditions the evaluation was undertaken. In addition to these foundational issues, credibility is also influenced by the depth and breadth of the study as well as whether the findings are based on a single study or conclusions drawn about the effectiveness of sets or types of interventions. In other words, much more goes into the judgment of the credibility of research than just the design. While we will discuss some of the broader issues related to credibility, we will concentrate mostly on how the design of the study affects its credibility, since this is the focus of the current debate over the gold standard for research and evaluation.

One aim of this chapter is to discuss elements of RCTs that increase or threaten credibility. This is a daunting task since we believe that credibility is highly subjective. Credibility is a perceived quality and does not reside in an object, person, or piece of information. Thus, what is called credible will be different for different people and under different situations. For assessing credibility in evaluation, we argue that there needs to be a consensus among persons recognized as experts in what they label credible. In this chapter, we will describe the elements of an RCT that make it more or less credible to determine causal relations.

It is important to note that the RCT's designation as the gold standard is based on theoretical or potential characteristics of RCTs. The chapter will describe some of the issues that arise when implementing an RCT that affect its credibility.

Causation, Epistemology, and Credibility

An important component of credibility is what is defined as knowledge and which methods are used to obtain, discover, or create this knowledge. For instance, in comparing qualitative and quantitative methods, the ontological, epistemological, and theoretical issues of what are "data," how they are analyzed, and what interpretations are drawn from them are viewed quite differently (Brannan, 2005). Although there have been some efforts to critique the quality, trustworthiness, and transferability of qualitative research (e.g., Rolfe, 2006) and similarly the quality and internal, external, statistical conclusion, and construct validity of quantitative research (Shadish, Cook, & Campbell, 2002), epistemological disagreements exist on both sides. Even those who utilize mixed methods acknowledge that the epistemological arguments remain (Howe, 2004; Onwuegbuzie & Leech, 2005).

Although epistemology is an important component of credibility, it is beyond the scope of this chapter. Discussing what qualifies as evidence or "truth" would take far more space than this book allows. Therefore, for the purpose of this chapter, we will focus solely on the credibility of studies utilizing quantitative methods. In particular, our discussion will examine claims that the "cause" resulted in the "effect" and whether RCTs should be the gold standard in quantitative program evaluation. While we limit this discussion to post-positivistic quantitative methods, we recognize that no single method can be used to address every question and that different methodologies may yield different answers.

The Cost of Making a Wrong Decision About Causality

We know that there are costs in making a wrong decision. To call a program effective when it is not means that valuable resources may be wasted and the search for other means to solve the problem will be hindered. Some programs may not only be ineffective but also harmful. In such cases, the costs of a wrong decision would be higher. On the other hand, falsely labeling a program as ineffective would mean that clients who would have benefited from the intervention will not have that benefit. Some examples illustrate the point. Imagine the identification of a drug as effective when it is not. Patients taking this drug would not have their condition improve and in some cases would continue to deteriorate. Further, if producing the drug takes hundreds of millions of dollars, the financial cost of this mistake is high. Conversely, if the drug were ineffective but costs only pennies to manufacture, there would be little waste of financial resources. While those taking the medication will not benefit from the treatment, the low cost would not inhibit the development of other medications. Thus, it is more likely that patients would receive effective medication in the future (assuming pharmaceutical research continues), although not as likely as if the drug was accurately labeled as ineffective. While mislabeling a drug as effective is problematic, this problem is exacerbated when the cost is high. The ramifications of the drug example above are somewhat straightforward, yet for most interventions the situation is not as clear. Most studies do not compute the costs of the intervention, let alone the cost of a wrong conclusion. Thus, credible research is needed to minimize wrong decisions and the subsequent human and financial costs. Later we will describe some actual medical decisions that were based on the use of a weak design.

The RCT as the "Gold Standard" of Evidence

RCTs are often thought of as providing more credible evidence than other research designs. This sentiment was demonstrated by the U.S. Secretary of Education's change in funding priorities in 2003 to give highest priority to RCTs.[2] While we agree that an RCT is a powerful research design, it is not immune to threats to validity. In fact, RCTs are just as vulnerable to threats to construct and statistical conclusion validity as other designs. Below we critique the validity and subsequent credibility of RCTs, with special attention to internal validity—that is, the cause-effect relationship.

Why RCTs Are High in Internal Validity

RCTs have high internal validity because each participant has an equal chance of being assigned to each group, which reduces the likelihood of a systematic bias in the selection and assignment of participants, the main threat to internal validity. Thus, random assignment rules out numerous rival hypotheses for the effects found that are based on initial participant differences. We will not describe all the threats to internal validity, as practically any book on program evaluation or research methods will list them. Instead, we will focus on the more visible threats and those that have not been widely discussed in relation to experimental designs.

More Visible Threats to Internal Validity That RCTs Share

While RCTs minimize some of the threats to internal validity, they are not immune from all. In fact, the majority of threats to drawing valid causal inferences remain. Some of these threats are well-known, such as experimenter effects, allegiance, history, and attrition, and others are less often acknowledged. First we will address the more often-cited threats.

Experimenter Effects

RCTs can be influenced by the behavior of the experimenter/evaluator. The most commonly acknowledged behaviors are experimenter expectancies in which the experimenter knows who is getting the intended treatment or "cause," and this either influences how the "effect" is recorded or how the participant is treated, thus influencing the observed effect. This threat is most often controlled for by using blinding or masking. The most common example of this is double-blinded drug studies in which both the participants and researcher do not know who is receiving the experimental drug or placebo. It is rare to have single-blinded let alone double-blinded RCTs in the social sciences (Kumar & Oakley-Browne, 2001). Moreover, although hundreds of studies have been conducted on experimenter expectancy effects (Rosenthal, 1976) and the broader term *demand characteristics* (Rosnow, 2002), it is not known how strong these effects are in the "real world" and under which conditions they will produce a significant bias in the results. A similar caution is expressed about the so-called Hawthorne effect, for which we believe there is no supporting evidence (Adair, Sharpe, & Huynh, 1989).

Allegiance Effects

Similar to experimenter expectancies is the bias caused by allegiance. Allegiance bias occurs when the experimenter develops or supports the treatment (intended "cause"), and this influences the observed or reported "effect." For instance, in the area of clinical psychology, Luborsky and colleagues (1999) compared 29 different individual therapies and found a correlation of 0.85 between differential investigator allegiances and differential treatment outcomes. Even if participants are randomly assigned to conditions, the experimenters' expectations and behaviors can systematically bias results. The allegiance effect can be controlled for rather simply by making sure that persons other than the originator of the program conduct the evaluation.

Local History

The validity of RCTs can be threatened when one group is exposed to external events that can affect the outcome, but not the other group. In these situations, it does not matter how people were assigned since a systematic bias is introduced to one group of participants and not the other. While it may be impossible for a researcher to prevent such an occurrence, the possibility of such an event requires the monitoring of both experimental and control conditions.

Attrition

One of the strengths of random assignment is its ability to minimize the effects of systematic initial differences among participants. However, this equivalence may be threatened when attrition occurs, especially if the attrition differentially affects one group and not the other. When attrition happens more in one condition than another, or if different types of attrition occur, then the experimental design is transformed into a nonequivalent comparison group design and the benefits of random assignment may be lost (Lipsey & Cordray, 2000). Systematic attrition—that is, attrition that is not at random—can have grave effects on the accuracy of causal inferences (Shadish, Hu, Glaser, Kownacki, & Wong, 1998), especially if the reasons for dropping out are inaccessible and how participants vary is unknown (Graham & Donaldson, 1993).

There are several approaches to diagnosing attrition (Foster & Bickman, 2000), but one of the more popular approaches to correcting the attrition problem is propensity scoring (e.g., Leon et al., 2006; Shadish, Luellen, & Clark, 2006; VanderWeele, 2006). Propensity scoring may also be useful even if differential attrition did not appear to occur. In these situations, propensity scores help account for differences that are not obvious (Rosenbaum & Rubin, 1983). However, the use of statistical equating techniques is not without controversy. Some question whether it can be done, while others argue about how it should be done (Baser, 2006; West & Thoemmes, in press). Moreover, there are important innovative approaches to strengthening the validity of quasi-experiments that do not use statistical adjustment but focus on designing more internally valid research approaches (Cook & Wong, in press).

Less Well-Recognized Threats to Internal Validity

When random assignment is feasible and well implemented, it can be an effective method for untangling the effects of systematic participant differences from program effects (Boruch, 1998; Keppel, 1991). However, random assignment alone is not sufficient to ensure high-quality evaluations with credible findings. As noted above, numerous other design, measurement, and implementation issues must be considered in order to make causal inferences. Some of these, which are described above, are commonly noted in the literature. Other threats to internal validity are not often acknowledged. Thus, we would like to draw your attention to a few.

Subject Preference Before Random Assignment

Since properly implemented random assignment ensures an equal chance of assignment to each group, it ignores individual preferences including individual decision-making preferences that might exist (McCall & Green, 2004; McCall, Ryan, & Plemons, 2003). For instance, drawing a sample from only those who are willing to be randomly assigned may not produce equivalent groups if participants have preferences for one condition over another. Suppose 80 people want condition A and 20 prefer condition B. Of the 50 people randomly assigned to condition A, the chances are that 80%, or 40, will end up in their preferred condition. Of the 50 people assigned to condition B, 20%, or 10, will be in their preferred condition.

Willingness to be randomly assigned and preferences for a treatment condition are clearly not the same. Faddis, Ahrens-Gray, and Klein (2000) experienced this problem in their effort to compare school-based and home-based Head Start services. In this study, researchers found that many families who were randomly assigned to home-based child care programs rather than Head Start (school-based) centers, never enrolled their children and when they did, they were more likely to attrite. Thus, the families that enrolled and remained in the evaluation may have been systematically different by condition from those families that did not complete enrollment. It would also appear from the attrition patterns of this study that some families prefer center-based Head Start to home-based Head Start services. These preferences may have affected how beneficial each type of program was to families and the conclusions drawn from the comparison.

Similar results have been found in mental health services research (Corrigan & Salzer, 2003; Macias et al., 2005). For instance, Chilvers and colleagues (2001) found that patients who chose counseling did better than those who received the services because of randomization. Similarly, in a review of the influence of patient and physician preferences in medical research, King and colleagues (2005) found evidence that preferences can influence outcomes; however, this effect was minimized in larger trials.

In order to address the effect of preference in RCTs, some have advocated for a patient preference RCT/comprehensive cohort design, or two-stage randomized design (Brewin & Bradley, 1989; Howard & Thornicroft, 2006). In the first two designs, some of the people with clear treatment preferences are enrolled in their desired treatment while the rest (those with and without strong preferences) are randomly assigned to a treatment condition. In the two-stage randomized design, all participants are randomized into two groups. The first group is able to select their treatment and the second group is randomized to the treatment condition. These variations of the RCT allow evaluators to estimate the degree to which a preference systematically biases results as well as assess how representative the randomized sample is to the general population (those with preferences and without). While this approach may "work," it is not feasible in most conditions since there are rarely the abundant resources, i.e., participants and money, needed to apply these designs.

Unmasked Assignment

Theoretically, RCTs should not have any selection bias because of the random assignment of participants to conditions. Unfortunately, sometimes the random assignment process breaks down. The potential breakdown may be suspected when the person doing the random assignment knows which condition will be used next. This is described as an unmasked trial. Berger and Weinstein (2004) found several instances of this problem in major clinical trials, and Greenhouse (2003) warns that finding significant baseline differences with an unmasked trial is clear evidence of the manipulation of random assignment.

Smaller Sample Size Than Expected

The reduction of selection bias due to random assignment is based on the notion that with a large enough sample, potentially biasing participant characteristics will be distributed evenly across groups. However, many studies do not include sample sizes large enough to truly protect against systematic bias. As Keppel (1991) warns, "we never run sufficiently large numbers of subjects in our experiments to qualify for the statistician's definition of the 'long run.' In practice, we are operating in the 'short run,' meaning that we have no guarantee that our groups will be equivalent with regards to differences in environmental features or the abilities of subjects" (p. 15). In small sample studies, the threat of selection bias is much greater regardless of random assignment of participants to conditions.

One-Time Random Assignment

If we took the same people and reassigned them to groups randomly, there would inevitably be differences in group means obtained, as "any observed comparisons between the outcome for the experimental group and the outcome for the control group confounds possible treatment effects with random variation in group composition" (Berk, 2005, p. 422). Thus, findings from an RCT only provide information on a specific configuration of people and do not necessarily apply if the people were regrouped. Thus, all single studies should be judged with caution. This is a reminder that in science all findings are provisional—regardless of the method used.

Threats to Between-Group Differences—Even in RCTs

There are other threats to the internal validity of randomized experiments found in almost any textbook on research design that seem plausible but appear to be without any empirical support, at least none we could find.

Resentful Demoralization

When the control group or a weaker treatment group knows that they are not getting the treatment, they may become demoralized and not perform as well. Thus, differences at posttest may be due to decreased performance of the control group and not enhanced performance of the treatment group. Unfortunately, it is difficult to demonstrate that the control group deteriorated while the treatment group held its own, rather than a real effect occurring. Blinding or masking helps protect against this. Moreover, we do not know if this artifact is rare or the magnitude of its effect.

Compensatory Rivalry—John Henry Effect

Knowledge of whether you are in the treatment or control group can also have the opposite effect of demoralization. Instead of losing motivation, the control group members may become even more motivated to perform, just to "show them." John Henry may have been a real person, but his relevance to research design is based on legend. John Henry was a "steel-driving man" who competed against a steam machine to drive spikes into the railroad cross ties. Although he won the race, he died soon after. Because of his knowledge of the machine's advantage, John Henry did not become demoralized but became more motivated to beat the machine.

In a similar fashion, a control group's members might compete more strongly against a more heavily resourced experimental condition to demonstrate their prowess.

Lack of External Validity in RCTs

While this chapter focuses on the credibility of RCTs in drawing causal inferences, we must note the most often-cited criticism of this design is its reduced external validity. Clearly, if the focus of an evaluation is whether a program is effective, then understanding for whom and under what conditions it is effective is important as well. Unfortunately, the nature of volunteerism and the evaluator's ability only to randomly assign those willing to be in any group can limit the generalizability of findings. This has led many to question whether causal inferences are enough of a benefit when RCTs may create artificial circumstances and findings that may not be generalizable to other settings, people, or times (Cronbach, 1982; Heckman & Smith, 1995; Raudenbush, 2002). Berk (2005) states this strongly by claiming, "It cannot be overemphasized that unless an experiment can be generalized at least a bit, time and resources have been wasted. One does not really care about the results of a study unless its conclusions can be used to guide future decisions. Generalization is a prerequisite for that guidance" (p. 428).

The validity of the RCT depends upon the investigators' intention to study the effectiveness of a "cause" in the real world or its efficacy in more of a laboratory context. While Cook and Campbell (1979) described internal validity as the sine qua non of research, external validity is essential for research in applied contexts. It is clear that the health sector values internal validity over external validity (Glasgow et al., 2006), as the research standards of the medical field (e.g., CONSORT) do not deal with external validity. Currently, it is likely that a "tightly designed" study that is high in internal validity is more likely to be published and a grant application approved even if it is low in external validity.

Judging the external validity is often more difficult than assessing internal validity. How are we to know if the results will apply in the future in some other context? Predicting the future is difficult under any circumstances, but it is especially difficult when we do not know what factors moderate the treatment. We agree that it is too limiting to focus solely on internal validity. The best way to assure external validity is to conduct the study in a setting that is as close as possible to the one that the program would operate in if it was adopted. We see the recent emphasis on research transportability and bridging science and practice to be a step toward valuing external validity.

Appropriateness of the Comparison

Another aspect of external validity beyond volunteerism is the use of the appropriate comparison. Some RCTs are well implemented but conceptually flawed due to the use of an inappropriate comparison group. When this occurs, the internal validity may be high but the utility of the study (i.e., external validity) is low. For instance, in a review of pharmaceutical-funded versus independent investigator–implemented RCTs, Lexchin, Bero, Djulbegovic, and Clark (2003) found that new drugs were typically compared to placebo conditions rather than another medication. As such, large effects were found yet the drugs' performance in comparison to current treatments was unexplored. Here, the RCTs were well executed but were not much of a contribution to science or human well-being. Thus, external validity is essential for the credibility if the findings are going to be applied.

Other Issues Raised With RCTs

Privileging Certain Types of Research

The belief that RCTs are indeed the gold standard of research implies that other studies employing other designs are weaker and thus, less credible. The implications of this are that research areas amenable to the conduct of RCTs are by their very nature more credible. This introduces an unintended side effect of championing the RCT. For example, it is much easier to conduct a randomized double-blind study of a psychotropic drug than to evaluate a type of psychotherapy. This implies that drug studies are more credible, on the average, than psychotherapy studies. In a similar fashion, total coverage or mandated programs cannot be feasibly evaluated using an RCT. In the former, everyone is receiving the treatment and thus none can be randomly assigned because it would be illegal to withhold the benefit. This does not mean that these programs are immune to study, only that they cannot be studied using an RCT. However, their findings can still be credible.

A similar issue of privileging research occurs when the use of RCTs promotes more investigation into a low-priority area resulting in resources being spent in less beneficial areas. For instance, in the area of HIV interventions, before truly potent antiretroviral therapy was discovered, 25 RCTs found spuriously significant effects for a variety of treatments of approved, controversial, and contraindicated medications. This resulted in what Ioannidis (2006) calls a domino effect when "one research findings being accepted leads to other findings becoming seemingly more credible as well. This creates webs of information and practices to which we assign considerable credibility, while they may all be false and useless" (p. e36).

Ethical Issues

There are ethical issues in using the RCT because of the possibility that effective treatments may be denied to some. There have been many discussions of the ethics of design (Boruch et al., in press; Fisher & Anushko, in press; Sieber, in press) and we will briefly summarize them here. First, if it is known with some degree of certainty that one treatment is better than another, then one must question why the study is to be conducted. It is only when we do not know the relative effectiveness that an RCT is called for. Second, in almost all cases a treatment group is compared to another treatment and not a no-treatment condition. This use of an active control is important for methodological as well as ethical issues. Some conditions are especially appropriate, from an ethical point of view, for using an RCT. When there are more in need than there are treatments, it seems especially fair to distribute the treatment by lot or randomly, thus giving everyone an equal chance of obtaining the experimental treatment.

Difficulties can arise and bias results when the clinical staff does not believe that the effectiveness of the treatment is unknown. Why select a treatment to test if it was not likely that it was effective? Another bias that may be introduced is when the clinician believes that the treatment will work better with a particular type of client. This is one reason why the investigator should maintain strict control over the random assignment process.

Sometimes the random assignment of participants would be unethical, making an RCT inappropriate. For instance, the recent attempted Children's

Environmental Exposure Research Study of the effects of pesticides on babies in Florida was halted due to national response to the questionable ethics of such a study to be carried out by the EPA (Johnson, 2005). Just because an RCT is possible does not mean it should be conducted. Smith and Pell (2003) make this point well in their satirical article, "Parachute Use to Prevent Death and Major Trauma Related to Gravitational Challenge: Systematic Review of Randomized Controlled Trials."

Multilevel/Cluster Designs

In addition to ethical issues, feasibility factors into whether the RCT is the best design to use. Randomized experiments where the unit of assignment is not an individual but a group such as a school or classroom offer a special challenge because of covariation due to nesting of units within other units. This research is most often found in educational research where the treatment may be introduced at the class, school, or even district level. In such cases, there is a strong consensus that the appropriate analysis is at the unit of random assignment. Thus, if schools are randomly assigned, then the school should be the unit of analysis. The major drawback to this position is the drastic reduction of degrees of freedom. In the not-too-distant past, researchers randomly assigning an intervention to, for example, eight schools with 500 students each would analyze the data as if there were 4,000 participants (8 × 500) instead of 8. By not considering nesting, the analyst is not taking into account the intercorrelation coefficient (ICC) between students and classes within a school. This ICC can seriously affect the statistical power of the design.

For instance, Varnell, Murray, Janega, and Blitstein (2004) reviewed 60 group- or cluster-randomized trials (GRTs) published in the *American Journal of Public Health and Preventive Medicine* from 1998 through 2002. The authors found that only nine (15.0%) GRTs reported evidence of using appropriate methods for sample size estimation. Of 59 articles in the analytic review, 27 (45.8%) reported at least one inappropriate analysis and 12 (20.3%) reported only inappropriate analyses. Nineteen (32.2%) reported analyses at an individual or subgroup level, ignoring group, or included group as a fixed effect. Thus, interclass correlations were largely ignored. In an attempt to deal with this problem, there are now Consort Standards (described later) that can be used in evaluating the quality of cluster designs (Campbell, Elbourne, & Altman, 2004).

Using the correct level of analysis has important implications for the design of RCTs. Now instead of counting students, we need to count schools. While there is not a one-to-one loss in statistical power, i.e., one student is equivalent to one school, it will typically take close to 40 schools to detect a small to medium effect size between two conditions. While this is a difficult requirement, it is more feasible in education than in other areas. For instance, in our current Institute of Educational Sciences–funded grant, it is feasible to randomly assign the necessary 60 schools out of the 120 in the school district. Fortunately, there are school districts that have many schools within them. However, this is not the case for areas outside of education. In the area of mental health, randomizing at the mental health center level is difficult. Currently, we are conducting an RCT using 40 different mental health sites. If we were not collaborating with the country's largest provider of mental health services for children, we do not believe the study could be conducted. Moreover, the expense of conducting these multisite studies is very high, especially compared to single-site research.

Do RCTs Have Different Outcomes From Other Designs?

While RCTs are often called the gold standard of research, one must question whether these designs yield different results from quasi-experimental designs. A recent and very visible example of an RCT producing findings that were different from those of a nonrandomized design is the research on hormone replacement therapy for women. Previous nonrandom trials indicated positive effects of the therapy, while a randomized trial found negative effects (Shumaker et al., 2003). Similarly, in a meta-analysis comparison of psychotherapy studies using RCTs and quasi-experiments, Shadish and Ragsdale (1996) concluded that under some circumstances a well-conducted quasi-experiment can produce adequate estimations of the results obtained from a randomized study; however, they concluded that randomized experiments are still the gold standard.

Since then, other studies have been completed comparing experimental and quasi-experimental designs. These studies have not produced consistent findings. Some research has found different outcomes favoring randomized experiments (e.g., Glazerman, Levy, & Myers, 2003), while others found that quasi-experiments produced outcomes of unknown accuracy (e.g., Rosenbaum, 2002). However, all the previous studies shared a flaw that made the results even less certain. All of them confound assignment method with other study variables. Shadish and Clark (2007), in an unpublished manuscript, used an innovative procedure to untangle these confounds by first randomly assigning students to either a random assignment condition or a self-selection procedure. The authors found that both the random assignment condition and self-selection condition produced similar results after adjusting the self-selection procedure with propensity scores. However, the authors caution that these results may not generalize since they were conducted in a college laboratory using college students as participants, and that the results appear to be sensitive to how missing data in the predictors are handled.

Approaches to Judging the Credibility of RCTs

There have been several approaches to evaluating the quality of an RCT. Probably the most widespread is the Consolidated Standards of Reporting Trials (CONSORT). Around 1995, two efforts to improve the quality of reports of RCTs led to the publication of the CONSORT statement. These standards were developed for medical clinical trials but can be used with some modification in any RCT. The CONSORT statement consists of a checklist and flow diagram for reporting an RCT. They were designed for use in writing, reviewing, or evaluating reports of simple two-group parallel RCTs. The standards apply to the reporting of an RCT but may be considered a proxy of the actual conduct of the study. This assumes that the published article accurately describes the methods. Huwiler-Müntener, Juni, Junker, and Egger (2002) found that methodological quality of published articles as rated by reviewers was associated with reported quality indicated by a subset of the CONSORT standards. Soares and colleagues (2004) compared the published quality of randomized controlled trials performed by the Radiation Therapy Oncology Group to the actual protocol used in each study. The authors found that the published version of the article underestimated the quality of the protocol used. Unfortunately, the authors only compared the absolute level of quality and not the correlation between quality of the reports and quality of the protocol.

The key aspects of the checklist that relate specifically to RCTs are summarized in Table 4.1.

There have been several studies in quite a few medical specialties that have examined whether research published in their journals has improved since the release of the standards. Kane, Wang, and Garrard (2007) examined RCTs published in two medical journals before and after the CONSORT guidelines were evaluated; one journal used the CONSORT statement (JAMA) and one did not (NEJM). The results indicated that reporting improved in both journals, but JAMA showed significantly more improvement in all aspects of RCT reporting. Several other studies found similar results (Moher, Jones, & Lepage, 2001; Plint et al., 2006).

The publication of the CONSORT standards has had a greater effect on research in medicine than on research in the behavioral sciences. For instance, Spring, Pagoto, Knatterud, Kozak, and Hedeker (2007) examined

Table 4.1   Key Aspects of the Checklist That Relate Specifically to RCTs

Section and Topic	Descriptor
Randomization	
a. Sequence generation	a. Method used to generate the random allocation sequence, including details of any restrictions (e.g., blocking, stratification).
b. Allocation concealment	b. Method used to implement the random allocation sequence (e.g., numbered containers or central telephone), clarifying whether the sequence was concealed until interventions were assigned.
c. Implementation	c. Who generated the allocation sequence, who enrolled participants, and who assigned participants to their groups.
Blinding (masking)	Whether or not participants, those administering the interventions, and those assessing the outcomes were blinded to group assignment. If done, how the success of blinding was evaluated.

SOURCE: Based on Moher, Schulz, and Altman (2001).

the analytic quality of RCTs published in two leading behavioral journals and two medical journals. One of the criteria used was intention to treat (ITT), where the analysis includes all participants kept in the assigned group regardless of whether they experienced the condition in that group. Not only did more reports in medical journals (48%) state that they were going to use ITT than in behavioral journals (24%), but more also used it correctly in the medical journals (57%) than in behavioral journals (34%). Moreover, the articles in the top psychology journals were less likely than those in medical journals to describe a primary outcome, give a reason for estimating study size, describe the denominators that were used in the analysis of the primary outcomes, and account for missing data in analyses.

In the area of social and behavioral research, the Society for Prevention Research (SPR) has established broader standards that provide criteria with which to judge the credibility of evidence for efficacy, effectiveness, and dissemination (Flay et al., 2005). These broader concerns require criteria dealing with the intervention, measures, analysis, and other aspects of research. We will focus on those standards related to determining the credibility of causal statements. These are

Standard 3: The design must allow for the strongest possible causal statements;

Standard 3.b: Assignment to conditions needs to minimize the statistical bias in the estimate of the relative effects of the intervention and allow for a legitimate statistical statement of confidence in the results; and

Standard 3.b.i: For generating statistically unbiased estimates of the effects of most kinds of preventive interventions, random assignment is essential. (p. 157)

SPR supports the use of nonrandomized designs when necessary, for example for total coverage programs or when ethical considerations do not allow such a design. The alternatives suggested are the interrupted time series and regression-discontinuity designs. The requirements of these latter two designs severely limit their use. A third design, matched case-control design, is viewed as acceptable only when there is a pretest demonstration of group equivalence. To be credible, this necessitates demonstrating equivalence by using sufficiently powered tests on several baselines or pretests of multiple outcomes and the inclusion of major covariates. The key is to provide convincing evidence that the lack of a random assignment process did not result in a correlation between unmeasured variables and condition.

Other Approaches to Establishing Causality

There are other research designs found to be scientifically acceptable in other disciplines that do not involve experiments, let alone RCTs. These disciplines include geology, astronomy, engineering, medical forensics, and medical laboratory testing. In some cases, it is impossible to conduct experiments, such as in astronomy. Like RCTs, approaches in these fields rely on observational methods. Extremely precise predictions, exacting measurement, and exceptionally large numbers of replications are what these fields have in common. While it is important to note that other observational methods are scientifically acceptable ways to establish causality, it is equally important to understand that they are credible only under conditions that rarely, if ever, occur in the social sciences.

An approach that is more suitable to the social sciences is known as the program theory, theory-driven, or pattern-matching method (Bickman & Peterson, 1990; Chen & Rossi, 1983; Donaldson, 2003; Scriven, 2005). These are nonexperimental, observational methods that use complex predictions to support a causal hypothesis. In some ways, they are like astronomical research without the precision. This approach is not in opposition to RCTs and has been used in RCTs and quasi-experiments as a way of understanding what is occurring in the black box of the program. We fully realize that RCTs can directly answer only a very limited number of questions, and we must depend on other approaches to fill the gaps.

While both experimental and quasi-experimental designs have numerous threats to the validity of conclusions drawn, the RCT, when implemented well, controls for more threats than nonexperimental designs (in the social sciences). As such, well-executed RCTs are more credible in determining causal relationships. However, the argument has been made that they are inherently less feasible, more costly, and more difficult to implement. Having conducted many RCTs and quasi-experimental designs, we do not agree.

Feasibility

RCTs have been criticized as being difficult to conduct and lacking feasibility. We would argue that the existence of so many RCTs belies that criticism. In a report to Congress, the Congressional Research Service cited the number of RCTs as of 2002 as 250,000 in medicine and 11,000 in all the social sciences combined (Brass et al., 2006). While the number is 20 times more in medicine, 11,000 is still a significant number of RCTs. Two other examples are the Cochrane Collaboration (www.cochrane.org), which has over 350,000 RCTs registered, and the Campbell Collaboration (Petrosino, Boruch, Rounding, McDonald, & Chalmers, 2000; www.campbellcollaboration.org), which contains over 13,000 RCTs in the social sciences (Boruch, 2005). While there are some specific conditions in which RCTs could not or should not be implemented, these appear to be rare rather than the modal situation.

Practical Issues in the Conduct of RCTs

Currently, we both are conducting RCTs in such areas as mental health, education, and parenting. In addition to these studies, the senior author has conducted over 20 large-scale RCTs in his career in several areas, representing over $20 million in external funding. Having worked with numerous types of designs, we have not found RCTs to be more difficult to implement than matched-comparison designs.

Limited Treatment Resources

The *Congressional Research Service Report* (Brass et al., 2006) suggests that RCTs take longer to conduct, are more expensive, and in general are more difficult to implement than nonrandomized designs. This is clearly true when RCTs are compared to pre-experimental designs such as the simple post only or pre-post designs. As noted earlier, the fair comparison is with designs that include a control group.

There are some conditions that are optimal for an RCT. If there are more people who want a service than can be provided for, then the fairest way to determine who receives the service is usually by lot or random assignment. Often, the service provider might insist that severity should serve as the criteria for admissions. It is possible to argue that within every measure of severity, there is a band of uncertainty within which random assignment could be done. However, this limits the power of the study as well as the external validity. In such cases, the regression-discontinuity design may be more appropriate.

Nonequivalent Control Group

Finding a comparison group can often be more difficult than randomly assigning participants to conditions. Assuming that such a group could be found, there is still the difficulty of convincing the control group organization to collect data when there is no benefit to the organization or clients for participating in the study. In addition, more analyses must be conducted to assess a pretest of group differences and, when possible, propensity for group assignment.

Cost Is Cost

As mentioned earlier, cost is often raised as a consideration in implementing an RCT. The cost of including a comparison group should be the same whether random assignment is used or not. However, in many quasi-experiments, the control group is not in the same location as the treatment group, often necessitating increased expenses either due to travel or the staffing of a remote site. If the experimenter is very confident of the randomization process (e.g., the sample is very large), then it is possible to do a posttest only design with the assumption that the treatment and control groups were equivalent before the study started. This would cut data collection costs in half! Hak, Wei, Grobbee, and Nichol (2004) found only one empirical study that looked at the cost effectiveness of different study designs testing the same hypothesis. However, it was not applicable to this discussion of RCTs because it compared a case-control design to a cohort design. We do not have empirical evidence that RCTs are more expensive.

Random Assignment

Negotiating for the use of an RCT, where it is ethical and legal, is not as difficult as some may make it appear. For instance, we have implemented random assignment in a study in which parents called to obtain mental health services for their children. While there was initially some resistance of one staff person, the random assignment apparently posed no problem to parents since 84% agreed to participate in the study.

One of the issues in implementing an RCT is the danger of crossover in which those assigned to the treatment group end up in the control group, usually because the organization did not provide the promised services, or when control group participants are exposed to the treatment (also known as contamination and diffusion). In some situations, physical separation of the participants reduces the probability of this problem, but in the above example the parents were all in the same community. Moreover, the service organization could not legally or ethically refuse to treat children. The latter issue was dealt with by asking parents, before they became clients, if they were willing to participate in the random assignment, with the incentive that their child would not be put on the waiting list if he or she was selected for treatment. All of the system-of-care clients received care in that system. In the control group, 6% of the cases received services from the system of care at some point in the study. Thus, crossover was not a problem in this particular study (Bickman, Summerfelt, & Noser, 1997).

Crossover problems may occur in educational experiments that are implemented at the school level and take more than a school year to conduct. In these cases, it is not unusual for some students to transfer between schools. In one of our current studies, 1.4% of the over 1,000 students changed to schools that had a different experimental condition in the first year and less than 1% changed schools in the second year.

The issue of crossover analysis can be dealt with in a conservative fashion by using an intention-to-treat approach in the analysis. In this case, the analysis is conducted using the original assignment, regardless of the condition the participant experienced. It is conservative because it will water down any potential treatment effects, but it maintains the advantages of the random assignment. A discussion of the intention-to-treat analysis may be found in Nich and Carroll (2002).

Resistance to random assignment may also be a problem. In our experience, we have not found it to be a significant issue. However, in an experiment we conducted on pediatrician diagnosis and treatment of ADHD, we found that the pediatricians took an extraordinarily long time to commit to participate. We think there was a conflict between their values as scientists and not wanting to be subjects in a study. Still, this would have probably occurred whether participants were randomly assigned or not.

Conclusion: So What Counts as Credible Evidence?

While RCTs may be prone to numerous threats to validity, they are nonetheless one of the most credible designs available to researchers. We have described many of the problems of RCTs, both in implementation and in concept. However, we still view them to be a credible choice for quantitative research. They are not really a gold standard, in the sense of being perfect, but to paraphrase what Winston Churchill said about democracy, we conclude, "For determining causality, in many but not all circumstances, the randomized design is the worst form of design except all the others that have been tried."

This chapter has explored the randomized control trial as the gold standard for credible research. As noted, credibility of research is determined by assessing if the findings are believable, trustworthy, convincing, and reliable. Specifically, judging credibility necessitates information about the research questions asked: what evidence was gathered to answer these questions, who asked the questions and gathered the evidence, how the evidence was gathered and analyzed, and under which conditions the evaluation was undertaken. In addition to these foundational issues, credibility is also influenced by the depth and breadth of the study as well as whether the findings are based on a single study or multiple studies. For assessing credibility in evaluation, we argue that there also needs to be a consensus among persons recognized as experts, on what they label credible.

While credibility is affected by what is viewed as knowledge, or truth, this chapter is limited to discussing only post-positivistic quantitative methods. As such, issues of credibility are influenced by statistical conclusion, and internal, construct, and external validity.

The RCT is as vulnerable to threats to statistical conclusion validity and construct validity as other methods. However, it is protected against one of the main threats to internal validity, selection bias. Even with this protection, there are several other well-recognized as well as less commonly acknowledged threats to internal validity. As described in the chapter, some of the well recognized threats include experimenter effects; allegiance effects; local history; and attrition, especially differential attrition. Less familiar threats include participant preferences prior to randomization, unmasked assignment, small sample size, and one-time random assignment.

When considering issues of external validity, RCTs may create an artificial situation in which the findings are not very generalizable. In such cases, credibility of the application of the evaluation is reduced. When conducting any RCT, it is important to use an appropriate comparison and to be sure that group random trials are used when making comparisons across settings or in situations where interclass covariation will influence results. While RCTs may still be prone to numerous threats to validity, this chapter has argued that they are still one of the most credible designs available to researchers and evaluators.

Notes

1. We will use the term RCT, known as a randomized clinical or control trial, to represent all randomized experiments, not just clinical trials.
2. While certain quasi-experimental designs were included in this priority, randomized designs were preferred when possible.

References

Adair, J. G., Sharpe, D., & Huynh, C. (1989). Hawthorne control procedures in educational experiments: A reconsideration of their use and effectiveness. *Review of Educational Research, 59*(2), 215–228.

Baser, O. (2006). Too much ado about propensity score models? Comparing methods of propensity score matching. *Value in Health, 9*(6), 377–385.

Berger, V. W., & Weinstein, S. (2004). Ensuring the comparability of comparison groups: Is randomization enough? *Controlled Clinical Trials, 25*(5), 515–524.

Berk, R. A. (2005). Randomized experiments as the bronze standard. *Journal of Experimental Criminology, 1*, 417–433.

Bickman, L., & Peterson, K. (1990). Using program theory to describe and measure program quality. In L. Bickman (Ed.), *Advances in program theory* (pp. 61–72). (Vol. 47 in the *New Directions for Evaluation* series). San Francisco: Jossey-Bass.

Bickman, L., Summerfelt, W. T., & Noser, K. (1997). Comparative outcomes of emotionally disturbed children and adolescents in a system of services and usual care. *Psychiatric Services, 48*, 1543–1548.

Bloom, H. S. (in press). The core analytics of randomized experiments for social research. In P. Alasuutari, J. Brannen, & L. Bickman (Eds.), *Handbook of social research methods.* London: Sage Publications.

Boruch, R. F. (1998). Randomized controlled experiments for evaluation and planning. In L. Bickman & D. Rog (Eds.), *Handbook of applied social research methods* (pp. 161–191). Thousand Oaks, CA: Sage Publications.

Boruch, R. F. (Ed.). (2005, May). Place randomized trials: Experimental tests of public policy [Special issue]. *Annals of the American Academy of Political and Social Sciences, 599.*

Boruch, R. F., Weisburd, D., Turner, H., Karpyn, A., & Littell, J. (in press). Randomized controlled trials for evaluation and planning. In L. Bickman & D. Rog (Eds.), *Handbook of applied social research methods* (2nd ed.). Thousand Oaks, CA: Sage Publications.

Brannan, J. (2005). Mixing methods: The entry of qualitative and quantitative approaches into the research process. *International Journal of Social Research Methodology, 8*(3), 173–184.

Brass, C. T., Nunez-Neto, B., & Williams, E. D. (2006, March 6). *Congress and program evaluation: An overview of randomized controlled trials (RCTs) and related issues.* Washington, DC: Congressional Research Service, Library of Congress. Retrieved May 18, 2007, from http://opencrs.cdt.org/document/RL33301.

Brewin, C. R., & Bradley, C. (1989). Patient preferences and randomised clinical trials. *British Medical Journal, 299,* 313–315.

Campbell, M. K., Elbourne, D. R., & Altman, D. G. (2004). CONSORT statement: Extension to cluster randomised trials. *British Medical Journal, 328,* 702–708.

Chen, H. T., & Rossi, P. H. (1983). Evaluating with sense: The theory-driven approach. *Evaluation Review, 7,* 283–302.

Chilvers, C., Dewey, M., Fielding, K., Gretton, V., Miller, P., Palmer, B., et al. (2001). Antidepressant drugs and generic counselling for treatment of major depression in primary care: Randomised trial with patient preference arms. *British Medical Journal, 322,* 772–775.

Cook, T. D., & Campbell, D. T. (1979). *Quasi-experimentation: Design and analysis issues for field settings.* Boston: Houghton Mifflin.

Cook, T. D., & Payne, M. R. (2002). Objecting to the objections to using random assignment in educational studies. In F. Mosteller & R. Boruch (Eds.), *Evidence matters: Randomized trials in education research* (pp. 150–178). Washington, DC: Brookings Institution.

Cook, T. D., & Wong, V. C. (in press). Better quasi-experimental practice. In P. Alasuutari, J. Brannen, & L. Bickman (Eds.), *Handbook of social research methods.* London: Sage Publications.

Corrigan, P., & Salzer, M. (2003). The conflict between random assignment and treatment preference: Implications for internal validity. *Evaluation and Program Planning, 26,* 109–121.

Cronbach, L. J. (1982). *Designing evaluation and social programs.* San Francisco: Jossey-Bass.

Donaldson, S. I. (2003). Theory-driven program evaluation. In S. I. Donaldson & M. Scriven (Eds.), *Evaluating social programs and problems: Visions for the new millennium.* (pp. 109–141). Mahwah, NJ: Erlbaum.

Faddis, B., Ahrens-Gray, P., & Klein, E. (2000). *Evaluation of Head Start family child care demonstration* (Final Report). Washington DC: Commissioner's Office of Research and Evaluation.

Fisher, C. B., & Anushko, A. E. (in press). Research ethics in social science. In P. Alasuutari, J. Brannen, & L. Bickman (Eds.), *Handbook of social research methods.* London: Sage Publications.

Flay, B. R., Biglan, A., Boruch, R. F., Castro, F. G., Gottfredson, D., Kellam, S., et al. (2005). Standards of evidence: Criteria for efficacy, effectiveness, and dissemination. *Prevention Science, 6*(3), 151–175.

Foster, E. M., & Bickman, L. (2000). Refining the costs analyses of the Fort Bragg evaluation: The impact of cost offset and cost shifting. *Mental Health Services Research, 2*(1), 13–25.

Glasgow, R. E., Green, L. W., Klesges, L. M., Abrams, D. B., Fisher, E. B., Goldstein, M. G., et al. (2006). External validity: We need to do more. *Annals of Behavioral Medicine, 31*(2), 105–108.

Glazerman, S., Levy, D. M., & Myers, D. (2003). Nonexperimental versus experimental estimates of earnings impacts. *The Annals of the American Academy of Political and Social Science, 589*, 63–93.

Graham, J., & Donaldson, S. (1993). Evaluating interventions with differential attrition: The importance of nonresponse mechanisms and use of follow-up data. *Journal of Applied Psychology, 78*(1), 119–128.

Greenhouse, S. W. (2003). The growth and future of biostatistics: (A view from the 1980s). *Statistics in Medicine, 22*, 3323–3335.

Hak, E., Wei, F., Grobbee, D. E., & Nichol, K. L. (2004). A nested case-control study of influenza vaccination was a cost-effective alternative to a full cohort analysis. *Journal of Clinical Epidemiology, 57*, 875–880.

Heckman, J. J., & Smith, J. A. (1995). Assessing the case for social experiments. *Journal of Economic Perspective, 9*(2), 85–110.

Howard, L., & Thornicroft, G. (2006). Patient preference randomised controlled trials in mental health research. *British Journal of Psychiatry, 188*, 303–304.

Howe, K. (2004). A critique of experimentalism. *Qualitative Inquiry, 10*(1), 42–61.

Huwiler-Müntener, K., Juni, P., Junker, C., & Egger, M. (2002). Quality of reporting of randomized trials as a measure of methodologic quality. *JAMA, 287*, 2801–2804.

Ioannidis, J. (2006). Evolution and translation of research findings: From bench to where? *PLos Clinical Trials, 1*(7), e36.

Johnson, S. L. (2005). *Children's Environmental Exposure Research Study.* Washington, DC: U. S. Environmental Protection Agency. Retrieved May 30, 2007, from http://www.epa.gov/cheers.

Kane, R., Wang, J., & Garrard, J. (2007). Reporting in randomized clinical trials improved after adoption of the CONSORT statement. *Journal of Clinical Epidemiology, 60*(3), 241–249.

Keppel, G. (1991). *Design and analysis: A researcher's handbook.* Upper Saddle River, NJ: Prentice Hall.

King, M., Nazareth, I., Lampe, F., Bower, P., Chandler, M., Morou, M., et al. (2005). Impact of participant and physician intervention preferences on randomized trials: A systematic review. *Journal of the American Medical Association, 293*(9), 1089–1099.

Kumar, S., & Oakley-Browne, M. (2001). Problems with ensuring a double blind. *Journal of Clinical Psychiatry, 62*(4), 295–296.

Leon, A. C., Mallinckrodt, C. H., Chuang-Stein, C., Archibald, D. G., Archer, G. E., & Chartier, K. (2006). Attrition in randomized controlled clinical trials: Methodological issues in psychopharmacology. *Biological Psychiatry, 59*(11), 1001–1005.

Lexchin, J., Bero, L., Djulbegovic, B., & Clark, O. (2003). Pharmaceutical industry sponsorship and research outcome and quality: Systematic review. *British Medical Journal, 326*, 1167–1170.

Lipsey, M., & Cordray, D. (2000). Evaluation methods for social intervention. *Annual Review of Psychology, 51*, 345–375.

Luborsky, L., Diguer, L., Seligman, D. A., Rosenthal, R., Krause, E. D., Johnson, S., et al. (1999). The researcher's own therapy allegiances: A "wild card" in comparison treatment efficacy. *Clinical Psychology: Science and Practice, 6*, 95–106.

Macias, C., Barreira, P., Hargreaves, W., Bickman, L., Fisher, W., & Aronson, E. (2005). Impact of referral source and study applicants' preference for randomly assigned service on research enrollment, service engagement, and evaluative outcomes. *American Journal of Psychiatry, 162*(4), 781–787.

Maxwell, J. (2004). Causal explanation, qualitative research, and scientific inquiry in education. *Educational Researcher, 33*(2), 3–11.

McCall, R., & Green, B. (2004). Beyond methodological gold standards of behavioral research: Considerations for practice and policy. *Social Policy Report, 18*(2), 3–12.

McCall, R., Ryan, C., & Plemons, B. (2003). Some lessons learned on evaluating community-based, two-generation service programs: The case of the Comprehensive Child Development Program. *Journal of Applied Developmental Psychology, 24*(2), 125–141.

Moher, D., Jones A., & Lepage, L. (2001). Use of the CONSORT statement and quality of reports of randomized trials: A comparative before-and-after evaluation. *JAMA, 285*, 1992–1995.

Moher, D., Schulz, K. F., & Altman, D. G. (2001). The CONSORT statement: Revised recommendations for improving the quality of reports of parallel-group randomized trials. The CONSORT Group. *JAMA, 285*, 1987–1991.

Nich, C., & Carroll, K. M. (2002). Intention to treat meets missing data: Implications of alternate strategies for analyzing clinical trials data. *Drug and Alcohol Dependence, 68*(2), 121–130.

Onwuegbuzie, A., & Leech, N. (2005). On becoming a pragmatic researcher: The importance of combining quantitative and qualitative research methodologies. *International Journal of Social Research Methodology, 8*(5), 375–387.

Petrosino, A., Boruch, R. F., Rounding, C., McDonald, S., & Chalmers, I. (2000). The Campbell Collaboration social, psychological, educational and criminological trials register (C2-SPECTR) to facilitate the preparation and maintenance of systematic reviews of social and educational interventions. *Evaluation and Research in Education, 14*(3), 206–219.

Plint, A. C., Moher, D., Morrison, A., Schulz, K., Altman, D. G., Hill, C., et al. (2006). Does the CONSORT checklist improve the quality of reports of randomised controlled trials? A systematic review. *Medical Journal of Australia, 185*(5), 263–267.

Raudenbush, S. W. (2002, February 6). *Identifying scientifically-based research in education.* Paper presented at the Working Group Conference, Washington, DC. Retrieved May 30, 2007, from http://www.ssicentral.com/hlm/techdocs/ ScientificallyBasedResearchSeminar.pdf.

Rolfe, G. (2006). Validity, trustworthiness, and rigour: Quality and the idea of qualitative research. *Journal of Advanced Nursing, 53*(3), 304–310.

Rosenbaum, P. R. (2002). *Observational studies* (2nd ed.). New York: Springer-Verlag.

Rosenbaum, P. R., & Rubin, D. B. (1983). The central role of the propensity score in observational studies for causal effects. *Biometrika, 70*(1), 41–55.

Rosenthal, R. (1976). *Experimenter effects in behavioral research* (Enlarged ed.). New York: Irvington.

Rosnow, R. L. (2002). The nature and role of demand characteristics in scientific inquiry. *Prevention & Treatment, 5.*

Rossi, P. (1987). The iron law of evaluation and other metallic rules. *Research in Social Problems and Public Policy, 4,* 3–20.

Scriven, M. (2005, December). *Can we infer causation from cross-sectional data?* Paper presented at the School-Level Data Symposium, Washington, DC. Retrieved May 28, 2007, from http://www7.nationalacademies.org/bota/School-Level%20Data_Michael%20Scriven-Paper.pdf.

Shadish, W. R., & Clark, M. H. (2007). *Can nonrandomized experiments yield accurate answers? A randomized experiment comparing random to nonrandom assignment.* Unpublished manuscript.

Shadish, W. R., Cook, T., & Campbell, D. (2002). *Experimental and quasi-experimental designs for generalized causal inference.* Boston: Houghton Mifflin.

Shadish, W. R., Hu, X., Glaser, R. R., Kownacki, R. J., & Wong, T. (1998). A method for exploring the effects of attrition in randomized experiments with dichotomous outcomes. *Psychological Methods, 3,* 3–22.

Shadish, W. R., Luellen, J. K., & Clark, M. H. (2006). Propensity scores and quasi-experiments: A testimony to the practical side of Lee Sechrest. In R. R. Bootzin & P. E. McKnight (Eds.), *Strengthening research methodology: Psychological measurement and evaluation.* Washington, DC: American Psychological Association.

Shadish, W. R., & Ragsdale, K. (1996). Random versus nonrandom assignment in controlled experiments: Do you get the same answer? *Journal of Consulting and Clinical Psychology, 64,* 1290–1305.

Shavelson, R. J., & Towne, L. (Eds.). (2002). *Scientific research in education* (National Research Council. Committee on Scientific Principles for Educational Research). Washington, DC: National Academy Press.

Shumaker, S. A., Legault, C., Rapp, S. R., Thal, L., Wallace, R. B., Ockene, J. K., et al. (2003). Estrogen plus progestin and the incidence of dementia and mild cognitive impairment in postmenopausal women: The Women's Health Initiative memory study: A randomized controlled trial. *Journal of the American Medical Association, 289,* 2651–2662.

Sieber, J. E. (in press). Planning ethically responsible research. In L. Bickman & D. Rog (Eds.), *Handbook of applied social research methods* (2nd ed.). Thousand Oaks, CA: Sage Publications.

Smith, G., & Pell, J. (2003). Parachute use to prevent death and major trauma related to gravitational challenge: Systematic review of randomised controlled trials. *British Medical Journal, 327,* 1459–1461.

Soares, H. P., Daniels, S., Kumar, A., Clarke, M., Scott, C., Swann, S., et al. (2004). Bad reporting does not mean bad methods for randomised trials: Observational study of randomised controlled trials performed by the Radiation Therapy Oncology Group. *British Medical Journal, 328,* 22–24.

Spring, B., Pagoto, S., Knatterud, G., Kozak, A., & Hedeker, D. (2007). Examination of the analytic quality of behavioral health randomized clinical trials. *Journal of Clinical Psychology, 63*(1), 53–71.

VanderWeele, T. (2006). The use of propensity score methods in psychiatric research. *International Journal of Methods in Psychiatric Research, 15*(2), 95–103.

Van de Ven, P., & Aggleton, P. (1999). What constitutes evidence in HIV/AIDS education? *Health Education Research, 14*(4), 461–471.

Varnell, S. P., Murray, D. M., Janega, J. B., & Blitstein, J. L. (2004). Design and analysis of group-randomized trials: A review of recent practices. *American Journal of Public Health, 94*(3), 393–399.

West, S. G., & Thoemmes, F. (in press). Equating groups. In P. Alasuutari, J. Brannen, & L. Bickman (Eds.), *Handbook of social research methods.* London: Sage Publications.

5

What Is Credible Evidence in Education?

The Role of the What Works Clearinghouse in Informing the Process

Russell Gersten

John Hitchcock

The What Works Clearinghouse (WWC) (http://whatworks.ed.gov), established in 2002 by the U.S. Department of Education's Institute of Education Sciences, endeavors to provide the public with a central and trusted source of scientific evidence regarding which instructional programs and practices are truly effective. It is an ambitious enterprise—in fact, some consider it an overly ambitious endeavor—based on the belief that educational research can and should be scientific and that findings from scientific research should inform educational practice. As several have noted—at least

AUTHORS' NOTE: This chapter represents the perspective of the authors. In no way does this reflect the official position of the Institute of Education Sciences or the U.S. Department of Education.

as judged by the number of available reports on the website—initial progress was slow. In addition, some have criticized the quality standards as far too rigorous (e.g., Viadero & Manzo, 2006), as not rigorous enough in terms of alignment of the interventions evaluated to specific outcome measures (e.g., Schoenfeld, 2006), or as a failure to include case studies of implementation difficulties along with the outcome evaluations (Confrey, 2006; Schoenfeld, 2006). Nonetheless, the WWC has produced and posted over 50 intervention reports to date, with more on the way, across a wide array of topic areas.

With the perspicacity of hindsight, it is easy to see how the initial research team underestimated the complexities of articulating a set of precise, explicit standards for assessing the quality of educational research studies. In addition, as the research teams began to assess individual research reports and articles, the teams grappled with a key, current issue in research design: the fact that until as late as 2001, many educational research studies failed to account for clustering or misaligned the unit of statistical analysis with the unit of assignment (these issues are complex and cannot be fully addressed here; references that describe these in detail include, for example, Raudenbush & Bryk [2002]).[1] Most commonly, the problem was that classes or schools might be assigned to various experimental conditions, yet the unit of statistical analysis was the individual student. The consensus of virtually all statisticians is that this is an improper technique in that it does not take into account the clustering that invariably takes place at the classroom or school level. In reviewing studies of the effectiveness of a wide array of mathematics curricula, the National Research Council (NRC, 2005) found that the percentage of experimental or quasi-experimental comparisons finding significant differences between curricula approaches shrunk when the appropriate unit of statistical analysis was included. For example, they dropped from 63% to 30% for elementary grades and from 40% to 1% for middle school. Thus, the research team was faced with the problem of developing a consistent methodology for handling the fact that many well-designed studies (often appearing in high-quality journals) presented inaccurate analyses and often labeled effects as statistically significant, when in fact they were not.

Although it is beyond the scope of this work to cover all coding scenarios, we do discuss these issues in more detail later in the chapter. We begin by discussing the purpose of the WWC and the type of research studies that, to date, have been analyzed.

The purpose of this chapter is to explain some of the thinking behind the WWC, especially focusing on the value the project places on randomized designs. We discuss the challenges faced in developing guidelines that could be employed consistently across studies (i.e., ways to address clustering concerns, what to do with studies with only one unit in a condition, and issues in rating studies and the overall evidence behind an intervention).

This chapter is most definitely an insider's perspective on the WWC. Both of the authors have been involved in the project from its very earliest phases, though we have hardly been key players in many of the major decisions made.

Purpose of the Clearinghouse and the Historical Context

Several events are critical for understanding the purpose of the clearinghouse, and the nature of the activities undertaken there. The first is the disillusionment with the quality of educational research that peaked toward the end of the last century (e.g., Kaestle, 1993). The second was the desire in Congress (beginning in the mid-1990s) to remedy this situation. Congress explicitly framed the No Child Left Behind Act of 2001 (NCLB, 2002) to promote use of findings from scientifically based research in schools with problematic reading performance. The act defined scientifically based reading research as

> Research that applies rigorous, systematic, and objective procedures to obtain valid knowledge relevant to reading development, reading instruction, and reading difficulties; and includes research that employs systematic, empirical methods that draw on observation or experiment; involves rigorous data analyses that are adequate to test that stated hypotheses and justify the general conclusions drawn; relies on measurements or observational methods that provide valid data across evaluators and observers and across multiple measurements and observations; and has been accepted by a peer-reviewed journal or approved by a panel of independent experts through a comparably rigorous, objective, and scientific review. (p. 7)

Shortly thereafter, in another serious effort to improve the rigor of educational research and evaluation activities, Congress created an Institute for Education Sciences (IES). Unlike its predecessors, it was intentionally created to support the conduct of rigorous scientific research in education (as opposed to a focus on "hot topics" regardless of methodological rigor). Like the National Institutes of Health, it is an independent institution rather than an agency within the U.S. Department of Education. The intent was to curtail direct political interference in the research conducted by the IES.

Another critical event of 2002 was the release of a report by the National Research Council of the National Academy of Sciences (NRC, 2002). The report made three major assertions. The first is that in order to establish causal claims (e.g., that approach X is an effective means to accelerate the English language development of English learners), we must resort to experiments that entail random assignment of participants to conditions. This was a reconfirmation of the insights of Campbell and Boruch (1975) and a critical wake-up call to the field. For decades, educators had argued that since schools were uncomfortable with the use of random assignment and budgets for educational research were tight, it was acceptable to conduct compromised experiments, often called quasi-experiments. The 2002 NRC report noted that large-scale, randomized trials can and should be conducted in education when the goal is to demonstrate effectiveness of a particular instructional program or approach to teaching.

The second major assertion—and the one that, to date, has received the most attention—is that there is a legitimate role for qualitative methods and descriptive research in the scientific endeavor. Qualitative inquiry is essential for developing a better understanding of educational problems and for interpreting patterns of findings. Such inquiry also is extremely important for understanding issues related to program implementation (NRC, 2005) and the interaction of curricula with teacher skill and knowledge of the content.[2] Qualitative inquiry can help us determine which questions are meaningful and thus needs to work in tandem with experimental inquiry. However, qualitative studies are not intended to be—and cannot be—credible evidence of program effectiveness.

The third assertion in the National Research Council (2002) report has yet to resonate with the general public. Yet, in many ways, it is the most important statement. The panel concluded that "it is possible to describe the physical and social world scientifically so that, for example, multiple observers can agree on what they see. Consequently, we reject the postmodernist school of thought when it posits that social science research can never generate objective or trustworthy knowledge" (p. 25). In other words, the NRC report clearly stated that there was no sound reason not to consider education as amenable to the scientific method that has led to so many advances in fields as diverse as medicine, public health, molecular biology, genetics, engineering, physics, welfare policy, clinical psychology, and treatment for substance abuse. The panel saw no credibility to the argument that rigorous, controlled research is impossible in education, as numerous education scholars have claimed. They also recognized that any scientific endeavor will be fraught with ambiguities and tensions and that a dynamic interaction between experimental research and all type of descriptive research is essential for the evolution of a scientific community.

Yet the report is consistent in its emphasis on the importance of randomized controlled trials (RCTs) as the critical lynchpin in the scientific enterprise. While acknowledging the difficulties of conducting RCTs in education, they note that there are also difficulties in conducting RCTs in areas such as medicine, health, counseling, and therapy. Moreover, only RCTs *"are the ideal* for establishing whether one or more factors caused change in an outcome because of their *strong ability to enable fair comparisons"* (p. 110, emphasis added). They go on to note that "randomized experiments are not perfect. . . . They typically cannot test complex causal hypotheses, they may lack generalizability to other settings, and they can be expensive. However, we believe that these and other issues do not generate a *compelling rationale against their use in education research"* (p. 125, emphasis added).

The NRC (2002) report argues for education research to move into the scientific research paradigm with the understanding that we will need to wait for consistent patterns of findings and we will need to be aware that each finding is fragile and dependent on specific aspects of the educational experiment. This relates to control over extraneous factors. This can be done either by rigorously controlling the study, or—and here is where the art of experimental design emerges—creating designs that ensure that no one extraneous factor can explain the results. Rigorous design includes careful attention to issues such as (a) who does the actual teaching (in a curriculum evaluation), (b) ensuring that a study never compares volunteer teachers to nonvolunteer teachers, and (c) making certain that no study of program effectiveness could simply be interpreted as different amounts of time given to each method. In analysis of research articles and reports, careful attention needs to be devoted to what efforts are made to ensure that the comparison and intervention groups are truly comparable, such as checking whether differential attrition is leading to spurious findings.

The WWC responded to several critical national needs. The first was the need to dramatically increase the number of rigorous RCTs in education to supplement descriptive and qualitative studies so that professional educators would have an evidence base for making decisions about selecting curricula, intervention programs for students with learning problems, selecting professional development approaches, and determining effective structures for establishing tutoring programs. The second was the need for serious review of research on topics of high relevance for the profession using clear criteria, while considering the various methodological flaws that occur in many studies. The third was development of a set of criteria that could also help educational researchers understand how to conduct such studies. The WWC plays a role in addressing each of these needs. It addresses the first and third indirectly and the second directly.

Major Focus of the What Works Clearinghouse

The purpose of the WWC effort is to give decision makers access to the highest-quality evidence available on educational interventions, and based on the above NRC position, this means identifying those interventions supported by high-quality RCTs, or at least designs that might approximate results that may be found via an RCT design. The reader should note that this is directly aligned to the goals set forth in the National Academy of Sciences (NRC, 2002, 2005) reports.

Grover (Russ) Whitehurst, the IES director, confirmed this focus after extensive meetings with school administrators. A recurrent question posed by administrators was, "What is the best curricula approach to use to teach mathematics or reading?" Whitehurst (personal communication, June 2004) noted that the situation in mathematics curricular decisions, for example, was often cited as a source of dismay and confusion. Different mathematics experts recommend very different types of mathematics curricula, and many administrators wanted clear guidance to choose products supported by a valid base of evidence as opposed to publisher-supported evidence claims.

An increasing body of research suggests the strong role curriculum plays in determining what teachers do and say, and thus is likely to strongly affect student learning (e.g., Ball & Cohen, 1996; Foorman, Francis, Fletcher, Schatschneider, & Mehta, 1998). Scholars such as Stahl (2000) have called for systematic, rigorous research on curriculum impacts. The WWC was aware that evaluating the quality of the research supporting effectiveness of various widely used curricula was likely to cause a good deal more controversy and unease than, say, decisions about the effectiveness of a theoretical position, such as the use of cooperative learning or cognitive strategy instruction. Developers are likely to react unfavorably to ratings of effectiveness that indicate the data are inconclusive or the quality of the evidence in support of their approach is weak. Nonetheless, as in other areas such as public health, this approach seemed to fit the demands of Congress and the needs of constituents.

A Brief Introduction to the What Works Clearinghouse

WWC's current focus is instructional interventions and practices on a wide array of topics. These topics include academic interventions for English Language Learners (ELLs) in grades K–6, beginning reading curricula, curricula for teaching elementary and middle school mathematics, dropout prevention programs, and character education programs. A principal investigator (PI) with extensive experience in conducting research in the area leads each review.[3]

The PI has some discretion in terms of setting the parameters for the review, although major decisions are typically done in consultation with experts. In the ELL review, for example, we engaged experts such as Catherine Snow, William

Saunders, Sharon Vaughn, and Robert Linquanti in discussions of whether to limit the review to only studies of students who are currently classified as ELL (i.e., are formally classified as limited in their English proficiency, the Rivera [1994] definition) or to also include students who are from homes where other languages are spoken, but are no longer classified as limited English proficient. We thought that the goal should be to include both groups, since they both require some type of specialized instruction, but wanted input from leading researchers in this area. Other parameters we set included developing a working definition of the domain[4] of English language development (i.e., determining what academic outcomes fall within this domain) and deciding to examine studies of reading, English language development, and mathematics. Finally, in order to give our work focus, we decided to include only studies of instruction in the elementary grades.

Once the parameters of the review were established, a study coding manual was developed and an exhaustive literature search conducted. Journals thought to focus on the topic area were hand searched ($n = 12$) back to 1983, the default time interval for WWC reviews (although again we obtained input from colleagues). In addition, multiple databases were covered using key search terms, related meta-analyses were perused to identify potentially eligible studies, and the public was asked to submit intervention names. Typical Internet search engines were also used. Over 700 citations (published and unpublished literature) of studies that potentially fit our parameters were gathered. Next, studies were screened for construct fit (e.g., ensuring the study included outcomes for ELLs in Grades K–6) and technical adequacy, the latter of which is perhaps the most rigorous and unique feature of the What Works Clearinghouse.

WWC Standards of Evidence and Technical Review

The WWC has endeavored to set clear criteria for determining whether a study produces credible evidence of effectiveness. There are two phases to the process. The first is to determine whether the design of the study is rigorous enough so that an educator can conclude that the effects found are not due to other extraneous factors, but due to the curriculum or intervention that is the focus of the study. As anyone involved in research synthesis or meta-analysis knows, development and refinement of standards is a demanding effort. The WWC utilized the expertise of some of the best statisticians and research design experts in the country. We hoped that the development and public posting of the criteria that determine a sound evaluation design would improve the quality of future curricular evaluations.

From the outset, the WWC thus had two goals for the standards: (a) to provide a consistent, publicly available set of standards for determining ratings of both the quality of the research design and the effectiveness of the intervention, and (b) to provide guidelines that researchers can use in designing intervention research. This in turn provides a foundation for an ancillary goal of the WWC—to provide consumers, developers, and professional evaluators with a sense of strong design features that promote causal inference. This is directly responsive to Congress's charge in NCLB to disseminate scientifically based research and is also responsive, for example, to the recommendation of the NRC (2005) that "the Federal Department of Education in concert with state educational agencies should undertake an initiative to provide local and district decision makers with training in how to conduct and interpret valid studies of curricular effectiveness" (p. 203).

The WWC (http://ies.ed.gov/ncee/wwc) is aware that no experimental design is perfect and that every design always involves a series of tradeoffs and balances. Therefore, the Standards, which have been developed over a period of several years, address evidence for the causal validity of instructional programs and practices according to criteria that appear on the website under Evidence Standards. The review process is succinctly described in a three-page summary of the methodological criteria used with additional detail provided in a set of Working Papers. A general discussion of these standards follows, but full description of details goes beyond the scope of the chapter.

In terms of initial screens, the WWC essentially utilizes a three-point rating system based on internal causal validity: (1) *meets evidence standards*, (2) *meets standards with reservations,* and (3) *does not pass screens.* In the project's vernacular, a study with strong causal validity "meets WWC standards." Studies with concerns about causal validity but that have taken steps to address these can "meet standards with reservations," although whether they do or not is based on several factors. The remaining studies do not pass evidence screens. RCTs are hence always considered worthy of review, and this is the only design that can meet evidence standards in the WWC system, but they can still be downgraded to "meets standards with reservations" if, for example, there is evidence of severe differential attrition. More severe problems with causal validity such as a confounding of the intervention with either school or teacher can prevent the study from passing evidence screens. (Some earlier efforts at research synthesis such as Greene's [1999] work on bilingual education erred in considering all RCTs as the "gold standard," regardless of the quality of the research design.)

Quasi-experimental designs (QEDs) are also considered worthy of serious review, but only if they control for pretest differences on a salient pretest variable (e.g., pretest scores, demographic variables, etc.). This is because they cannot account for all of the unmeasured factors that may be at work in a study, such as differential motivation to perform well (see, for example, Boruch, 1997; Shadish, Cook, & Campbell, 2002), whereas a randomized trial can (assuming the trial did not experience problems such as severe attrition or contamination between treatment and control groups). This position is supported not only by underlying theory and logic, but also empirical evidence. Recent studies compared the results from randomized trials to results that would have been obtained if QEDs had been used. The results indicate that even superior QEDs should not be assumed to replicate RCT findings and, in some cases, may not even approximate them (Wilde & Hollister, 2002). Hence, only RCTs without design problems are judged to meet the project's standards without any qualifiers, and even the strongest QEDs that provide empirical evidence of group equating prior to the onset of an intervention are at best rated as "meets standards with reservations."

Again, specific criteria for assessment of problems with attrition and randomization are described in detail in a set of technical working papers, but we summarize this section by listing the major reasons for excluding studies:

1. Confounding of intervention with either teacher or school (i.e., there is only one teacher per condition, or one school per condition)[5]

2. Failure to provide pretest information on a salient pretest variable (for quasi-experiments only)

3. Differential attrition between intervention and control groups or extremely high attrition (without an adequate attempt to account for this factor in data analysis procedures) will downgrade an RCT and will lead to a "does not pass" rating for a QED.

Effect Direction, Magnitude, and Significance Ratings

Studies that "meet evidence standards" or "meet evidence standards with reservations" are further reviewed by researchers with content area expertise. The review team determines whether (a) the study used a valid outcome measure (focusing only on content validity, not on psychometric coefficients of criterion-related validity), (b) the extent to which relevant people and settings are included in the study, (c) the adequacy of statistical analysis and reporting of the data, and (d) statistical reporting. If these features are acceptable, the WWC *recomputes* the direction, magnitude, and statistical significance of the effect.

Recalculation is often necessary for two reasons: The first is to correct for any errors due to misalignment of the unit of analysis with the unit of assignment (Donner & Klar, 2000; Raudenbush & Bryk, 2002). The WWC uses the correct unit of analysis and corrects for clustering using a technique that assumes a (default) intra-class correlation (ICC)[6] of .20 for academic outcomes (.10 for behavioral); both values are based on ICCs found in recent large-scale evaluation research conducted by IES. The second reason is that many studies conduct multiple comparisons with the same sample, and thereby run a risk of elevated (Type 1) error rate. When this occurs, the Benjamini-Hochberg correction is applied, which in most applications is a more liberal correction than the better-known Bonferroni procedure but essentially accomplishes the same end (Benjamini & Hochberg, 1995; Benjamini & Yekutieli, 2001). As a result, readers will see many instances on the WWC website where the authors of the report found statistical significance, but WWC calculations do not confirm the significance.

After statistical significance is addressed, estimates of effects are calculated. The default approach is to calculate a standardized mean difference, which is the difference between treatment and control mean outcomes divided by the pooled within-group standard deviation of the outcome measure.[7] Studies with effects that are not statistically significant (i.e., could be due to chance) but are greater than .25 standard deviation units are considered *substantively important*. Effects are then characterized as *statistically significant positive*, *substantively important positive*, or *indeterminate*. (There are similar categories for studies with negative program impacts.)

Once effect sizes (ES) are obtained, studies of the same intervention are pooled into an intervention report and assigned a rating; these ratings are an assessment of the cumulative evidence of studies that pass standards (with or without reservations) so should thus not be confused with the aforementioned study-level assessments. When there are multiple effect sizes within an academic domain (e.g., reading, mathematics), the WWC takes an average value but also reports the range of effects toward the beginning of reports and lists them individually in appendices. Intervention ratings include *Positive Effects* (two or more studies with statistically significant positive effects, one of which possesses a *strong* design) or *Potentially Positive Effects* (at least one study showing a statistically significant positive effect or an ES of +0.25 or more). Intervention ratings can also be negative, which are more or less mirror images of the above (e.g., *Potentially Negative Effects*). Other ratings include *Mixed Effects* (i.e., the presence of both positive and negative outcomes) or *No Discernible Effects* (i.e., ES's are so small that there appears to be no impact).

Application Example: Interventions for ELL Students

To concretize some of the above ideas, we offer an overview of the ELL review and walk the reader through an intervention rating. Again, the focus of the review was on replicable academic interventions for K–6 ELL children in the United States.

Two recent studies by Vaughn and colleagues (Vaughn, Cirino, et al., 2006; Vaughn, Mathes, et al., 2006) focusing on a new intervention entitled Enhanced Proactive Reading (EPR) were included in the review. These were intensive interventions for first-grade English learners who were deemed at risk for experiencing difficulties learning how to read. The authors defined EPR as

> a comprehensive, integrated reading, language arts, and English language development curriculum . . . targeted to first-grade English language learners experiencing problems with learning to read through conventional instruction. The curriculum is implemented as small group daily reading instruction, during which English Language Learners instructors provide opportunities for participation from all students and give feedback for student responses. (http://ies.ed.gov/ncee/WWC/reports/english_lang/epr)

The curriculum is implemented as small-group, daily reading instruction by trained teachers. Small-group activities also include approximately 10 minutes of English language development activities based primarily on a read-aloud activity. Teachers use a read-aloud approach to teach students the conventions of academic English, build listening comprehension and receptive skills, and encourage expressive vocabulary. The appendix at the end of the chapter provides details on where to download the report and provides additional details about EPR.

Vaughn, Cirino, et al. (2006) randomly gave the students access to the same amount of reading instruction without EPR. A similar design was used in the Vaughn, Mathes, et al. (2006) study of 41 ELL students. Both studies used similar reading outcome measures, were conducted in similar settings (in four Texas schools), and used comparable teacher training; only the lowest one or two students in each class were selected to participate.

Evidence Screening

The main differences between the two investigations were largely based on methods, and understanding these gives a sense of WWC coding methodology. As it turned out, Vaughn, Mathes, et al. (2006) reported there were 10 cases of failed randomization that occurred due to scheduling conflicts. The authors therefore replaced these students on a nonrandom basis. Although the authors were careful to empirically examine the impact of this replacement, the WWC could not be sure if some unmeasured variables may have existed that might undermine causal validity of the design. Randomization is viewed in the strictest of terms, so the study was downgraded to a QED. This work also experienced differential attrition. If left unchecked, the combination of failed randomization and attrition would cause the study to not meet evidence screens. The WWC does, however, use procedures to gather additional information, and the authors were able to demonstrate post-attrition equivalence on the analytic sample. Hence, the design was viewed as a QED with attrition, which was corrected, and thus met standards with reservations. Estimates of effects and statistical procedures were calculated. The study by Vaughn, Cirino, et al. (2006), by contrast, was rated as an RCT that met WWC standards without reservations. This is because students were randomly assigned to conditions, procedures were described in reasonable detail, and there was no mention of problems with the assignment process.

Outcomes of the Review

Given the pattern of findings, the WWC rated EPR as having potentially positive effects in the reading domain on the basis that the overall ES was substantively positive (several ES's were reported and the overall average was +0.49, greater than 0.25), at least one of the two studies met WWC criteria without reservations, and there was no contrary evidence. There were also outcomes in a second academic domain, English language development. The average effect across the studies was slightly negative and very small (the one ES for the QED was +0.13, and the other study yielded an ES of −0.17, for an average of −0.02); hence, the *No Discernable Effects* intervention rating was applied. Even though the program demonstrated effects in English language development in one study, these effects were not replicated in the methodologically stronger study. Thus, the WWC rated the EPR intervention as having potentially positive effects in the reading domain, and no discernible effects in the English language development domain. It seems the intervention is a promising one and should be further studied while considering outcomes for English language development.

The degree to which these findings might be generalized is a question that is left largely to the judgment of readers. Clearly, the intervention focuses on first graders with serious potential problems in reading, so those interested in the intervention may wish to think twice about attempting to implement the work in other grades. The sample on which findings were based was drawn from several urban schools with high percentages of ELL students. Combining this with the use of two strong designs, one can be reasonably confident that the intervention is likely to have positive impacts when working with similar groups. Of course, there are always qualifiers if the evidence is based on only two studies. In addition, teacher training was extensive.

How the What Works Clearinghouse Can Contribute to the Progress of the Field of Program Evaluation

Readers should not conclude—and hopefully have not concluded—that program evaluation should only encompass rigorous outcome evaluations using RCTs or the highest-caliber quasi-experimental designs. Rather, our belief is that

1. The portfolio of educational research is severely underweighted in this type of investment. As in fields like public health, psychiatry, psychology, and welfare reform, progress and true reform require this type of research to be an active part of the research portfolio in educational research. The need is critical in educational evaluation research.

2. The "age of excuses" for why the educational system cannot possibly afford the temporary deprival of services that RCTs require should be over. The quality of evidence that emerges when rigorous design and the rules for rigorous outcome evaluation are followed is well worth the occasional sacrifice. The sacrifices of a teacher or student being deprived of an exciting-sounding innovation are minuscule compared to the benefits gained by rigorous evaluation research.

3. Studies such as those reviewed on the WCC website can serve an educational purpose for the professional education community. Those contemplating design of a research study can look at the flaws that led to downgrading of various studies and try to ensure that they do not commit the same mistakes in their current research.

4. The database on the What Works Clearinghouse provides a serious resource for school districts and schools as they encounter claims from vendors that research supports their program. As can be seen on the website for topics as diverse as elementary mathematics, and beginning reading and language and literacy instruction for ELLs, many widely touted curricula, at the current point in time, display no discernible impact on student achievement. This is critical information for the public to possess.

Conclusion: So What Counts as Credible Evidence?

The What Works Clearinghouse is an ambitious enterprise meant to provide independent and high-quality reviews of studies that test the effectiveness of replicable educational interventions (e.g., products such as curricula or textbooks and practices such as replicable tutoring approaches). These reviews aim to inform consumers of educational interventions about the evidence that supports the use of evidence by assessing its causal validity against published standards. Should a study of relevant interventions demonstrate adequate causal validity, the WWC estimates the magnitude of the impact the intervention has relative to a counterfactual condition (i.e., effect size) and summarizes available research so that consumers can make informed decisions about what instructional materials to adopt. A key point here is that the WWC endeavors to be a trustworthy source of information and thus remains an independent body with no stake in what interventions are purchased, and studies are evaluated against publicly available standards.

This chapter has provided an insider's perspective on WWC criteria and processes for screening studies, coding ones that are relevant and then summarizing evidence for publicly available reports. This perspective was provided by describing general principles and then offering examples via publicly available documents. With that said, the report authors were not key players on major decisions and the WWC is an ever-evolving project. Hence, it is important that readers understand that the chapter does not necessarily represent the views of the U.S. Department of Education and may well not contain the most current information about the WWC.

The chapter began with an overview of purpose and then provided some historical context for the work of the WWC. After describing the major focus of the project, methods for identifying relevant studies, evidence standards, and some technical details on estimating program impacts were described. The chapter closed with an example taken from one of the WWC topic areas: interventions for English Language Learners in Grades K–6. That is, the chapter provided some explanatory material for an intervention report that is available on the WWC website and walked the reader through the application of rating criteria and processes used to estimate the impacts of the intervention.

In the end, readers should have a better understanding of WWC processes (as implemented at the time of this writing) and, more generally, important criteria to consider when designing and reporting about studies that attempt to determine if a given intervention appears to make a difference in academic achievement. Although the chapter did not focus on technical matters in the way that texts of research design and analysis might, the insider's perspective may help concretize the importance of randomization, baseline equivalence between treatment and control groups, clustering, and experimenter error rates when trying to understand the impact of educational interventions.

Notes

1. Briefly, most educational data are "clustered" in that students are nested in groups such as classrooms, which are in turn nested in schools, and then districts. This is a concern because individual observations such as student test scores are generally correlated within a cluster (i.e., students within a given unit such as a classroom are similar to each other) for reasons that are unrelated to a given treatment condition. For example, students in a school may be somewhat similar to each other because they come from the same neighborhoods. Students within a classroom may also be similar because of how the classroom was formed (consider how classroom similarity occurs when schools "track" students and thereby assign them based on academic ability). Different teachers of course have different impacts on learning, which will also increase score similarity. Statistically speaking, these scenarios violate the assumption that scores are independent, which is important in techniques such as analysis of variance. When this assumption is violated, it is often the case that statistically significant findings (e.g., $p < .05$) are in fact not. Multilevel (also called hierarchical linear) models can correct for clustering, but many studies in education research have failed to use these techniques, especially prior to the time when they became more widely understood.

2. Given the WWC focuses on program impacts within an experimental framework, no effort has been made to address features of other types of designs commonly used in education research. Readers interested in other designs (e.g., qualitative and single-case) are referred to Gersten et al.'s (2005) and Odom et al.'s (2005) work on quality indicators of research design, and Kratochwill and Shernoff's (2004) review of evidence-based practices.

3. The PI for the ELL strand is the senior author of this chapter; the coauthor is Deputy Director of this same strand.

4. The term *domain* has particular meaning within the WWC because outcomes are categorized within them for reporting purposes; details are provided below, in the appendix.

5. This seems to be all too common in education research, where assignment (be it random or otherwise) occurs at higher-order units (e.g., schools, classrooms) and there is only one such unit in a condition. Studies of this type do not pass evidence screens because if, for example, two teachers are assigned randomly to two conditions, one cannot separate out teacher effects (e.g., skill, motivation) from intervention effects.

6. The degree of nonindependence in clustering (see endnote 1) can be expressed as an ICC. A zero ICC is equivalent to saying observations are independent; the value is calculated by dividing the variance attributable to clusters by the total variance of observed data. If classroom groupings alone can explain 50% of the variation, then the ICC = .50. Note that even a small ICC (e.g., .05) that is unaccounted for in an analysis can have a large impact on Type 1 error rate.

7. There are more details about effect size calculations provided on the WWC website.

References

Ball, D. L., & Cohen, D. K. (1996). Reform by the book: What is—or might be—the role of curriculum materials in teacher learning and instructional reform. *Educational Researcher, 25*, 6–8.

Benjamini, Y., & Hochberg, Y. (1995). Controlling the false discovery rate: A practical and powerful approach to multiple testing. *Journal of the Royal Statistical Society, Series B (Methodological), 57*, 289–300.

Benjamini, Y., & Yekutieli, D. (2001). The control of the false discovery rate in multiple testing under dependency. *The Annals of Statistics, 29*, 1165–1188.

Boruch, R. F. (1997). *Randomized experiments for planning and evaluation: A practical guide.* Thousand Oaks, CA: Sage Publications.

Campbell, D. T., & Boruch, R. F. (1975). Making the case for random assignment treatments by considering the alternatives: Six ways in which quasi-experimental evaluations in compensatory education tend to underestimate effects. In C. A. Bennett & A. A. Lumsdaine (Eds.), *Central issues in program evaluation* (pp. 195–296). New York: Academic Press.

Confrey, J. (2006). Comparing and contrasting the national research council report "on evaluating curricular effectiveness" with the What Works Clearinghouse approach. *Educational Evaluation and Policy Analysis, 28*, 195–213.

Donner, A., & Klar, N. (2000). *Design and analysis of cluster randomized trials in health research.* London: Arnold Publishing.

Foorman, B. R., Francis, D. J., Fletcher, J. M., Schatschneider, C., & Mehta, P. (1998). The role of instruction in learning to read: Preventing reading failure in at-risk children. *Journal of Educational Psychology, 90*, 37–55.

Gersten, R., Fuchs, L. S., Compton, D., Coyne, M., Greenwood, C., & Innocenti, M. S. (2005). Quality indicators for group experimental and quasi-experimental research in special education. *Exceptional Children, 71*, 149–164.

Greene, G. (1999). Mnemonic multiplication fact instruction for students with learning disabilities. *Learning Disabilities Research and Practice, 14*, 141–148.

Kaestle, C. F. (1993). The awful reputation of education research. *Educational Researcher, 22*, 26–31.

Kratochwill, T. R., & Shernoff, E. S. (2004). Evidence-based practice: Promoting evidence-based interventions in school psychology. *School Psychology Review, 33*, 34–48.

National Research Council. (2002). Scientific research in education. In R. J. Shavelson & L. Towne (Eds.), *Committee on Scientific Principles for Educational Research.* Washington, DC: National Academy Press.

National Research Council. (2005). *On evaluating curricular effectiveness: Judging the quality of K–12 mathematics evaluations.* Washington, DC: National Academy Press.

No Child Left Behind (NCLB) Act of 2001, Pub. L. No. 107–110, § 115, Stat. 1425 (2002).

Odom, S. L., Brantlinger, E., Gersten, R., Horner, R. H., Thompson, B., & Harris, K. R. (2005). Research in special education: Scientific methods and evidence-based practices. *Exceptional Children, 71*, 137–148.

Raudenbush, S.W., & Bryk, A. S. (2002*). Hierarchical linear models: Applications and data analysis methods* (2nd ed.). Thousand Oaks, CA: Sage Publications.

Rivera, C. (1994). Is it real for all kids? *Harvard Educational Review, 64*, 55–75.

Schoenfeld, A. H. (2006). What doesn't work: The challenge and failure of the What Works Clearinghouse to conduct meaningful reviews of studies of mathematics curricula. *Educational Researcher, 35*(2), 13–21.

Shadish, W. R., Cook, T. D., & Campbell, D. T. (2002). *Experimental and quasi-experimental designs for general causal inference.* Boston: Houghton Mifflin.

Stahl, S. (Chair). (2000, April). *Jeanne S. Chall: Memories and legacies.* Symposium conducted at the 2000 AERA Annual Meeting, New Orleans, LA.

Vaughn, S., Cirino, P. T., Linan-Thompson, S., Mathes, P. G., Carlson, C. D., Cardenas-Hagan, E., et al. (2006). Effectiveness of a Spanish intervention and an English intervention for English Language Learners at risk for reading problems. *American Educational Research Journal, 43*, 449–487.

Vaughn, S., Mathes, P., Linan-Thompson, S., Cirino, P., Carlson, C., Pollard-Durodola, S., et al. (2006). Effectiveness of an English intervention for first-grade English Language Learners at risk for reading problems. *Elementary School Journal, 107*, 153–180.

Viadero, D., & Manzo, K. K. (2006). Tutoring program found effective, despite cold shoulder under Reading First. *Education Weekly, 26*, 1–2.

Wilde, E. T., & Hollister, R. (2002). *How close is close enough? Testing nonexperimental estimates of impact against experimental estimates of impact with education test scores as outcomes* (Discussion Paper No. ED462524). Madison: University of Wisconsin, Institute for Research on Poverty.

Appendix: An Overview of WWC Intervention Reports

This appendix is meant to walk readers though the primary sections of a WWC intervention report. The authors chose to continue to work with EPR, which as of this writing can be downloaded from http://ies.ed.gov/ncee/wwc/reports/english_lang/epr.

Each WWC intervention report has two primary sections, a front piece and technical appendices. The front part of the report provides an overview about the program, information such as scope of use and cost, research that meets WWC standards and associated effects, and the overall intervention rating. The appendices cover details about characteristics (i.e., participants, setting, intervention and comparison group details, primary outcomes, and teacher training) of each study that informed the report. In addition, details about WWC-calculated ES's and estimates of statistical significance are listed for each outcome related to the review, and intervention ratings for each domain are discussed. In the case of EPR, the front piece notes that there are no current cost data available since the intervention was only recently developed at the Vaughn Gross Center for Reading and Language Arts.

As of this writing, the WWC leaves it to the reader to make decisions about the generalizability of findings. The intervention was carried out across several cities and two studies, which suggests that one might have some confidence in terms of generalization. On the other hand, only first graders were included in the study, which was indeed the focus of the intervention, hence the reader would probably consider EPR for that grade only. Overall, the report comments heavily on the strength of internal validity (i.e., the degree to which differences between intervention and comparison groups are a result of the intervention and not alternative explanations) and the magnitude of impacts. Whether the program impacts are likely to translate to a grade or context in which a teacher is currently working is a decision left to the reader.

6

Evaluation Methods for Producing Actionable Evidence

Contextual Influences on Adequacy and Appropriateness of Method Choice

George Julnes

Debra Rog

Philosophers have long struggled with what it means for evidence to be credible (Weinberg, 1973). For this volume, the focus is on understanding what constitutes credible evidence for informing policy and program decisions, especially in the public sector. Our pragmatic approach extends the concept to suggest that for evidence to be useful, it not only needs to be credible but "actionable" as well, deemed both adequate and appropriate for guiding actions in targeted real-world contexts (Julnes & Rog, 2007). Certainly credibility helps evidence to be actionable, but the level of credibility necessary or useful to guide action depends on the situation. Further, evidence can be credible in the context studied but of questionable relevance for guiding actions in other contexts (Argyris, 1996).

Many factors influence whether a given set of evidence is judged as actionable for a particular purpose and in a specific context. Our interest in this chapter is with those factors related to methodology: To what extent are certain inquiry methods better suited for yielding actionable evidence and, more specifically, what role does the particular setting and situation play in determining whether the evidence generated by a particular method is considered actionable? We address this question for one type of evidence of interest in evaluation—evidence about the causal impacts of programs and policies that we can use to improve them and judge their worth. The methods we consider are the design methodologies, either qualitative or quantitative, that support our confidence in these causal conclusions.

As background, although there is general agreement that different methods are more suited to different contexts, conflict comes when developing specific recommendations about which particular methods fit the needs of particular contexts. This lack of consensus at the level of specifics has a long history in evaluation (see Reichardt & Rallis, 1994) and currently is present in the discussion over the relative value of random assignment experimental methods compared to a host of other techniques. The U.S. Department of Education (ED) helped to raise the issue by establishing priorities for random assignment experimental methods for one class of evaluation questions, specifically those addressing the causal impacts of policies and programs. Because of this initiative to promote random assignment experiments, there has been a debate over what methods should be used in government-sponsored evaluations and, in turn, this has led to some conflicting views about the value of randomized studies. As a case in point, while many saw the ED's priority as an appropriate contextual stance (see Lipsey, 2007), much of the heated reaction against these priorities came from those who saw the department as promoting a near-exclusive emphasis on experimental methods, independent of relevant contextual factors.

This chapter addresses this controversy over method choice and reviews areas where there is at least some consensus, in particular with regard to the key factors that make one method more or less suitable than others for particular evaluation situations. We consider four questions: How are methods related to the questions that stakeholders want addressed? What contextual factors condition the evidence needed to support causal conclusions? How are we to judge the adequacy of methods for providing the needed evidence? and When is it appropriate to use particular methods of causal analysis? Although there may not be full agreement on how we address these questions, we believe that framing the current controversy in terms of these questions is one way to move the debate forward.

How Are Methods Related to the Questions That Stakeholders Want Addressed?

Primary among those factors influencing method choice are the questions and purposes that stakeholders want the evaluation to address. Scriven (1967) made an early attempt at providing a framework that distinguished formative and summative purposes for evaluation, with formative focused on improving programs and summative on supporting judgments of value. The implication is that more exploratory methods are appropriate for formative evaluation, while the more rigorous experimental designs might be called for in summative evaluations. Mark, Henry, and Julnes (2000) continued this approach by distinguishing four purposes of most evaluations—oversight and accountability, program and organizational improvement, assessment of merit and worth, and knowledge development. Making explicit connections among these purposes and appropriate methodologies, the conclusions were again that rigorous experimental designs would likely not be appropriate for the first two purposes in that list but might be called for in assessment of merit and worth (intended as the purpose of summative evaluation) or for some efforts at knowledge development. (This last purpose is a broad category that includes efforts to learn about the mechanisms responsible for program effectiveness as well as lessons about evaluation capacity building.)

There is not full agreement on either of these frameworks. Some continue to believe that experimental designs are being promoted too promiscuously and that other methods are relevant for some of the same evaluation questions and purposes. One approach to addressing the core of the controversy may be to clarify the specifics of what is needed in an evaluation, including the *tasks* needed to complete the evaluation, the *levels of conclusions* to be addressed in the evaluation, and the *form of causal conclusions* desired by stakeholders. Our hope is that this greater specificity will illuminate and support greater consensus on the relationship between stakeholder questions and the need for rigorous experimental evaluation methods.

Multiple Evaluation Tasks

A standard frame for organizing evaluation questions is in terms of the tasks that need to be accomplished to address them. Because the current method controversy is primarily about conducting summative evaluations, or evaluations with the purpose of assessing merit and worth, we focus here on the different tasks that are typically required in well-designed summative evaluations.

Organizing evaluation tasks. To illustrate the relationships between evaluation questions and the tasks that address them, consider the 14 evaluation questions offered by Weiss (1998, p. 273), as organized in Table 6.1, in terms of five traditional evaluation tasks—implementation evaluation, outcome assessment, impact evaluation, assessment of worth, and critical review (compare these with the related evaluation tasks delineated by Rossi, Lipsey, & Freeman, 2004). Building on the framework offered by Mark et al. (2000), evaluations conducted for the purposes of oversight and program improvement, for example, generally depend on one or both of the first two tasks, implementation evaluation and outcome assessment, with valuative judgments sometimes included.

Table 6.1   Weiss's Evaluation Questions, Organized by Evaluation Tasks

A. Implementation Evaluation
  - What went on in the program over time?
  - How closely did the program follow its original plan?

B. Outcome Assessment
  - Did recipients improve?
  - Did recipients do better than nonrecipients?

C. Impact Evaluation

  1. Aggregate Program Impacts
     - Is the observed change due to the program?

  2. Disaggregated Impacts
     - What characteristics are associated with success?
     - What combinations of actors, services, and conditions are associated with success and failure?

  3. Causal Explanation (Assessment of Causal Mechanisms)
     - Through what processes did change take place over time?

D. Valuation
  - What was the worth of the relative improvement of recipients?

E. Critical Review
  - What unexpected events and outcomes were observed?
  - What are the limits to the findings?
  - What are the implications of these findings? What do they mean in practical terms?
  - What recommendations do the findings imply for modifications in program and policy?
  - What new policies and programmatic efforts to solve social problems do the findings support?

A summative evaluation, on the other hand, often requires all five of the tasks listed in Table 6.1. There is generally a need to document and make judgments about the quality of implementation, monitor as many of the relevant outcomes as practical, develop conclusions about the contributions of the program in influencing changes in these outcomes, support judgments about the relative or absolute value of these program influences, and foster critical review about both the evaluation and the broader consequences of the program.

Implications of tasks for methodology. If summative evaluation is the main battleground in the current method conflict, and if summative evaluations often require all five of the tasks delineated in Table 6.1, which tasks are most problematic in debating the value of rigorous evaluation designs over other designs? For this, note that the first two tasks—implementation evaluation and outcome monitoring—begin with representing what is observed, whether it is the program activities or outputs (e.g., the number of training modules provided to teachers), or the outcomes of interest (e.g., student scores on state exams). Both the qualitative and quantitative approaches have recommended practices and standards for ensuring the reliability and construct validity of these representations.

Impact evaluation begins with this representation of activities and outcomes but requires also making judgments about causal impacts. This indeed is the kernel of the current controversy, as it requires judgments about the unique impacts of the program as distinguished from all other likely influences. Most in the evaluation community would acknowledge that failure to tease apart the program influences from other influences and confounds generally leads to invalid conclusions about program impacts. A range of methodologies, especially experimental and quasi-experimental designs, but some qualitative approaches as well, attempt to address these other influences, either through control or detailed explanation. How well these methodologies succeed in distinguishing the possible influences is a matter of debate. As such, the most fundamental difference in viewpoint in the methodology controversy is over the *adequacy* of these different designs to answer questions on causal impacts, such as those listed in part C of Table 6.1.

Multiple Levels of Conclusions

A second way to frame the variation in evaluation questions is in terms of what can be called the level of conclusion. In line with our focus on the impact evaluation task, the levels of conclusions can be understood by building on the distinction of three types of questions that Weiss suggests in the area of impact evaluation. The most basic of Weiss's (1998) impact questions in Table 6.1 is the following: "Is the observed change due to the program?" A more general form of this question is "What are the impacts due to the program?" This reflects a concern with the magnitude of program impacts, which may differ from the observed change when, for example, selection bias has resulted in program participants who are more disadvantaged or at risk than those in a comparison group.

In addition to estimating overall program impacts, impact evaluation often addresses, as indicated in Table 6.1, two related questions. First, evaluators are often concerned with moderated relationships wherein the size of the impact of a program is dependent on other factors. A second ancillary question addresses what are believed to be the underlying mechanisms responsible for the observed outcomes. Gathering evidence about those mechanisms, or processes, allows one to reassess the theory that guided the program and to suggest modifications to the program theory.

As background, it is useful to note that these three groups of questions—the overall aggregate questions, the questions about moderated relationships, and those focused on inferences about some underlying reality—apply to much that we do in evaluation. For example, when representing outcomes (section B in Table 6.1), such as the prevalence of homelessness in the United States, aggregate statistics are often made more meaningful through disaggregation across time or across geographical regions. Inferences about underlying constructs come to the fore in discussions on different definitions of homelessness, particularly in characterizing different "types" of homeless individuals (e.g., those without any shelter versus those staying with family). Similarly, the results of cost-benefit analysis as an approach to valuation (section D of Table 6.1) are generally presented both in the aggregate (overall net/present value) and disaggregated by major stakeholder groups. The focus on an underlying reality comes when, often through critical review, we consider whether real human needs are being met by programs and are reflected in the analyses.

Our concern in this chapter, however, is with the causal analysis required in impact evaluation and the associated method controversy. Accordingly, we discuss in more detail, as presented in Table 6.2, these three levels for the causal questions of impact evaluation.

Aggregate description. The exemplar of aggregate causal analysis in evaluation is the random assignment experiment that finds the treatment group has higher average scores on some desired outcome than the control group. For example, a random assignment experiment could be conducted to demonstrate an overall impact of calculator use on scores on a standardized mathematics exam (e.g., the NAEP). Based on such an experiment, we would feel justified in concluding that using the calculator caused the difference in

Table 6.2   Analysis of Methods Addressing Causal Questions in Evaluation

	Impact Evaluation
Aggregate Description	Causal description of impacts (internal validity); e.g., "The supportive housing program improved the housing stability of families compared to families that did not participate in the program."
Disaggregation	Generalized causal inference (including external validity); e.g., "The program improved the mental health outcomes of women, but had its greatest effect for women with higher clinical needs."
Inferences of Underlying Phenomena	Causal explanation based on underlying mechanisms; e.g., "The program was effective because it provided access to housing assistance while families were in the homeless shelter."

average scores for the two groups. This is an important piece of knowledge, representing what Shadish, Cook, and Campbell (2002) call a descriptive causal conclusion. It is descriptive in the sense of claiming that something about the treatment caused the observed difference but not trying to explain how the impact occurred. This is the classic domain of internal validity, distinguishing the "treatment as a package" from other causal factors, such as history and selection bias.

Sometimes fairly simple methods are sufficient for identifying causal impacts. For example, monitoring outcomes can, under select circumstances, seem sufficient for supporting conclusions on impacts and thus guiding action. However, in many of the contexts faced by evaluators, measured outcomes provide only ambiguous evidence of impacts and more formal approaches to supporting causal analysis are seen as having distinct advantages. Even when the methods used seem adequate, however, there are limits to what aggregate descriptive causal conclusions can tell us, leading scholars such as Cronbach (1982) to claim that internal validity is trivial. In general, such limits are addressed by disaggregated analyses and analyses that seek to identify underlying causal mechanisms and attribution to interventions of interest.

Disaggregation. Disaggregation for causal analysis can result from separate analyses for different groups, but also often makes use of moderated relationships yielded by including interaction terms in the analysis. For example, the calculator use described above might have the greatest impact on certain subsets among those taking the mathematics exam, such as helping most those with prior training in calculator use. Quantitative analyses of moderated relationships typically make use of interaction terms in multiple regression and ANOVA, in multilevel models such as hierarchical linear models, or in survival models that can examine outcomes over time. For case study methods, Yin (1994) describes how multiple-case designs in case study research can reveal how outcomes are dependent on moderated relationships.

Inferential analysis: Underlying constructs and causal mechanisms. The inferential level for causal analysis involves methods that go beyond descriptive conclusions to say something about the underlying causal mechanisms that are responsible for the descriptive causal relationships. In this sense, we are trying to "explain" the observed causal relationship. For example, we might use research in cognitive science to understand how calculator use helps on exams (e.g., reducing time required for computation, helping students try out different solutions, or helping students focus on the conceptual elements of the question). This understanding can then support the goal of disaggregation described above, such as allowing us to understand better the types of questions or the types of students that should benefit from calculator use.

The point for this inferential analysis is that though we might be grateful to have an accurate understanding of the descriptive causal relationship, we are rarely satisfied for long with this alone. We generally, though not always, would like to understand the mechanisms that are responsible for the observed causal impact. In traditions such as regression analysis and structural equation modeling, the study of mechanisms is the study of mediated relationships, or causal linkages, that relate the program activities to the targeted outcomes. An emphasis on logic models, program theories, and the search for underlying generative mechanisms is consistent with this focus on mediated relationships. The use of mixed methods, with qualitative accounts of the reasons underlying observed outcomes, is of particular use in both validating and deepening the understanding of our findings.

Implications of levels of conclusions for methods. Having agreed that the current method debate is focused on supporting the causal analysis required for impact evaluation, we now see that there are several levels of causal questions likely to be of interest. This is relevant here, as the value of random assignment experiments in specific settings varies according to which level of conclusion is of greatest concern.

Among those who accord some value to random assignment experimental designs for evaluation, there is broad agreement that such designs are particularly appropriate for aggregate causal questions, such as estimating the overall effect of a program or policy innovation. Indeed, the prototypic justification for RCTs (randomized controlled trials) is in providing somewhat definitive answers to this aggregate-level question.

The assessment is more complicated when considering the value of random assignment experiments in revealing the moderated relationships that underlie efforts to disaggregate results. On the one hand, reasonable sample sizes and the availability of fairly standard demographic data can allow evaluators to identify differential program effects on different groups of program participants. Experimental methods, for example, often make use of random assignment within subgroups, using strata or blocking variables, to support strong conclusions about the strength and importance of these factors in demonstrating moderated relationships.

Other types of disaggregation can be more difficult in experiments. For example, if, after data are collected, it becomes clear that implementation varied across the different settings, it can be misleading to attribute differences in outcomes to differences in implementation. Similarly, conversations with program participants might suggest differing impacts on different outcomes, only some of which were measured. In contrast, qualitative methodologies make it easier to learn about different outcomes of interest as the program and evaluation progress.

Understanding the underlying causal mechanisms via experimental methods is at least as difficult as supporting disaggregated conclusions. Critics contend that experimental methods are incapable of identifying causal mechanisms (Pawson & Tilley, 1997), but the relative virtues of experiments are more subtle than that. Note first that the experimental method in social sciences such as psychology is employed primarily when there are theories about underlying mechanisms, and the series of studies in an experimental research program are designed with modifications that progressively clarify the nature of those mechanisms. So it is that an experimental evaluation of disability policy, for example, will likely involve policy variations that reflect presumed psychological mechanisms that influence the willingness of people receiving disability-based public benefits to increase their earnings (Silverstein, Julnes, & Nolan, 2005). On the other hand, it is certainly true that experimental methods can only address a small number of presumed mechanisms and can offer limited insight on how multiple mechanisms interact. Adding qualitative methods in a mixed methods approach can provide the needed insights about complex mechanisms, but it is also true that the rich understanding that results can make the a priori experimental contrasts seem ill-advised at best.

Thus, experimental methods are argued as appropriate for strengthening impact-evaluation conclusions, but the value of these methods is dependent on the level of conclusions being addressed. While some stakeholders will in general be more interested in aggregate conclusions (e.g., those responsible for federal policy) and others more in the results of disaggregated analyses (e.g., state or local policy makers concerned with appropriateness for their contexts) or analyses of underlying mechanisms (e.g., program developers), being explicit about these multiple levels will help clarify what are claimed as advantages of one method over another in specific settings.

Desired Form of Causal Conclusions

Even if it is agreed that an evaluation planned for a specific setting needs to yield valid aggregate causal conclusions, there is another consideration that affects the value of different methodologies. This final frame builds on a distinction made by Dawid (2000) that concerns whether relevant stakeholders are interested primarily in determining the causes of known effects (e.g., what was responsible for improved education test results) or in identifying the effects of a known cause (e.g., what happens to employment and earnings when there is a change in Social Security Disability Insurance policies). The first question is often addressed with case comparison methods (e.g., looking at those who experienced a serious side effect from a drug and trying to understand how they differ from those who did not experience that side effect) and the second with experimental manipulations (Shadish et al., 2002).

The typical debate around this is between those arguing for the adequacy of qualitative methods for the first question (you can spot this when you hear phrases like "establishing causality" or "modus operandi method") and those insisting that only rigorous quantitative methods can provide unbiased answers to the second (as in, "estimating program impacts"). Without distinguishing the two causal questions, the debate is never really engaged. A reasonable clarification is that both quantitative and qualitative methods can be effective in establishing causality, but quantitative experimental methods have a distinct advantage for estimating the magnitude of program and policy impacts, particularly when it is possible to employ random assignment and make population estimates based on sampled data.

Summary of Relationships
Between Questions and Methods

The analytic framing presented above is intended to highlight the distinctions between the different types of evaluation questions and their implications for method choice. At the end of this unpacking of the four frames, our conclusion, which we believe is acknowledged by most in the evaluation community, is that rigorous designs such as RCTs are primarily valuable *when stakeholders want an evaluation to yield valid population estimates of the magnitude of program or policy impacts.* This entails wanting to assess the merit and worth of a program and conducting an impact evaluation that can be trusted to distinguish program impacts from the impacts of all other relevant influences. It also suggests a primary importance of aggregate conclusions, as well as perhaps the moderating influence of a limited number of demographic variables.

Our posited consensus on the particular set of questions that call for rigorous quantitative designs is not intended or expected to foreclose debate, merely to clarify it. Some may argue that primary stakeholders are rarely concerned with questions on the magnitude of unique program impacts. To the extent that proponents of random assignment experiments cannot show that their stakeholders are interested in these questions, they should acknowledge the limited appropriateness of experimental methods. Our experience in working with stakeholders in federal agencies and in large foundations, however, is that they are often very interested in establishing credible estimates of the magnitude of program or policy impacts. They are interested in these estimates of magnitude primarily because the actuaries in the federal government responsible for estimating the budget impacts of policy changes (such as OMB, the Office of Management and Budget) are often interested in little else. Before authorizing a policy change, officials want and need some sense of the financial implications, and this often requires some estimate of policy benefits, such as the number of people who will benefit to the point of not requiring further government assistance. So, the space of stakeholder questions for which RCTs are almost uniquely adequate may be quite small, yet one can still conclude that there is a need to increase the capacity in government and in the evaluation community to conduct such rigorous designs.

Relegating RCTs to a small space in the realm of stakeholder questions leaves substantial evaluation territory open to proponents of other designs. However, if opponents of random assignment methods believe that other methods are as good or better at answering questions about the magnitude of program impacts, they need to make their case more explicitly and effectively than has been done to date. Similarly, if proponents of RCTs wish to argue for the superiority of such designs for a much expanded space of stakeholder questions, they, too, need to make their case in ways not yet done. We do not expect these persuasive arguments to be forthcoming and thus hope that our framing of the stakeholder questions helps avoid spurious debates in which opposing sides are referring to different questions when critiquing available methods.

In sum, our multiple framing of these questions offers hope of a more informed dialogue on which methods are best able to yield actionable evidence that requires first considering the stakeholder questions of interest. However, we must also then consider the contextual factors that affect the adequacy and appropriateness of alternative methods for answering these questions. In the next section, we address how context affects what constitutes actionable evidence for guiding program and policy decisions.

What Contextual Factors Condition the Evidence Needed to Support Causal Conclusions?

We have connected decisions about evaluation design to the questions of primary interest to identified stakeholders. However, here again, context matters. Even when it is agreed that estimating program impacts is the main concern, factors such as the policy context and the nature of the phenomena being studied will affect the need for rigorous designs.

Policy Context

Efforts to advance our understanding of what constitutes actionable evidence need to consider multiple perspectives, not simply those of evaluators. This suggests a political context that includes the degree of confidence that policy makers and other stakeholders feel that they need before taking action, and also the relative importance of knowledge production and knowledge accumulation for the range of stakeholders.

Degree of desired confidence. Some situations call for greater confidence in the conclusions that result. For example, it is generally accepted (see Mark et al., 2000) that efforts to improve programs through incremental program changes require less confidence in causal conclusions (e.g., that hiring more staff will "cause" a reduction in client dissatisfaction and complaints) than do efforts to help determine which of two alternative programs should be funded (e.g., an assessment of the relative worth of two approaches to teaching English as a second language) or whether to continue or expand a program. Not only are incremental improvement efforts better able to rely on previous evidence of effectiveness, there is also the expectation that incremental changes can be reversed more easily if subsequent evidence supports very different conclusions.

This variation in desired confidence in causal conclusions occurs in the context of other priorities, including understanding the degree to which the program impacts can be expected to generalize to other settings. While the tension between strong causal conclusions (internal validity) and generalizability is not inevitable or absolute, trade-offs between the two are common in practice. Other priorities that often compete with the accuracy and precision of the findings include timeliness, cost of the evidence that is to result, and whether there are opportunity costs for conducting one study as opposed to another, all considered below under evaluation constraints.

Knowledge production and accumulation. Deciding what method to use to address a particular question depends, in part, on the state of knowledge in that area. Evidence that might appear weak and unworthy of confidence in one situation can be judged actionable in others. For example, early in a public health emergency, such as the HIV/AIDS crisis of the past quarter-century, anecdotal evidence can play a role in guiding action that would not be appropriate in the context of better evidence and greater understanding. Conversely, for emerging problem areas where little is known about a phenomenon, it may be premature to mount an experimental study. There may not be adequate information on the population in need, the nature of the interventions, and so on to warrant a study or risk the chances of it failing.

In addition, for an evaluation to produce knowledge that can have cumulative force, it is necessary to be aware of the understanding already attained in an area. For example, as Boruch (2007) notes, if current knowledge is limited such that the solution to an issue is extremely debatable, a randomized study may be warranted; otherwise, other methods may suffice. There is also often a responsibility to learn as much as possible about the phenomenon as one is evaluating solutions to deal with it. Thus, the depth of underlying knowledge in an area may influence the methods that are appropriate to promote knowledge accumulation.

With this focus on accumulation, the question of the relative importance of confidence in causal conclusions changes in that the pool of relevant stakeholders telescopes to include those who will make use of the evaluation evidence at some point in the future. This increases the incentive to strengthen the technical adequacy of the knowledge produced. Whereas improvements in the technical adequacy of methods are unlikely in themselves to resolve the debate over evaluation methodology, they can reframe the debate by showing us how to retain rigor while also moving beyond some standard design solutions to strengthen causal conclusions. That is, there will always be cogent and passionately held differences in opinion about how evaluators can and should best contribute to the social good in particular contexts. This is good—debates between strong positions in evaluation (e.g., between Campbell and Cronbach) have yielded much that is to be valued. However, it is also the case that failure to understand technical advances already available can prolong debates unnecessarily (Shadish, 2002).

The need for defensible knowledge, especially in charged policy situations, requires us to continue these advances.

Nature of Phenomena Studied

Another contextual determinant of the information needed to address causal questions is the nature of the phenomena under study, such as school dropout rates among transitioning at-risk youth or weight change among those with eating disorders. Aspects of the phenomena studied discussed below are the complexity of the mechanisms responsible for change, the complexity of the system dynamics involved, and the expected patterns of change.

Complexity of mechanisms studied. One key method-related aspect of the phenomena studied is the degree to which the presumed causal mechanisms can be easily identified. As an example, contrast the differing implications of studying school dropout rates, as noted above, with studying waiting times in airport security lines under different inspection procedures. The relevant mechanisms are likely understood better in this latter category than in the school dropout example, affecting the methods needed to maintain confidence in causal conclusions.

One difference is that the notion of "mechanism" is quite different in physical systems from how it is used in human psychological and social systems (Mohr, 1996). This is the point made by Boruch (2007), citing as an example the testing of bullet-protective material on pigs. The outcome of shooting pigs with the protection does not require establishing the "counterfactuals" of shooting a pig without such protection—we know that the pigs would be seriously or mortally wounded. However, when we are considering volitional behavior or complex systems with many confounding factors, it is more difficult to think of situations when the counterfactuals are as clear as they are with physical systems.

Complexity of the system-context dynamics. The sheer complexity of some phenomena, like comprehensive reforms (Yin & Davis, 2007), questions the applicability of some evaluation designs including random assignment. Conducting a set of mini-studies to try to answer the central questions also is often misplaced, as they often miss the critical questions about the initiatives as a whole. A number of authors (Connell, Kubisch, Schorr, & Weiss, 1997; Fulbright-Anderson, Kubisch, & Connell, 1998; Rog & Knickman, 2004) note the challenges in evaluating comprehensive reforms, such as the role and dynamics of the context; the evolutionary nature of the initiatives and the fact that they are often designed from the bottom up; variations in what they do, who they serve, and where they take place; the difficulty in quantifying and measuring the goals (e.g., increasing community efficacy, systems change); and the fact that, because they often encompass entire communities or neighborhoods, there are often few places that lend themselves for comparison. Finally, the "system" under study and its context are typically often hard to distinguish, with boundaries blurred (Yin & Davis, 2007).

Patterns of change. A third aspect of the phenomena relevant for method choice is the manner in which change in the outcomes of interest can be expected. The greater the latency between the onset of an intervention and changes in measured outcomes, the more difficult it is to rule out alternative causal explanations. On the other hand, if the outcomes most relevant in judging program effectiveness are likely to improve quickly after the onset of the intervention, degrade quickly after the intervention is discontinued, and improve again after reinstatement of the intervention, then independent manipulation of the intervention without a comparison group (as in an ABAB design), and certainly without one based on random assignment, might be adequate for confidence in causal inferences (Shadish & Rindskopf, 2007). Unfortunately, such responsive patterns of change are more likely with less complex mechanisms in less complex systems.

How Are We to Judge the Adequacy of Methods for Providing the Needed Evidence?

Even if we can agree on the information, or evidence, needed to address identified stakeholder questions, there is considerable controversy over the degree to which specific evaluation methods are adequate for providing the needed information. Complicating a resolution to this controversy is the lack of consensus on how we determine what is adequate.

Varieties of Actionable Evidence About Methodology

Just as we advocate for evaluations to produce "evidence" to guide program and policy decisions, we should be guided by evidence or data in our work—specifically, in what methods we choose to use in specific situations. Table 6.3 provides an overview of three general sources of evidence for method choice that we propose to guide method choice based on others' work—outcome-based, practice-based, and critical review (see Boruch, de Moya, & Snyder, 2002, p. 52). In this section, we discuss criteria for judging each type of evidence for determining methods to use, and offer conclusions about the value and shortcomings of each.

Table 6.3   Sources of Actionable Evidence for Informing Policies on Method Choice

Outcome-Based Evidence: What is the impact of method choice on evaluation outcomes? Major concerns include
- O Accuracy and precision of findings
- O Reliability and validity of the outcomes/findings
- O Depth of findings and explanatory power

Practice-Based Evidence: Is there wisdom and evidence of effectiveness in practice? Major concerns include
- O Agency policies and preferences
- O General quality of implementation
- O Use and persuasiveness of the findings

Critical Review as Evidence: What are the broader social impacts of methodological choices? Major concerns include
- O Analysis of ethical implications
- O Reflection on broader social consequences

Outcome-based evidence. Outcome-based evidence implies assessing alternative research designs by the outcomes produced, with respect to their accuracy and precision and their persuasiveness and influence. This is the standard approach used in quantitative studies wherein, for example, the outcomes of interest might be the calculated effect sizes that result from a random assignment design as compared to the average effect sizes produced when using nonrandomized comparison groups. Boruch (2007) marshals this type of evidence in describing systematic studies of the effect of method choice on study outcomes.

For qualitative studies, the parallel concern would be whether different approaches yield different conclusions when applied in similar settings. One might be interested, for example, in whether a case study approach using semistructured interviews applied to one facet of school reform yields different outcomes from an ethnographic approach based on ongoing observations and interactions with program participants.

This issue of corroboration highlights the importance of criteria for outcome-based approaches when there are differences in study findings across different designs. Specifically, if different designs tend to yield different assessments of program effectiveness, we need to make sense of these differences. For many quantitative and qualitative designs, there are established criteria determining the reliability and validity of the data collection, with measures of reliability (inter-rater, internal consistency, and test-retest) and validation procedures (criterion-related validity, but also the more general construct validity paradigm). For quantitative designs as well, however, there is also a long tradition of assessing the adequacy of internal validity in terms of ruling out alternative mechanisms that might be responsible for program-related outcomes. Illustrating that these criteria transcend the traditional comparison group paradigm, Shadish and Rindskopf (2007) make the case that single-subject research has developed corresponding ways of strengthening our confidence in conclusions derived without large samples or distinct comparison groups.

There are less established bases for determining the accuracy and precision of the evidence from qualitative designs or those that lack comparisons. Designs that employ triangulation incorporate the ability to judge the significance of particular outcome data. In addition, designs that build in "contrarian" and alternative views allow one to determine if even divergent perspectives yield convergent findings or results. However, standards differ across various designs and approaches and, in some instances, are absent. It is in this context that the work of Robert Yin (1994; Yin & Davis, 2007) has been particularly helpful in developing criteria for judging the adequacy of case study research and evaluation.

Accuracy and precision are not, however, the only outcome-related criteria generally used in assessing the value of evaluations. The extent to which an evaluation can provide answers to the "why" and "why not" questions that revolve around outcome findings also operates as criteria for determining whether a particular methodological approach will provide actionable evidence. The affinity toward logic models and program theory is in part guided by a need to understand the elements within a program that may be key ingredients causing the outcome as well as generative mechanisms that are linking agents to the ultimate outcomes of interest. Growth in the attention to moderators and mediators in our evaluation designs and analyses is responsive to the need to understand not only if something made a difference, but also for whom and under what conditions. Studies that have simplistic designs that can be easily analyzed with ANOVA may not be suited to the complex program and policy situations we are asked to evaluate.

Practice-based evidence. Another source of justification for matching a method to a situation is to assess them in terms of the method preferences and practices of various agencies. The rationale for using this type of evidence is that over time one expects some form of environmental pressure to lead people to use those practices that meet their needs and provide the best information. To the extent that this dynamic does indeed select for more useful, and more context-sensitive, methodologies, one can talk of there being "wisdom in practice" that needs to be explicated.

Examples of this source of practical evidence include formal agency policies regarding preferred methodologies for different types of studies, actual historical trends in the use of alternative methodologies, and patterns of current use (Boruch et al., 2002). One might hope that adaptive selection would also be sensitive to the quality with which the various methodologies are often implemented. If a random assignment design is excellent in the abstract but is rarely implemented effectively in certain contexts, this might be taken as evidence of its limited appropriateness in such contexts. Lois-ellin Datta (2007) documents potential examples of "wisdom in practice," noting, for example, that agencies that make the most use of qualitative evaluation may have particular needs that are addressed less well by quantitative approaches. Further, she delineates several factors, both institutional and personal, that might account for these patterns of practice. In particular, she notes differences among agencies with varying cultural needs that respect, value, and demand different ways of knowing.

Another practice-based concern is whether the methods did in fact produce actionable evidence that were put to use by policy makers and administrators. It might be, for example, that the questions best addressed by random assignment designs constitute a narrower set than what policy makers want answered for informing policy. On a related note, Judith Gueron (2002) emphasizes the greater persuasiveness of the results of random assignment studies, but the stories of actual people collected through qualitative inquiry are often held up as particularly important to policy makers. Either way, the work by Carol Weiss (1988, 1998; Weiss, Murphy-Graham, & Birkeland, 2005) and many others (e.g., Cousins, 2004; de Lancer Julnes, 2006; Kirkhart, 2000) on the utilization of evaluation highlights the difficulties in using some measure of "influence of findings" as a yardstick to measure the appropriateness of the approaches used. First, the latent nature of how studies often have an effect and the rare instances of immediate "instrumental" use challenge our ability to measure the true impact findings have. Moreover, the nature and receptivity of the results, the extent to which a "policy window" exists, and competing priorities have as much to do in determining whether an evaluation is successful in affecting public policy as does how the results were derived.

The challenge for accepting actual practice as evidence of best practice alone is that practices can and do persist without necessarily being the "best choices." Some of the factors identified by Datta (2007) can lead to suboptimal practices as well as particularly effective ones. Accordingly, practice-based evidence is rarely persuasive by itself for those interested in understanding the desired fit between method and context. Conversely, neglecting patterns of practice puts a greater burden on the other sources of evidence in trying to understand the contextual nuances that should condition use of different methods in different circumstances.

Critical review as evidence. A third source of evidence about method choice can be discussed under the general label of critical review. The issue for critical review is whether our current policies and practices for method choice are taking us where we want to go as a society (Henry & Julnes, 1998). One focus of critical review for evaluation is to consider the ethics of the evaluation practices. For example, one might make use of ethical analysis to argue that a particular methodology, such as random assignment to experimental or control groups, leads to undesired social consequences for particular groups of those affected by a study. This seems to be Lincoln's (2004) view when, in reviewing the Cook and Payne chapter in Mosteller and Boruch (2002), she points out that random assignment designs might be more acceptable with willing adults than with the small children who are often the focus of educational evaluation.

A related point for this ethical analysis is that experimental methodologies may be used in an elitist mode that neglects the values and voices of those being studied (e.g., Greene, 2007; Schwandt, 2007; Smith, 2007). In the disability policy arena, for example, the phrase "not about me without me" is often used to express the right of a person with a disability to be involved in research that claims to represent the issues affecting him or her (Julnes, McCormick, Nolan, & Sheen, 2006). On the other hand, ethical analyses could also lead to the conclusion that random assignment is the most just way of allocating scarce resources in particular settings (Boruch, 2007). In addition, in highly political situations, having more defensible data that fit agreed-upon standards of accuracy and precision may be more defensible and provide stronger evidence to support change in areas that have been heretofore resistant.

Critical review can also involve a consideration of other long-term consequences of using particular designs. For example, while cognizant of the criticisms of experimental methods, the thrust of the critique by Cook and Payne (2002) of the long-term failure to advance our understanding in education is that there has been an overreliance on less-effective (i.e., nonrandom assignment) designs. Tharp (2007) addresses the balance of methods from a developmental perspective, arguing that it is the *process* of development that must be supported and that different methods are valuable at different stages in organizational and social development. This is a reminder that context-appropriate method choice is a means to an end and that the desired "end" is better viewed as an ongoing process than as some fixed and final outcome (Julnes, Pang, Takemoto-Chock, Speidel, & Tharp, 1987). The larger point for critical review is that policy debates on method choice take place within the broader governmental arena of competing interests and competing values (Julnes & Foster, 2001), some consistent with our notions of social betterment, some not.

When Is It Appropriate to Use Particular Methods of Causal Analysis?

Beyond the *adequacy* of different methods is the *appropriateness* of using those methods in specific situations. On the one hand, situational constraints might result in evaluations that could be misleading; on the other hand, we need to recognize the ethical implications of method choice.

Evaluation Constraints

Even if there is consensus that a more controlled, randomized study is the best technical choice to address the questions of interest, there are often practical, political, and conceptual constraints that function as hurdles that must be surmounted before an experimental design is accepted as appropriate. One way to understand these constraints and to determine if they can be surmounted is through the conduct of an *evaluability assessment* (see, for example, Wholey, 2004)—an evaluation planning tool designed to judge the readiness of a program for rigorous evaluation. Among its features are an assessment of program readiness (examination of the logic of the program as designed and as implemented, the stakeholder agreement with logic, and the program stability and potential for impact) and evaluation capacity (requisite capacity for measurement and other conditions, such as appropriate control groups) to conduct a study that is feasible, appropriate, and has the requisite rigor to guide discussion. Finally, by determining the extent to which decision makers agree upon the desired outcomes from a program and can articulate how they would use the potential evaluation results, evaluability assessment directly unearths and confronts any political tensions and constraints that may exist that need to be eliminated before an evaluation can produce actionable evidence.

Degree of program readiness. Evaluation theories have long addressed the need for the primary evaluation questions and preferred methods to change as the focus moves from initial pilot demonstrations to established programs or policies. For the evaluability model, issues affecting method choice include the degree to which there is clear program logic, the extent to which stakeholders agree on that logic, and the extent to which there is consistency between what is designed and what is implemented.

1. *Clear and Appropriate Program Logic.* The internal logic of a program or policy is too often assumed and not examined before a study is designed and mounted. The lack of a good program theory tying the program to the intended outcomes can render an evaluation meaningless and indicate the need for greater attention to informing the redevelopment of a program.

The program logic, however, needs to be in line with resources. For example, a program may be designed to be staffed by 10 professionals, but resource cuts now mean that only four professionals and four paraprofessionals can be hired. How does this change affect the program's ability to achieve the outcomes? Are there different outcomes that should be considered? The program logic needs to be adaptable to such changes.

2. *Degree of Program Maturity and Stability.* As Weiss (1998) points out, a concern of evaluability assessment is whether the program "operates as intended" and is "relatively stable" (p. 73). This is particularly important to discern before mounting an intensive evaluation that seeks to estimate program impacts. Indeed, one of the major criticisms of randomized experiments, accepted fully even by proponents of experiments, is that they are conducted before programs are ready for this type of inquiry (see Datta, 2007; Lipsey, 2007; Tharp, 2007). Related to this readiness, some programs are quite dynamic in their orientation and their stability may be greatly influenced by outside factors (e.g., funding, weather conditions). This fluctuation can necessitate design features that track and measure these changes and incorporate them into both conceptual and analytic models. This need is even more pronounced when conducting multisite evaluations, where each site may have fluctuations that need to be examined, and judgments need to be made about the suitability of including the site in the outcome evaluation and design features to add to understand these contextual dynamics.

Evaluation capacity. There may be additional issues with the evaluation and measurement capacity of a program and the overall environment that make certain designs less possible. There may not be the conditions in place for a randomized study or the data system in place to examine "dosage" of services provided. In addition, as Datta (2007) notes, in program areas such as Head Start, it may not be feasible to construct a no-treatment comparison group due to the spread of early intervention. Being able to obtain enough participants to yield a sufficient sample size is a related problem. Some programs may lack a sufficient pool of possible program participants in the community that meet the study eligibility criteria; some may lack the staffing capacity to serve clients in the study period given the number of clients that can be served by each staff member, the amount of time they are expected to receive program services, and so on. For other programs, there may not be the systems in place to monitor programs over time, and thus circumstances would not be conducive for ongoing performance monitoring. Time is also a critical capacity issue often not taken into consideration (or ignored because the funding time frame is set) when examining the plausibility of achieving stated outcomes; often those outcomes agreed upon by stakeholders are well outside what is plausible to achieve within the evaluation time frame, and the more proximal and intermediate outcomes that the program could achieve have not been considered or delineated.

Political constraints. As noted above, political constraints, especially those unattended to, can undermine the potential value of an evaluation. In particular, understanding how the stakeholders of a program view its purposes and intended outcomes can be important to developing an evaluation that is accepted and produces findings that have influence. Where evaluators differ is on which stakeholders should be included and the priority their views should be given. Evaluators with a focus on social justice believe too much attention has historically been given to decision-making stakeholders and too little attention has been given to the beneficiaries of programs and others affected by their consequences. The implication of this belief for method choice is that resource-intensive methods are less defensible when there is insufficient consensus on a program's purposes and intended outcomes on the part of those it affects or when there is only a limited chance of the results being used to inform future practice that could benefit those a program serves.

Ethical Considerations

The final domain addressed here, though it might be the first constraint to consider in practice, concerns the range of ethical considerations that can lead us to choose one design over another, even if they are in conflict with some of the other information obtained. For randomized studies in particular, Boruch (2007) has suggested a list of questions at one level of ethical thinking that guide whether a randomized study is ethically warranted.

Protecting human subjects. Whatever design is chosen, there are ethical implications for study participants. For example, the 1978 Belmont Report charged Institutional Review Boards with protecting human subjects of research in terms of three principles: respect for persons (protecting personal dignity and autonomy), beneficence (maximizing anticipated benefits and minimizing possible risks), and justice (making sure the benefits and burdens of research are distributed fairly).

Respect for persons includes the requirement of informed consent and the need to respect the values of participants—without intending harm, being included in a study can hurt participants in many ways, some of which are only poorly understood when informed consent documents are signed. Beneficence requires that the evaluation be expected to yield real benefits (i.e., the problem being studied is serious and the findings are likely to guide future decisions) and entail only the minimal risks necessary to achieve this benefit. If, for example, an experimental evaluation design results in more defensible findings than other approaches and is found to have more influence in guiding policy decisions than other approaches, this would argue for use of that design in similar situations as long as there were only a minimal risk to participants. The concern with justice includes whether it is ethical to withhold treatment from those assigned to the control groups (e.g., those denied treatment perhaps bearing an unacceptable burden for the benefits to others that might result). However, in most current-day evaluations, the control groups are not "no treatment" groups but rather continue to receive any treatment or services as usual. The case can be made that if a treatment is in fact known to be better than receiving other services, then it is not an obvious candidate for summative evaluation.

Promoting social justice. In addition to justice as it relates to protecting participants, there is also a broader concern with social justice. In particular, there may be subtle or not-so-subtle consequences of method choice that work against the interest of some stakeholder groups. As Lois-ellin Datta (2007) noted, some federal agencies, such as the Bureau of Indian Affairs, might need to be especially sensitive to cultural issues that might not be addressed well with rigorous designs, such as with randomized field trials. A related point is that different stakeholder groups might want and need different sorts of information from an evaluation, and so prioritizing the needs of one group could be in conflict with the needs of others. Indeed, maximizing the utility of the findings for one stakeholder group may make them relatively useless or, worse, insulting for other stakeholders. Social justice requires that those least advantaged not be further disenfranchised by focusing only on the information needs of those with the greatest resources. This latter concern may not suggest one method over another, but rather the conduct of multiple or mixed methods in instances where the information needs are varied and diverse. It might also mean that in the evaluation planning/evaluability assessment phase, the evaluator has the obligation to share these various stakeholder perspectives, especially with the decision-making stakeholders, in an early effort to bridge some of these differences and help develop a constructive approach to the evaluation.

Attending to procedural justice. There are several concerns related to procedural justice in evaluation. One is the concern that many have with the federal government imposing standards on others. While part of this concern is that federal standards tend to be too uniform to meet different needs in different contexts, in this instance there is also simply the procedural concern with maintaining autonomy in decision making with regard to evaluation methodology (see Chelimsky, 2007). This procedural concern applies also to those who are the intended targets or recipients of the programs to be evaluated. Federal policies may make it more difficult for these program consumers to have input into the evaluation methodologies to be used. For example, persons with disabilities, in line with the phrase "not about me without me," are asking for and expecting more input into the design and implementation of evaluations of disability policies and programs as well as the interpretation and application of their results (Julnes et al., 2006).

Discussion

This chapter has presented the value of different methodologies in generating actionable evidence in addressing various evaluation questions. Our goal in this chapter was to approach the topic of method choice from a pragmatic perspective, one that can guide the choice of research designs to produce findings that in turn guide action. We begin this concluding discussion, therefore, with a review of the pragmatic elements of our contribution, then summarize the contextual factors that influence method choice, and finally suggest some steps that can be taken to continue to inform the variety of perspectives on evaluation methodology.

Pragmatic Framework for Method Choice

One point of agreement among many commentators on the current methodology debate is that it can at times be fueled by ideology. Although many qualitative and quantitative methodologists have a deep appreciation of a wide range of methods, too often proponents of one approach construct extreme images of opposing approaches as dogmatic and insensitive to context. Taking the knocking down of such caricatures as support for one's own position, this approach, with its *reductio ad absurdum,* makes it too easy to conclude that one's own approach is (almost) always preferred to other approaches and, hence, too difficult to promote meaningful dialogues on this controversy.

The pragmatic approach is to focus on the contextual contingencies that make our various research designs and methods more or less useful. Cornel West (1995) emphasizes this contextual step in clarifying our thinking by noting that "To demythologize is to render contingent and provisional what is widely considered to be necessary and permanent" (p. 314). Our sense is that the dialogue on what methods are appropriate and adequate would be more productive if the claims made in favor of and against specific methods were more contingent and provisional.

Contingent view of "best" evidence. As the chapters in this volume make clear, there will always be different views of what is required for evidence to be judged credible, but this shift to judging evidence not just on the methodological rigor with which it is derived but also based on what we and others view as persuasive is important and necessary. We need to remind ourselves, however, that evidence is not to be viewed as credible in some universal, abstract sense. In the area of measurement theory, measures, such as an intelligence test, are not judged as valid in general; instead, one speaks of the validity of particular conclusions derived from the measure as employed under specific conditions. So it is with judging credibility: the same evidence might be judged as credible under some conditions but not others. Failure to acknowledge this contextual nature would leave us with a dimension of credibility, ranging from low to high, on which some evidence is better than others and some is even viewed as the "best" as in a gold standard for evidence.

Therefore, our approach has been to emphasize "actionable" rather than "best" evidence to add to the contextual frame for judging the value of evidence. The value of evidence in such settings is dependent not only on whether evaluators judge it as credible but also on the degree to which the evidence is considered relevant to both the major stakeholder questions and to the contexts in which the actions of policy or program change are to take place.

Contingent view of best methodology. Just as there is little hope of defining what would be the best evidence independent of specific settings, so there is consensus that we should avoid holding up one methodology, such as the randomized experiment, as the gold standard or best methodology without regard to context. The label of gold standard has inflamed the controversy unnecessarily with its implication of a best methodology to be aspired to or approximated by many, if not all. This in turn distracts attention from the important task of matching methods with the needs of particular situations.

But if we know that methods must be selected to meet contextual needs, then perhaps we can organize our understanding of context into a decision-analytic framework that considers the many contextual factors and recommends the best methodology for that specific context. For example, given stakeholder concerns, available resources, and a few other considerations, it may be reasonable to conclude that a particular design is to be recommended. We support efforts in this direction but are skeptical that any final product will yield automatic choices of methodology. Not only is it difficult to consider so many factors at once, but there will also be little consensus on how to weight the various factors in selecting the best methodology. Some will likely apply greater weight to stakeholder questions than many other evaluators would; others will view ethical issues as trumping other factors more often than is typical among evaluators. Thus, efforts to consider context in identifying best methodologies represent an improvement over universal claims, but ultimately the same issues apply and situated judgments will always be of some value.

Context-based decision rules. Although unable to specify best methods in the abstract, we can at least identify and organize the factors that need to be considered in matching methods to specific contexts. In this chapter, we have offered what might be seen as the first steps in such a project by identifying the relevant contextual factors. Specifically, Table 6.4 summarizes the factors addressed. We note that RCTs are particularly valuable when (1) stakeholder questions require population estimates of the magnitude of program or policy impacts; (2) a high degree of confidence is desired in causal conclusion about impacts and the current knowledge is ambiguous and controversial; (3) the phenomena of interest do not allow for alternative approaches of estimating the counterfactual (what would have happened in absence of the intervention) because of the complexity of the presumed mechanisms involved, and the time lag of intervention impact complicates using an ABAB design; (4) the program appears to be at near-optimal functioning and there are sufficient resources to implement the necessary components of the RCT methodology; and (5) there are no major ethical concerns with implementing the RCT methodology.

In sum, as our theories and methods are tools, so are the frameworks offered in this chapter and elsewhere in this book to help guide method choice in evaluation and research. Accordingly, we have discussed and organized an array of factors that reasonable people will and should consider in deciding the appropriateness of different methods in specific situations. We have, however, resisted the temptation to offer anything as prescriptive as a decision model that takes our discussed factors as inputs and yields as an

Table 6.4   Review of Factors Influencing the Value of RCTs

Contextual Factor	Conditions Favoring RCTs
Stakeholder questions	When questions about the merit and worth of programs are foremost, particularly if interested in estimating the aggregate impacts for populations of interest
Policy context	When high levels of confidence about causal impacts are desired, particularly when current knowledge about these impacts is ambiguous or controversial
Nature of phenomena studied	When the mechanisms affecting outcomes are complex and it is difficult to estimate the "counterfactual" outcomes that would have occurred without the program
Evaluation constraints	When resources are sufficient to conduct a rigorous RCT and the program to be evaluated is stable and operating at what is believed to be near its peak level of functioning
Ethical considerations	When conducting the RCT would not compromise the rights of participants and would not contribute to social or process injustice

output the appropriate methodology for an evaluation in a specific setting. Rather, we seek to be systematic in understanding the factors that should influence method choice but are realistic in expecting that this issue will continue to be debated as government policies are advanced to guide method choices.

Process Implications for Promoting Appropriate and Adequate Evaluation Methods

Given the arguments developed above about the need to inform a debate that is not likely to end, we suggest several ways to promote an emphasis on conducting quality evaluations.

Embrace the "gray" in a black and white debate. Part of what has led to less-than-productive dialogues over methodology is the tendency to oversimplify opposing positions. This was seen in prior qualitative-quantitative debate where those criticizing the qualitative position bolstered their own position by ascribing a disbelief in causality to qualitative evaluators. Qualitative evaluators returned the favor by labeling quantitative evaluators as "positivists," a philosophical position that had been abandoned a half-century earlier. This human tendency to overrepresent our own views and oversimplify the opposing view is relevant to current debate over the methods needed to yield actionable evidence. On the one hand, opponents of efforts to promote RCTs (e.g., the ED published priorities) see attempts to enshrine experimental methods as a gold standard to be pursued whenever feasible; on the other hand, proponents of RCTs see a resistance to ever funding experimental methods. Our approach has been to find the "gray" commonality in this black and white debate so as to foster dialogue and help determine when certain methods are indeed agreed upon to be the more useful and pragmatic choice.

Pursue consensus where it can be found. The points above about a developmental model of inquiry apply as well to other areas with potential consensus. In this chapter, we have developed a set of factors that most would acknowledge as relevant in assessing the adequacy and appropriateness of different methods. This potential for partial consensus highlights the potential of pushing this consensus as far as it can go. In contrast, agreeing on which methods to use in specific settings is likely to be more problematic and likely less satisfying in the short run.

Relatedly, we might have more success reaching consensus on the criteria used to judge the value of different methods than we do in applying those criteria for actual method choice in specific settings. Outcome-based evidence, though most compelling, is generally best suited for quantitative designs, specifically randomized studies. Standards of quality for judging other designs are lacking and need to be developed. In particular, there is a need for standards in assessing the quality of a study's conceptualization, and how a study is implemented. The same applies for the analyses used in qualitative studies; in particular, they need a level of transparency that allows for critical review and assessment of accuracy.

Adopt a process orientation to methodology. Affirming evaluators as serving an inquiry process that is itself in service to social betterment, we affirm that our primary loyalty is to the quality of evaluation rather than to any particular methods or ideologies underlying these methods. From this view, it is well accepted that evaluation needs evolve over the life cycle of a program, beginning with exploratory attempts to improve implementation and understand how the program might address the targeted needs, and much later moving toward a full summative evaluation to assess and document overall effectiveness. Tharp (1981) made this point a quarter-century ago, using an ecological metaphor to argue for a natural progression of methods applied during the life of a program, current texts (e.g., Rossi et al., 2004) offer systematic conceptions of these evolving needs and associated methods, and government agencies (e.g., the U.S. Government Accounting Office) offer concrete recommendations that relate appropriate methodology to the program life cycle.

There are, however, other process issues that could improve the methods used in evaluation. One issue is that our views of effective methods in particular settings may change faster than our capacity to execute effectively evaluations based on these methods. Thus, even if there is a need to conduct more RCTs in certain evaluation areas, we might not have enough appropriately trained evaluators to implement the designs successfully. This would affect our judgments about the value of RCTs in general rather than their value given the current lack of capacity. The alternative conclusion would be that RCTs hold promise but require more capacity building in the sense of training in experimental methods, experience in running experimental evaluations, and dialogues on lessons learned among those who have been involved with experimental methods.

A second process-related point is that we do not want to presume enduring answers to questions about methodology. As new techniques are developed, designs and approaches formerly viewed as inadequate can be strengthened to yield evidence accepted as actionable. For example, statistical controls (e.g., adding control variables in multiple regression analysis) have generally been judged as less adequate than design controls (e.g., employing experimental and control groups), but recent advances in propensity scoring have resulted in "empirical studies that suggest that they can provide estimates of effects that are as good as those from randomized experiments" (Shadish, 2007).

Strive to fight fair. If we accept that our methods are tools and we will always be revisiting and renegotiating the value of different methods in different situations, it behooves us to approach this never-ending process in more productive ways. While such advice is obvious in the abstract, there may be much to learn from other traditions for dealing with conflict. For example, there is a tradition of family and marriage counseling that emphasizes learning to "fight fair" when addressing family conflicts. Focusing on the specific application of methods and designs and agreeing ahead of time upon criteria for assessing "design fit" can, we believe, help develop a "fairer" playing field than one that is based solely on ideological vs. pragmatic grounds.

Conclusion: So What Counts as Credible Evidence?

Interest on the part of government in using evidence to inform decision making has increased the potential for program and policy evaluation to contribute to improved governance and, more generally, to social betterment. This increased interest, however, has also cast a brighter light on evaluation methods and their adequacy in yielding evidence worthy of guiding decision making. This, of course, requires some consensus on the desired qualities of the evidence used to inform program and policy decisions.

This volume seeks to advance our understanding of this issue by asking, "What constitutes credible evidence?" Our chapter contributes to this discussion in two ways. First, we argued that in the evaluation context, as opposed to theory-building research, the "worthiness" of evidence is better framed as whether it is "actionable" rather than "credible." While, in general, more credible evidence is more worthy of guiding action, this reframing makes the quality of evidence less a matter of logic and more one that is concerned with the needs of actual managers, policy makers, and other interested stakeholders.

Second, we developed the notion that the worthiness of evidence, whether the focus is on being credible or actionable, cannot be judged in the abstract but rather only in terms of the needs and constraints of specific situations. We make no claim that this is an original insight; indeed, we would argue that everyone understands that different types of evidence are needed for different decisions. We do claim, however, that this general platitude has been underdeveloped, that much of the conflict over methodology in government-sponsored evaluations could have been managed better if we had elaborated in greater detail the factors that condition the adequacy of evidence in different contexts. It is to this second point that we devoted most of our chapter, framing the issue in terms of four questions: How are methods to be related to the questions that stakeholders want addressed? What contextual factors condition the evidence needed to support causal conclusions? How are we to judge the adequacy of methods for providing the needed evidence? and When is it appropriate to use particular methods of causal analysis?

How Are Methods to Be Related to the Questions That Stakeholders Want Addressed?

We began by affirming the primacy of the evaluation stakeholder questions in influencing the types of evidence needed in guiding decisions. Here, however, we have gone beyond traditional distinctions (e.g., program improvement questions vs. program continuation questions) to progressively localize the conflict in terms of

- The *tasks* required in addressing evaluation questions (representation, causal inference, and valuation), with a focus on the controversy over causal inference;
- The *level of analysis* (aggregate description, disaggregation, and inferences about underlying phenomena) of causal inference desired by stakeholders; and
- The *type* of causal conclusion of most interest (identifying the causes of a known effect or identifying the effects of a known cause).

What Contextual Factors Condition the Evidence Needed to Support Causal Conclusions?

This delineation of evaluation questions and implications for methodology might suggest guidelines for which methods produce credible or actionable evidence for specific questions, but the method implications are more complex and subtle than that. Equally important are a number of contextual factors that further condition the nature of the evidence needed to guide action. For example, relevant aspects of the policy context include the desired degree of confidence (decisions that can be reversed easily require less evidence than those with more permanent implications) and the nature of existing knowledge on the topic (weaker evidence can be actionable when little else is known; conversely, evidence consistent with a large body of existing evidence is reasonably judged as more credible than evidence without such corroboration).

The nature of the phenomena being studied is also relevant in that some causal relationships are sufficiently simple that even casual observational evidence is sufficient to establish the relationship (e.g., the Boruch example recounted above of pigs not being hurt when covered with protective material before being shot). Conversely, the more complex the system relationships in the domain being studied (as in evaluating the impact of a new curriculum in school districts also participating in other school policy experiments and in neighborhoods targeted by various social policy initiatives), the more important it is that multiple sources of evidence support the resulting conclusions.

A third evidence-relevant aspect of the phenomena studied is the pattern of change that can be established. If an organizational policy affects employee behavior in a way that corresponds to the implementation, rescinding, and subsequent re-implementation of the policy (as in a classic ABAB experimental design), then the causal contribution can be established through outcome monitoring. When the impacts of a policy change can take years to reveal themselves (e.g., employment outcomes in response to changes in Social Security Administration policies), confident conclusions require evidence that other causal factors were not responsible.

How Are We to Judge the Adequacy of Methods for Providing the Needed Evidence?

Having addressed the types of program-related evidence desired in different contexts, how are we to assess evidence on the adequacy of available methods for yielding quality evaluation evidence? The standard approach has been to examine the conclusions that result from different methodologies. For this approach to be definitive, however, there needs to be an accepted yardstick against which to judge the results of other methods. That random assignment experiments were accepted as this yardstick, and hence given the "gold standard" label, has further inflamed the method controversy and increased interest in other standards for judging methods. Accordingly, in addition to the traditional focus on outcome-based standards, we argued for considering practice-based standards that view the patterns of use of different methodologies in different agencies and contexts as evidence of potential effectiveness. In addition, we promote the importance of conducting critical reviews of the adequacy of alternative methodologies.

When Is It Appropriate to Use Particular Methods of Causal Analysis?

On what basis do we judge it appropriate or not to use particular methods? In some cases, we have experience with the conditions or requirements that must be met for more involved methods to be useful. In other cases, it is an ethical frame that determines our views on appropriateness. Our chapter has addressed the contextual requirements from the perspective of evaluability assessment, discussing the elements needed for a program to be ready to be evaluated (clear program logic and program maturity), the needed evaluation resources (financial, organizational, and timing), and the political constraints (degree of stakeholder engagement and likelihood of evaluation evidence having a meaningful impact). Ethical considerations include the importance of protecting human subjects, the concern with promoting social justice, and the need to consider as well the implications for procedural justice.

Pragmatic Implications of Our Analysis

Our analysis of the different types of evidence needed in different contexts and of the adequacy and appropriateness of methods for providing this evidence is consistent with Greene's (2007) conclusion that method choice in evaluation should be "contextual, contingent, and political" (p. 111). We have tried to clarify the relevant contextual contingencies but have also cautioned against simple frameworks that drive method choice in a somewhat automatic fashion based on a couple of these factors. Instead, our hope is to promote greater consensus on the implications of the factors we identify so that greater clarity in deliberations can support more informed judgments on method choice in political public policy environments.

References

Argyris, C. (1996). Actionable knowledge: Design causality in the service of consequential theory. *Journal of Applied Behavioral Science, 32*(4), 390–406.

Boruch, R. (2007). Encouraging the flight of error: Ethical standards, evidence standards, and randomized trials. In G. Julnes & D. J. Rog (Eds.), *Informing federal policies on evaluation methodology: Building the evidence base for method choice in government-sponsored evaluation* (pp. 33–73). (Vol. 113 of *New Directions for Evaluation* series). San Francisco: Jossey-Bass.

Boruch, R., de Moya, D., & Snyder, B. (2002). The importance of randomized field trials in education and related areas. In F. Mosteller & R. F. Boruch (Eds.), *Evidence matters: Randomized trials in education research* (pp. 50–79). Washington, DC: Brookings Institution.

Chelimsky, E. (2007). Factors influencing the choice of methods in federal evaluation practice. In G. Julnes & D. J. Rog (Eds.), *Informing federal policies on evaluation methodology: Building the evidence base for method choice in government sponsored evaluation* (pp. 13–33). (Vol. 113 of *New Directions for Evaluation* series). San Francisco: Jossey-Bass.

Connell, J. P., Kubisch, A. C., Schorr, L. B., & Weiss, C. H. (Eds.). (1997). *New approaches to evaluating community initiatives: Concepts, methods, and contexts*. Washington, DC: Aspen Institute.

Cook, T. D., & Payne, M. R. (2002). Objecting to the objections to using random assignment in educational research. In F. Mosteller & R. F. Boruch (Eds.), *Evidence matters: Randomized trials in education research* (pp. 150–178). Washington, DC: Brookings Institution.

Cousins, J. B. (2004). Minimizing evaluation misutilization as principled practice. *American Journal of Evaluation, 25*, 391–397.

Cronbach, L. J. (1982). *Designing evaluations of educational and social programs*. San Francisco: Jossey-Bass.

Datta, L-e. (1994). Paradigm wars: A basis for peaceful coexistence and beyond. In C. S. Reichardt & S. F. Rallis (Eds.), *The quantitative-qualitative debate: New perspectives* (pp. 53–70). (Vol. 61 of *New Directions for Evaluation* series). San Francisco: Jossey-Bass.

Datta, L-e. (1997). A pragmatic basis for mixed-method designs. In J. C. Greene & V. J. Caracelli (Eds.), *Advances in mixed-method evaluation: The challenges and benefits of integrating diverse paradigms* (pp. 33–45). (Vol. 74 of *New Directions for Evaluation* series). San Francisco: Jossey-Bass.

Datta, L-e. (2007). Looking at the evidence: What variations in practice might indicate. In G. Julnes & D. J. Rog (Eds.), *Informing federal policies on evaluation methodology: Building the evidence base for method choice in government sponsored evaluation* (pp. 35–54). (Vol. 113 of *New Directions for Evaluation* series). San Francisco: Jossey-Bass.

Dawid, A. P. (2000). Causal inference without counterfactuals. *Journal of the American Statistical Association, 95,* 407–424.

de Lancer Julnes, P. (2006). Performance measurement: An effective tool for government accountability? The debate goes on. *Evaluation, 12*(2), 219–235.

Fulbright-Anderson, K., Kubisch, A. C., & Connell, J. P. (Eds.). (1998). *New approaches to evaluating community initiatives: Theory, measurement, and analysis* (Vol. 2). Washington, DC: Aspen Institute.

Greene, J. C. (2007). Method choices are contextual, contingent, and political. In G. Julnes & D. J. Rog (Eds.), *Informing federal policies on evaluation methodology: Building the evidence base for method choice in government sponsored evaluation* (pp. 111–113). (Vol. 113 of *New Directions for Evaluation* series). San Francisco: Jossey-Bass.

Gueron, J. (2002). The politics of random assignment. In F. Mosteller & R. Boruch (Eds.), *Evidence matters.* Washington, DC: Brookings Institution.

Henry, G. T., & Julnes, G. (1998). Values and realist valuation. In G. T. Henry, G. Julnes, & M. M. Mark (Eds.), *Realist evaluation: An emerging theory in support of practice* (pp. 53–72). (Vol. 78 of *New Directions for Evaluation* series). San Francisco: Jossey-Bass.

Julnes, G., & Foster, E. M. (2001). Crafting evaluation in support of welfare reform. In G. Julnes & E. M. Foster (Eds.), *Outcomes of welfare reform for families who leave TANF* (pp. 3–8). (Vol. 91 of *New Directions for Evaluation* series). San Francisco: Jossey-Bass.

Julnes, G., McCormick, S., Nolan, R., & Sheen, J. (2006). *Experiences and outcomes of the Utah Medicaid Work Incentive Program.* Technical report submitted to the Utah Department of Health.

Julnes, G., Pang, D., Takemoto-Chock, N., Speidel, G., & Tharp, R. (1987). The process of training in processes. *Journal of Community Psychology, 15,* 387–396.

Julnes, G., & Rog, D. J. (2007). Pragmatic support for policies on methodology. In G. Julnes & D. J. Rog (Eds.), *Informing federal policies on evaluation methodology: Building the evidence base for method choice in government sponsored evaluation* (pp. 129–147). (Vol. 113 of *New Directions for Evaluation* series). San Francisco: Jossey-Bass.

Kirkhart, K. E. (2000). Reconceptualizing evaluation use: An integrated theory of influence. In V. J. Caracelli & H. Preskill (Eds.), *The expanding scope of evaluation use* (pp. 5–23). (Vol. 88 of *New Directions for Evaluation* series). San Francisco: Jossey-Bass.

Lincoln, Y. S. (2004). High modernism at the National Research Council: A Review of F. Mosteller and R. Boruch's *Evidence Matters. Academe, 90*(6), 110–111, 113–115.

Lipsey, M. W. (2007). Method choice for government evaluation: The beam in our own eye. In G. Julnes & D. J. Rog (Eds.), *Informing federal policies on evaluation methodology: Building the evidence base for method choice in government sponsored evaluation* (pp. 113–115). (Vol. 113 of *New Directions for Evaluation* series). San Francisco: Jossey-Bass.

Mark, M. M., Henry, G. T., & Julnes, G. (2000). *Evaluation: An integrated framework for understanding, guiding, and improving public and nonprofit policies and programs.* San Francisco: Jossey-Bass.

Mohr, L. B. (1996). *The causes of human behavior: Implications for theory and method in the social sciences.* Ann Arbor: University of Michigan Press.

Mosteller, F., & Boruch, R. (2002). *Evidence matters.* Washington, DC: Brookings Institution.

Pawson, R., & Tilley, N. (1997). *Realistic evaluation.* Thousand Oaks, CA: Sage Publications.

Reichardt, C. S., & Rallis, S. F. (Eds.). (1994). *The qualitative-quantitative debate: New perspectives* (Vol. 61 of *New Directions for Program Evaluation* series). San Francisco: Jossey-Bass.

Rog, D. J., & Knickman, J. (2004). Strategies for comprehensive initiatives. In M. Braverman, N. Constantine, & J. Slater (Eds.), *Foundations and evaluations: Contexts and practices for effective philanthropy* (pp. 223–235). San Francisco: Jossey-Bass.

Rossi, P. H., Lipsey, M. W., & Freeman, H. E. (2004). *Evaluation: A systematic approach,* (7th ed.). Thousand Oaks, CA: Sage Publications.

Schwandt, T. A. (2007). Thoughts on using the notion of evidence in the controversy over method choice. In G. Julnes & D. J. Rog (Eds.), *Informing federal policies on evaluation methodology: Building the evidence base for method choice in government sponsored evaluation* (pp. 115–119). (Vol. 113 of *New Directions for Evaluation* series). San Francisco: Jossey-Bass.

Scriven, M. S. (1967). The methodology of evaluation. In R. W. Tyler, R. M. Gagne, & M. S. Scriven (Eds.), *Perspectives of curriculum evaluation* (pp. 39–83). (Vol. 1 of AERA Monograph Series on Curriculum Evaluation). Skokie, IL: Rand McNally.

Shadish, W. R. (2002). Revisiting field experimentation: Field notes for the future. *Psychological Methods, 7,* 2–18.

Shadish, W. R. (2007, November 7–11). *The renaissance of quasi-experimentation.* Paper presented at the Annual Meeting of the American Evaluation Association, Baltimore, MD.

Shadish, W. R., Cook, T. D., & Campbell, D. T. (2002). *Experimental and quasi-experimental designs for generalized causal inference.* Boston: Houghton Mifflin.

Shadish, W. R., & Rindskopf, D. M. (2007). Methods for evidence-based practice: Quantitative synthesis of single-subject designs. In G. Julnes & D. J. Rog (Eds.), *Informing federal policies on evaluation methodology: Building the evidence base for method choice in government sponsored evaluation* (pp. 95–109). (Vol. 113 of *New Directions for Evaluation* series). San Francisco: Jossey-Bass.

Silverstein, R., Julnes, G., & Nolan, R. (2005). What policymakers need and must demand from research regarding the employment rate of persons with disabilities. *Behavioral Sciences and the Law, 23,* 1–50.

Smith, N. L. (2007). Judging methods. In G. Julnes & D. J. Rog (Eds.), *Informing federal policies on evaluation methodology: Building the evidence base for method choice in government sponsored evaluation* (pp. 119–123). (Vol. 113 of *New Directions for Evaluation* series). San Francisco: Jossey-Bass.

Tharp, R. G. (1981). The meta-methodology of research and development. *Educational Perspectives, 20,* 42–48.

Tharp, R. G. (2007). A developmental process view of inquiry and how to support it. In G. Julnes & D. J. Rog (Eds.), *Informing federal policies on evaluation methodology: Building the evidence base for method choice in government sponsored evaluation* (pp. 123–126). (Vol. 113 of *New Directions for Evaluation* series). San Francisco: Jossey-Bass.

Weinberg, J. (1973). Causation. In P. P. Weiner (Ed.), *Dictionary of the history of ideas* (pp. 270–278). New York: Scribner.

Weiss, C. H. (1988). Evaluation for decisions: Is anybody there? Does anybody care? *Evaluation Practice, 9*(1), 5–20.

Weiss, C. H. (1997). Theory-based evaluation: Why aren't we doing it? In D. Fournier & D. J. Rog (Eds.), *Progress and future directions in evaluation: Perspectives on theory, practice, and methods* (pp. 41–55). (Vol. 76 of *New Directions for Evaluation* series). San Francisco: Jossey-Bass.

Weiss, C. H. (1998). *Evaluation: Methods for studying programs and policies.* Upper Saddle River, NJ: Prentice Hall.

Weiss, C. H., Murphy-Graham, E., & Birkeland, S. (2005). An alternate route to policy influence: How evaluations affect DARE. *American Journal of Evaluation, 26*(1), 12–30.

West, C. (1995). Theory, pragmatism, and politics. In R. Hollinger & D. Depew (Eds.), *Pragmatism: From progressivism to postmodernism* (pp. 314–325). Westport, CT: Praeger.

Wholey, J. S. (2004). Evaluability assessment. In J. S. Wholey, H. P. Hatry, & K. E. Newcomer (Eds.), *Handbook of practical program evaluation* (2nd ed., pp. 33–61). San Francisco: Jossey-Bass.

Yin, R. K. (1994). *Case study research: Design and methods* (2nd ed.). Thousand Oaks, CA: Sage Publications.

Yin, R. K., & Davis, D. (2007). Adding new dimensions to case study evaluations: The case of evaluating comprehensive reforms. In G. Julnes & D. J. Rog (Eds.), *Informing federal policies on evaluation methodology: Building the evidence base for method choice in government sponsored evaluation* (pp. 75–93). (Vol. 113 of *New Directions for Evaluation* series). San Francisco: Jossey-Bass.

PART III

Nonexperimental Approaches for Building Credible Evidence

7

Demythologizing
Causation and Evidence

Michael Scriven

Myths grow up around all great institutions and grand dreams, from the Greek gods and the master race, to democracy and the American West, and science is no exception. They are usually based on some over-simplified claim about the nature of science: that it's essentially quantitative, or concerned only with general claims, or only with claims that are falsifiable, or that are intersubjectively testable, and so on. Refuting them is mainly an exercise for the philosophy of science journals. But there are times when we need to separate the myths from reality in a wider forum, and this is the time to separate the current myths about causation and evidence from the reality, because the issue is no longer a merely academic dispute. The lives and welfare of huge numbers of human beings now hang in the balance, and we need to bring our best thinking to bear on settling the issues.

AUTHOR'S NOTE: My thanks to Ryoh Sasaki for raising some problems with an earlier draft of this overview that I hope to have resolved in this version.

134

Commonsense Science

The current mythology receiving most public attention would have it that scientific claims of causation or good evidence, either optimally or universally, require evidence from randomly controlled experimental trials (RCTs).

The truth of the matter—the reality—is very different, as many readers with good general scientific knowledge will realize upon reflection. If you think of the domain of science as represented by a map of the United States, the concepts of causation and evidence are ubiquitous, and normally used with great care and precision throughout the region. On this map, the Eastern Seaboard represents the area where RCTs rightly rule, including, for example, pharmacology and some parts of clinical medicine and applied psychology; in the Midwest, that approach is often an option, but in the rest of the country RCTs are completely irrelevant to the scientific work of the region, though for slightly different reasons in different areas.

For example, the South on our map represents the domain of mathematical physics where laws rule. There have been efforts, for example by Bertrand Russell, to outlaw the notion of cause from science, based on the observation that mathematical laws, which he thought represented the ideal form to which all science should aspire, do not employ the term *cause*. Commonsense prevailed, since those laws, the moment they are applied to any real case, provide an excellent basis for causal claims without invoking experiments. For example, in astrophysics we have no difficulty in providing causal explanations about the motion of bodies like comets and meteorites moving under gravitational forces, although we are obviously not able to do any experiments with those bodies.

In the Mountain West, where geology is king, we don't have any mathematical laws, but we have some good models of causal processes—for example, in explaining the formation of the Rockies, or Meteor Crater in Arizona, or, for that matter, the craters on the moon. Again, no experiments were or will be called for in support of these claims, although plenty of empirical research in the field provides the evidence to back them up. On the Central Pacific Coast, we find the domains of anthropology and ethnography, where it's considered just plain unacceptable to experiment with one's subjects— but the scientists seem to have no problems about recording their observations of tribal warfare in which one person injures another, or domestic activities where people make things or do things, all of these being causal claims. In the Pacific Northwest, the home of epidemiology, where the cause of epidemics like lung cancer, obesity, or food poisoning are the hot topics, or in the Southwest, where the forensic sciences reside, and where we find plenty of autopsies aimed at determining the cause of death or studies by the National Transportation Safety Board (NTSB) on the cause of airline disasters or the collapse of bridges, there seems to be no mention of control groups. The scientists at work in the West, or the South, are not dreaming of the day when things will get better so that they can run "true experiments"— they are just getting their jobs done, and finding no intrinsic barriers to drawing causal conclusions.

In short, much of the world of science, suffused with causal claims, runs along very well with the usual high standards of evidence, but without RCTs. We all know this very well, once we are reminded of it.

So it's just a myth that science does better, if its work in support of causal claims is based on experiments, although the way many of us were taught science, with an emphasis on the great experimental sciences of physics and chemistry and the parts of biology that make good projects at science fairs, tends to foster that illusion.

Where is the battle being fought, and why is it a battle at all? These questions bring us to the Midwest, which is another story. This is the land of bipolar allegiance, and there are many localities there where dominance has alternated between the experimental and the nonexperimental forces, with some areas remaining loyal to the midstream party of the quasi-experimentalists. The crusaders from the conservative Northeast are trying to take over the domains of education, psychology, sociology, social work and penology, international affairs, and parts of medicine that occupy this territory, along with other domains, and it's true that in some areas their takeover has led to improvements—people had been using less sound approaches when RCTs could have been used. But in many other cases, the attempted takeover is just forcing the issue, and the force used often causes more grief and distortion than benefits. For these are the areas where "it all depends"—that is, the right choice of investigative methodology depends on whether one can get the resources needed, the permissions required, the time window stretch, and so forth, that the demanding RCT model must have.

In such cases, to insist that we use an experimental approach is simply bigotry—not pragmatic, and not logical. In short, it is a dogmatic approach that is an affront to scientific method. Moreover, to wave banners proclaiming that anything less will mean unreliable results or unscientific practice is simply absurd. Look west, young man, or look south, and you'll see there are other ways to go that are just as scientific, just as capable of coming to causal conclusions that are beyond reasonable doubt. Those methods can be used in the Midwest, often are, and are frequently the best choice.

Before we leave our map, let's add something about what Canada is supposed to represent. That vast stretch of territory represents the proper use of causal language outside science. The two eastern provinces represent its use in history, by professional historians, who would have some difficulty arranging control groups with long-dead figures but have no difficulty—other than those involved in due diligence—in supporting causal explanations of many historical events. The two western provinces represent its proper use in the law, where it often meets the required standard for conviction of felonious acts, that is, establishing the facts "beyond reasonable doubt." And the central provinces of Saskatchewan and Manitoba represent its proper use in ordinary language and technology where we can say with complete confidence that we *know* that the reason our car just slowed down was *because* we pushed on the brake pedal, or that we lost the draft manuscript *because* we hit Delete at the wrong moment.

The overall picture the map represents is one in which RCTs stand in the grand sweep of causal usage. They own a small slice of it, and often there is a case for them to be granted a lease in another significant slice, although there they have to earn their place and are often not the best choice.

Logical Building Blocks for an Understanding of Causation

Let's see if we can get the elements of this issue set out plainly, to see how a safe path can be laid between the patches of quicksand that abound. There are really just five matters we need to be clear about.

First, it is crucial to understand the difference between the case for using RCT designs in a wider range of studies in the Midwest, which was underestimated for a while and is indeed well worth considering, and the case for insisting that it is the only legitimate causal design in that entire area; that is, the area where it is theoretically feasible. The first is good practice; the second is methodological imperialism, a kind of program that could only be justified if the RCT myth about causation were true instead of being a fantasy. In this situation the RCT myth, like the Aryan myth, has costly consequences in human terms: for example, where it has been believed (the World Bank appears to be the latest proselyte), it has jeopardized the funding of many large humanitarian projects that think they should not be evaluated using an RCT design—usually for ethical reasons (i.e., unwillingness to have some applicants prevented from receiving aid)—by supporting the view that this means they cannot be shown to be worth funding.

Second, we need to be clear how we acquire causal language, for that is where it gets and retains its essential meaning. It will be argued here that this investigation shows our original understanding supports bulletproof demonstrations of causal connections based purely on direct observation.

Third, we need to understand the standards of confidence that apply to causal claims, and how they can be met. It will be shown that the highest relevant standards for scientific purposes are readily attainable by many alternative designs in many cases.

Fourth, we need to be clear about what RCTs do that other designs do not, and how this bears on meeting high standards of scientific confidence. In particular, we need to look at half a dozen of the alternative approaches rather carefully, to see whether they are in fact inferior in terms of their ability to substantiate causal claims *and* the respects in which they will sometimes have significant advantages over RCTs (e.g., completion speed, resulting confidence level, cost, burden on subjects, generalizability, ethicality, level of expertise required for implementation, and side effects, if any). It will be shown that the usual claimed intrinsic advantage of the RCT design is only a theoretical advantage, and its actual achievements are easily matched in practice by many other designs; that even such a theoretical advantage is not present in the RCT designs currently being advocated because they are not in fact true RCT designs; and that, nevertheless, there are real advantages for a near-RCT approach in some circumstances, although they can only be determined by weighing its comparative merits on (at least) the eight listed considerations (see Sundry Notes section, later in this chapter) that bear on the merit of a research design.

Fifth, we need to be clear that there *is* a "gold standard" of experimental design for causal investigation, although it is not the RCT; it is the logical underpinning of the RCT and the many competing designs. This is the *general elimination method* (GEM), quite easily understood and more easily taught than the RCT.

In the following discussion, we do not segregate the above points, since the overlap and interaction among them is extensive, but all will receive solid support.

The Origin of Causal Concepts

The first of the two foundation stones to be laid in constructing the logic of causation is the proposition that causation is directly and reliably—indeed, trivially and universally—observable. It is perhaps best to approach the proof of this by looking at how we acquire the concept of causation. It is developed in the child's brain before language skills are well developed, and it springs from the palmar ("grip") reflex, which soon develops considerably: into the child's realization that he or she can manipulate the environment by shaking a rattle to make a noise, the recognition and manipulation of crayons for producing marks on paper, and the discovery that squeezing the cat makes her scratch. These are all cases of understood causation and indeed, by the age of 3 years, the average child has discovered some things that are much more sophisticated, beginning with how to cause others to do things upon request—and indeed becomes notably "bossy" about such demands. Also acquired are the basic notion of responsibility for his or her actions, resulting in blame when the child is bad and praise when he or she is good, and the denial of responsibility for "bad" actions (e.g., knocking something over) when the wind or a sibling did it. Soon there is language to express all of this, and the youngster rightly claims to see others do things, and is also able to get others to do things. In other words, their experience now includes the management as well as the observation of causation, and the evaluation of consequences. Maturation simply brings greater range and sophistication to these basics, so there's nothing essentially new about such claims as the adult makes (e.g., that the brakes are working well in his or her car), every datum for this generalization being a (tactile) observation of causation.

The Cognitive Process of Causal Inference vs. Observation

Despite the commonplace use of our language to the contrary, Tom Cook (personal conversation) and many well-trained social scientists and educational researchers, following Hume, find it hard to accept the notion of observed causation. They appear to favor the idea that we are "really" inferring it. But that's like saying we "really" infer that this person we see in the crowd meeting the passengers from our plane into San Francisco is our spouse. Of course, the neural net is, in some sense, putting bits and pieces together, but that's part of what happens in perception; the end result of these neural machinations is pattern recognition, not pattern inference. Hume's pitch was seductive because we don't see causation in quite the same way that we see color and motion. Causation, like many other complex predicates, refers to a learned holistic feature of a configuration, not just to a learned element in it. That configuration is what enables the billiards player to say, in suitable circumstances, that he did indeed see the cue ball strike the object ball, and thus cause the latter to head for the pocket. Once one learns how to see this kind of example of causation, it becomes part of the perceptual vocabulary, like the myriad instances of your friend's face, or even part of perceptual evaluation, for example, what makes a "good seat" in an equestrian event, or good style in a dismount from the parallel bars in gymnastics.

This epistemic status of causal claims as observable is fully recognized in the one place outside science where doubts are best respected, the court of law. Eyewitness testimony, especially but not only if it meets all the well-defined standards (normal vision, good lighting, clear field, propinquity, recency, corroboration, absence of motive to lie, etc.), is treated there as in science, as an appropriate datum in the court of last resort for establishing a case. The examples of it regularly include testimony that causation was observed in the standard cases such as battery, vandalism, and shooting. Causation is part of the language of observed acts, and as part of the language of observation, in suitable circumstances, it is established as having occurred with all the credibility that observation deserves, in science as in law.

So the first key conclusion here is that the simplest and probably the most reliable of all ways to establish causation is by critical observation. (I use the term "critical observation" here as shorthand for observation subject to the usual checks for the usual sources of error, including reflection on the likelihood of those.)

Interestingly enough, close study of the bible on quasi-experimentation, by Cook and Campbell (1979), turns up a passage in which this view is conceded, although its implications for causal methodology were never developed there: "we do not find it useful to assert that causes are 'unreal' and are only inferences drawn by humans from observations that do not themselves directly demonstrate causation" (p. 33).

This position leads us to the second foundation stone for the logic of causal inquiry.

Scientific, Legal, and Practical Certainty

One of the main attractions of the RCT approach is that it appears to provide a greater degree of certainty than alternatives. There are circumstances in which this is true, but it is not true across the board for several reasons, of which the first is that even causal claims based on direct critical observation can attain the benchmark level of certainty, and it's very hard to find an RCT that matches that standard. The "benchmark level" in scientific research, as in criminal law, and in common practice where important matters are at stake, is simply "beyond a reasonable doubt." This is the standard required to establish a case in criminal law, and is traditionally and extensively distinguished from "the balance of evidence," which is the criterion for establishing the occurrence of misdemeanors. This concept of certainty is part of the common language of science, so that in the lab or field, the observer or reasoner knows when to make and how to understand a claim that someone is certain that he or she did, or saw, or calculated, that something occurred or was the case.

This is not careless use, or abuse, of the term; it is the proper use of the term. It illustrates what the term does in fact mean. Some strands of perfectionist argument in epistemology here, as with perception and causation, have sought to persuade us otherwise, pushing us in this case toward the idea that the proper use of "certain" refers to the complete impossibility of error as in definitional claims and mathematical theorems. But "certain" is a contextually defined term and the proper standards for its use in the context of empirical discussions is empirical support beyond reasonable doubt, not the same standards as apply in talking about the realm of deductive proof. One might as well argue that the term large is improperly used to describe an emu's egg, or an elephant, or anything smaller than the universe. The perfectionist move is just an example of bad linguistic analysis. The law courts remind us that there is a well-established body of rules for the proper use of terms like *observe* and *certain* beyond what is sometimes scoffed at as the imprecision of ordinary usage. The courts define the hard core of ordinary use, since that is what the juries understand, and that is what good scientific use employs. Even Tom Cook (2001) concedes, in his magisterial review of the arguments for and against the RCT design, when talking about case studies (where we often rely on reported observations of causation), "I do not doubt that these procedures sometimes reduce all reasonable uncertainty" (p. 38). And that is just the conclusion we need to establish, for that is all that can be reasonably required of any scientific method for establishing causation.

The Alleged RCT Advantage

RCT designs do have an edge, although not the edge that is often claimed for them. As Tom Cook (2001) goes on to say in the quote begun above,

> I do not doubt that these procedures sometimes reduce all reasonable uncertainty, though it will be difficult to know when this has been achieved. However, I do doubt whether intensive, qualitative case studies can reduce as much uncertainty about cause as a true experiment. That is because such intensive case studies rarely involve a totally credible causal counterfactual. Since they typically do not involve use of comparison groups, it is difficult to know the group under study would have changed over time without the reform under analysis.

The first problem with this passage—and with this position, which is the basic argument for the superiority of the RCT (a.k.a. "true experiment") design—is that the RCT design, as used in the cases under discussion here, does *not* support a counterfactual. The RCT design as used in traditional pharmacological research does have this property. But in educational and community interventions, the design is crucially weakened and is no longer a double-blind, as it is in the drug studies. It is not even a single-blind. That is, both the subjects and the researchers know who is in the experimental group, and usually both know which subjects are in the control group. This leaves open a gap through which the Hawthorne effect (and its converse) can slip in. (I refer to this situation as a "zero-blind" or "unblinded" condition.) As Cook and the texts define the RCT design, the key point about it is that after randomization (and assuming adequate group size), the only relevant difference between the two groups is the treatment; but in the context we are discussing, there is another difference, namely the difference in the beliefs of the subjects and experimenters, which we know can cause effects of the type and size we are finding from treatments, and so we cannot conclude that differences in outcomes must be due to the treatment.

So the intensive case study (and the same applies to good quasi-experimental designs and critical observations) is not essentially disadvantaged against the RCT; both leave open, in principle, other explanations of whatever effects are claimed.

Might it not still be argued that the RCT has an edge in only having this one loophole, whereas in the other designs there are, at least typically, more possible counterexplanations? This is not as telling a point as it might appear, since the total probability of the alternative explanations is not additive based on the number of their descriptions; it is entirely situation-dependent. There will be situations where the Hawthorne possibility is more threatening to the RCT than the totality of the alternatives is to a case study or quasi-experimental design; this will be quite common in the case of the regression-discontinuity design, for example, but also will occur in many other cases. So the RCT edge, significant though it is when the design is double-blind (although even then not a unique edge on validity), is entirely situation-dependent in the normal context of social and educational inquiry. It will still be significant in special cases, but nonexistent or negative in others.

The second problem with the quoted argument for the RCT's superiority is that causation may occur in the absence of support for a counterfactual, as it does in cases of overdetermination. I have discussed these cases at some length elsewhere and will only remark that it is a significant although not crucial weakness of RCTs for the purposes of the present discussion that they will not have any advantage at all in such cases, whereas case studies (and some other approaches, e.g., those based on theory) will do so.

The bottom line here is that the advantage of RCTs is by no means general and must be established in the particular case, a nontrivial task. It remains true that there are cases, including important ones, where the RCT design will settle the issue of causation and no alternative approach will do so as well. However, the same is true for many other designs. The conclusion for researchers is simple: each case needs to be highly specified, including not just the exact question we need answered and the degree to which we want to be able to generalize the answer, but also the exact constraints on time and resources and social context, before one can decide on the optimal design for an investigation. That analysis is obviously not best done by those who specialize in RCTs alone; it must involve serious discussion by a panel including those experts in alternative approaches of several if not all of the kinds listed earlier. As Cook (2001) stresses, relying on a single approach is a methodological error and a serious one, and relying on the wrong one compounds the felony. Using a panel that favors just one approach would be a further felony in itself.

The Other Contenders

Every child acquires a repertoire of possible causes for a large number of effects before reaching school age; for example, children know that the vase on the table by the window can be knocked over by the wind, the shades, the cat, a sibling, a playmate, or a grown-up. When they encounter the effect, they begin to sift that list and check for indicators, either immediately observable or quickly accessible, that will eliminate one or more candidates and eventually may identify the responsible cause. This is the basic case of hypothesis creation and verification and it is the essential element, even if subliminally and non-inferentially, in all careful causal explanations.

There is a background assumption for this enterprise—the assumption that everything has a cause. The truth of that assumption in the macro domains of everyday experience and scientific investigations is unaffected by the discovery of micro uncertainty, not because the latter phenomenon cannot manifest itself at the macro level—indeed, it can—but because it has a sufficiently small incidence at that level to leave the deterministic principle unaffected as a methodological guide.

The two key components in the basic procedure outlined are the list of possible causes (LOPC), based of course on memories of prior personal or reported observations, and the general elimination methodology or algorithm (GEM). Both become increasingly complex as the individual's experience and learning expand—for example, by the addition of theories about possible causes that are extrapolations, or extensions by analogy or speculation, from a human's direct experiences. Take, for example, the theory of tectonic plates that added to the list of possible causes for mountain ranges. No one saw those plates collide and raise the Rockies or the Urals, but we all can visualize what happened on a smaller scale, and once conceived, we add it to the LOPC and can readily project the kind of clues in the geologic record that would confirm this etiology, thus kicking in the GEM process that in fact confirms the hypothesis.

When the hypothesis is about the formation of star clusters, we begin to move beyond models that are based on analogies with ordinary experience, and instead create formal models that extrapolate from those models or even from models that seem to have worked in other areas beyond direct experience. So the piggybacking continues, stretched to its limits with string theory at the macro limit and boson-hadron models at the micro limit. In all of these realms, however, the concept of causation continues, usually unchanged by the changes in the forms to which it applies, except for quantum uncertainty, where it, too, must be modified significantly. And in all these areas, for all these kinds of causal claims, the same procedures of investigation apply—that is, the process of LOPC identification and GEM application to whittle the list down in particular cases.

This vast web of theory-driven causation is essentially independent of any direct experimental confirmation, since it deals with entities that are largely beyond the range of manipulation. The large hadron collider at Geneva (a giant particle accelerator used by physicists to study the smallest known atomic particles), which was first fired up in 2008, is the culmination of the main exception to this segregation, the zone of experiments with fundamental particles. But even there, where the term "experiments" is always used, it does not refer to experiments with randomized controls, but to those ruled by simple pre-post design, entirely adequate in those circumstances to establish the conclusions to the satisfaction of the Nobel Prize committees. It is simply absurd to suggest that the conclusions arrived at in these circumstances do not deserve to be called "evidence-based" because there is no RCT in sight. To avoid tilting at windmills, it seems that we should modify the overgeneralized claims of the more enthusiastic supporters of RCT and allied terminology so as to retain a reasonable position to consider.

The Limited RCT Position

These controversial terms should be flagged in some way to indicate when they are not intended to be taken in their normal, all-contexts sense, so we'll add the prefix "limited" to their use in these restricted senses. This has the effect of converting positions that are absurd into ones that can be argued against without using such language as "absurd." Instead of saying, as the head of the Institute for Educational Science has pronounced, that there is no scientific basis for any causal claim that is not based on RCT studies, we'll take that as meant to apply to zero-blind (a.k.a. limited) RCTs used to investigate current (i.e., limited) issues about *the effect of typical large-scale interventions in areas such as education, health, and social services.* Correspondingly, we'll take the term "evidence-based," which is often said to be justified only for the results of RCT studies, to be intended to apply to limited RCT studies, *only* when talking about the effects of that kind of limited intervention in those limited kinds of areas.

The thrust of the preceding arguments is then that the limited claims are nevertheless wrong, even if not absurd. That is, even the view that only (limited) RCTs can establish limited causal claims is wrong, since they can be perfectly well established beyond a reasonable doubt in other ways and the limited RCTs aren't bulletproof themselves. Similarly, the view that the only (limited) evidence-based claims are those supported by RCT studies is wrong, since even limited evidence-based claims (that is, claims about typical current types of intervention in health, education, and social services) can be established by quasi-experimental, observational, and theoretical studies. Finally, the claim that "experiment" means a design with random allocation to the two groups should also be modified to the formulation, "limited experiments are those in which subjects are randomly allocated to groups."

This triple modification prevents what many have seen as an extremely tendentious, if unconscious, attempt to hijack an important slice of the scientific vocabulary.

Quasi-Experimental Designs (QEDs)

Let's walk through the consequences of the preceding arguments, using a common "lower-class" QED, the pre-post design with comparison groups. The argument given here would be much stronger with what is commonly thought of as a fancier or more robust design—for example, the interrupted time series design with bounded randomization of the intervals between applications. The example we'll use is of the highly interactive paradigm (HIP) for large introductory lectures at the college level, with enrollments in the low three-digit category. We divide the entering class in about half, in some convenient but not random way, such as by taking the morning class as the treatment group in the first semester of the experiment and using the afternoon class for the second semester of the experiment (this is a one-semester class). The experimental group receives the new treatment, and the others get the same approach that has been used for several years; the same instructor teaches both classes and teaches the control group just as he has for some years. That claim of approximate constancy in treatment is verified by an experienced colleague who visits a few times unannounced, and by a TA who's done that job previously and now works for both classes. Let's add that we have an experienced pair of instructional researchers independently look for other differences and find none to remark on. Each class gets the same pretest and posttest; they match closely on the pretest but on the posttest, where the control group shows about one sigma of improvement, the HIP group scores about two sigmas better than that. This effect recurs on two reiterations, the only two that are done as of report time for the 3-year experiment.

Now, did HIP have any effect? Given that you know the important "local knowledge" fact that it's extremely hard to kick a sigma difference out of any variation in instructional method, and that two sigmas is considerably more than twice as hard to get as one, the answer has to be yes, HIP made a big difference. Clearly the size of the difference is crucial here, as is often the case. Conclusion: there are situations where non-RCT designs will provide support for causal claims, beyond a reasonable doubt. If you now reflect on exactly what it would take to convert this study into even a limited RCT study, and on the fact that you are not very interested in small differences because they have a track record of never showing up on the replications at distant sites, you should be willing to buy the conclusion that the pre-post comparison study design is better than the RCT here. (That is, you use it knowing that it's a net that will catch only big fish, but you don't want little fish.)

There are a dozen variations on this kind of case, ringing the changes on such matters as dealing with cases where you are only interested in generalizing to the native population in Uganda, but the native population won't give permission for putting their children into the control group; or you can't afford the cost of measurement and monitoring for the control group of ex-addicted homeless people, and the memory effects of vitamin shots are small, so interrupted time series will work well.

The bottom line is that there are many cases where non-RCT designs will be better than RCT ones for the cases of interest, cases where they will indeed achieve results beyond a reasonable doubt, and even more cases where they will be better than limited RCT designs, the only ones we're really talking about. The limited strategy, which protects the RCT position from absurd overstatement, still cannot save it from being beaten on its own ground—that is, on ground where it can be used. Like a good two-wheel drive car, it can be driven in snow, but it's easily overmatched by the four-wheel drives in those conditions.

The fundamental logic of causal investigation, that is, the rules of inference required for establishing any causal conclusion, is not the use of experiments in the limited sense; it is the use of a critically developed list of possible causes together with critically applied general elimination methodology, required even for the justification (although not the occurrence) of critical observation.

Funding Strategies

It is now time to turn from the logic of grading and ranking experimental designs to the distribution of resources among them. The first lesson to be learned about the logic of portfolio construction is that the best single investment—better than every alternative though it may be—is not the best bet for the whole portfolio budget. Investment managers know very well that the rule about not putting all one's eggs in one basket is not just valid for the medieval housewives who inspired the adage and their successors. Provided only that one's second and third choices still meet the minimum acceptable standards for good eggs, they are better choices than further investment in the top pick for at least half the portfolio.

In research funding, a much-better-than-minimum-acceptable standard is the ability to produce conclusions that are beyond a reasonable doubt, so even if RCTs were superior in their ability to yield such results across the board (which is itself a true counterfactual), it would be highly unscientific to back them across the board since they, like all other designs, can go wrong, badly and completely wrong, in a way that is usually not reversible even if detected, and is not always detectable at midstream.

But in scientific research, there are two distinct further reasons for the heterogeneous strategy besides protection against failure. It may be helpful to think of the analogy with an investor who decides to put some money into the stock of companies who are working on a new oil field. She could put all her money into one company that has an excellent production hole that is currently the best on the field and is planning to drill more wells on that site. But she knows that a single site can peter out, hit an artesian aquifer that drowns the wells, or run into labor trouble; so for simple safety reasons—our first consideration—she will buy into at least one other outfit. She's covering herself against the possibility of failure. But there's another reason to do so: wells that begin with a less-than-stellar rate of production sometimes hit another pocket below the first and do much better later. So there's a chance of doing better by approaching the formation from two directions, even if the second one is less productive at first. That's the possibility of *superiority* via backing an independent approach. And there's a third reason, too, probably enough reason to justify investment in a third wildcatter. This is the chance to get a better overall picture of the layout of the field, which will be invaluable in guiding further action or withdrawal. This third consideration of course corresponds to getting some information about generalizability—external validity. Safety, possible superiority, and generalizability—three reasons for avoiding the monolithic strategy. The analogy carries over completely to the issue of funding research, a point that Cook stresses in the paper previously cited.

This argument does not dismiss the possibility of doubling the investment in the best option, it just recommends not restricting all investment to it. Doubling in the research case would make especially good sense if combined with slight variations in the research personnel and population used. But it still comes further down the list than variations in the primary strategy. Somewhere in between these two major paths to enrichment of a single design approach, there is the use of the superbly ingenious list of ways to match the comparison group without using random allocation, a list developed and provided by Cook (2001).

The argument given makes an invincible case for the indefensibility of the present situation in which, according to the extensive testimony from members of the review panels that have talked about it, there is no serious consideration of using non-RCT designs instead of RCTs. That strategy is largely based on bad reasoning about the superiority of what are in fact flawed RCT designs, which even if peerless would be no better than many others and clearly worse in many cases. This bad reasoning is combined with the fallacy of assuming that such superiority, if it did exist, would justify a monolithic strategy.

The present ill-based practice is also too often combined with denial of the existence of the monolithic strategy, sometimes accompanied by a gesture in the direction of regression discontinuity funding. If there is any doubt that an essentially monolithic strategy is de facto in place, it would be easy enough to establish the facts by doing a survey of funding over the past 2 years, using a contractor with a team from both sides. It is certainly long past time for a meta-evaluation of the success of the new emphasis on RCT funding, and the absence of any movement toward doing that surely shows a serious lack of interest in finding out the truth about the claims for improvement before proceeding still further with the takeover, especially in the latest area where it has established a beachhead, the evaluation of international aid.

It is important that the reasons against the monolithic strategy apply even if, per impossibile, the RCTs were superior across the board in the certainty with which they can determine causation. It is an argument designed to be acceptable to both camps.

Cooperation Combined With Competition

It would be unrealistic to suppose that the causal wars will cease in the light of the above treatment of the underlying differences between the competing positions. But it would be good to see some recognition of the very considerable range of cases where both parties can benefit from using the skills of the other. Tom Cook, in the article cited, lists many such cases, although not with quite the spin I'm putting on them, and I'll sum it up in my way by saying that it seems clear that the effective execution of RCT studies depends very heavily indeed on skills that are highly developed in qualitative researchers and extremely rare in the training of quantitative researchers. The converse position is also clear: there is still a considerable area in qualitative research where the skeptical reflexes of the trained quantitative researcher need to be heeded very carefully, not because their usual dismissive judgment is justified, but because by heeding their concerns, the design can be greatly improved, including its credibility to a wider audience—a worthwhile consideration in itself—and also, often enough, in its validity. But let's take a final moment to look at the need for qualitative research skills in managing RCTs. We can begin with the two great threats to the validity of the (already limited) RCT design: differential attrition and cross-contamination. No one denies that some very expensive RCT efforts in the past have been completely brought down by these weaknesses. If these flaws are detected very early, it is sometimes possible to stop them in their tracks, before validity is hopelessly compromised. How can an early-warning system for them be set up?

The answer is almost always through a continual process of interviews, both with groups and face-to-face, with both students and staff, with parents and with administrators—a program that not only seeks by intelligent and systematic questioning to pick up the warning signs, but also builds trust and cooperation in what is, after all, a project with potential benefits for all.

Interestingly, there is a double reward from this activity. It provides not only good insurance for the validity of the study, but also vital evidence about the process whereby the causal agent—and any inhibitors of it—operate, which provides key clues to the possibility of generalizations in some dimensions and the improbability of generalizations in other directions, and often strong supportive evidence for the causal connection under investigation. Cook gives a long list of the valuable information that can be picked up by these observers in the source cited.

And who has the training for this kind of observation and interaction? Of course, it is a job description for a qualitative researcher. These are high skills, not often taught as having top importance in quantitative training programs. Cook (2001) actually gives as his reason for abjuring the term "gold standard" for RCT designs the fact that these skills are of great importance, are hard to acquire, and are rarely available. The bottom line is that RCTs are really hybrid designs—mixed method in the sense of having essential quantitative and qualitative components.

So I end on this note. A marriage of the warring parties is not only possible but would provide a win-win solution, with major winning side effects for those in need around the world. The prenuptial agreement should include (i) recognition of the place of duties for both parties; along with (ii) funding for non-RCT studies where they are better fitted to task and context than RCTs, with skilled quantitative researchers collaborating to cover both sharpening the design and analyzing the numerical data; plus (iii) at least one collaborative meta-evaluation panel funding proposals from both parties; and (iv) another one evaluating the success of contracts of both kinds. Serious concern with research standards (and human welfare) suggests that we should shortly see some proposals like this and/or signs that such proposals would be funded.

Conclusion: So What
Counts as Credible Evidence?

Myths are grand stories, fictions that achieve cult status, and they spring up around all powerful structures, whether structures of knowledge or political or market entities. Some of the myths about science occasionally acquire enough of a cult following to materially alter policy, as for example the myth about the inheritance of acquired characteristics altered agricultural policy in the Soviet Union at one stage. The currently popular myths about causation and evidence have now achieved this kind of potentially dangerous cult status. Those who stand to suffer include those who have been served by giant philanthropic programs that are now being attacked as based on inadequate evidence of efficacy. This chapter attacks these myths, mainly by reminding readers of their general commonsense and general scientific knowledge.

People are usually led to believe myths by charismatic evangelists who have been misled by and promulgate some set of near-truths. In the present case, the evangelists are a group of distinguished scientists, many on the faculty of great universities, and they remind us that scientific excellence is highly compartmentalized. Not only do leading scientists often promulgate highly implausible political or religious doctrines, but—as in this case—they can make mistakes of overgeneralization about science itself, thinking that excellent designs for demonstrating causation or providing evidence in their own sphere are definitive for the whole of science. We have often seen this when good physicists, for example, proclaim that the search for general laws expressed in exact quantitative terms is the key task of science and that the behavioral or educational sciences need to be reformed by rigorous efforts to find and report these. Similarly, good mathematicians reacted negatively to the suggestion that statistics should be admitted to the Parthenon of respectable mathematics. In the present case, good scientists have been entranced by the paragon of experimental design, the randomly controlled trial or RCT, and illicitly generalized this into a required standard for all good causal investigation. It is suggested here that this view is completely refuted by a careful look at the way that astronomy, epidemiology, engineering, geology, field biology, and many other sciences establish causal conclusions *to the highest standards of scientific (and legal) credibility.*

The situation in this myth-busting episode is in fact worse, since the grounds for refutation are as follows: Causation is a key component of much of science (pure and applied), as well as other disciplines outside science (especially history and law). In everyday life, history, and law, causal claims on which lives depend are frequently established conclusively without any need for RCTs, sometimes (e.g., Hume) by direct observation.

So this chapter tracks the way in which we acquire causal concepts in infancy, in the law courts, in scientific field studies, and in the engineering lab, in order to support the counterclaim about the epistemological and commonsensical status of RCTs.

The general position here is extended to suggest that (i) the attempted takeover of the terms *evidence* and *cause* is partly inspired by the false dichotomy between *experiment* and *quasi-experiment,* and (ii) the whole effort is closely analogous to the attempted annexation of the concept of *significance* by *statistically significant.* While the motivation for both assaults was the highly commendable one of improving rigor in the applied social sciences, which was certainly needed, the way to do that is by increased care in picking the right tool for each job and using it properly, not by an oversimplification of the task. It is to be hoped that repelling this invasion, and recovery from the attempt, takes less time and costs less in human as well as scientific terms than the earlier debacle.

Sundry Notes

- For an example of observations that, mediated by a theory, demonstrated causation, think of the observations of the solar eclipse of 1919 that showed sunlight was refracted by gravity as predicted by the general theory of relativity.

- The eight methods for detecting causation are those based on (i) direct observation, e.g., visual, affective, tactile; (ii) reported observation, e.g., case studies; (iii) eliminative inference, e.g., autopsy, engineering breakdown; (iv) theoretical inference, based on use of an analogy/theory, e.g., physics, geology, astronomy; (v) direct manipulation e.g., in the kitchen and lab; (vi) "natural experiments," e.g., meteorology, epidemiology; (vii) quasi-experimentation, e.g., medicine, pedagogy; (viii) RCTs, e.g., pharmacology.

References

Brinkerhoff, R. O. (2003). *The success case method*. San Francisco: Berrett-Koehler.

Cook, T. D. (2001). A critical appraisal of the case against using experiments to assess school (or community) effects. *Education Next*. Available online at http://www .hoover.org/publications/ednext/3399216.html.

Cook, T. D., & Campbell, D. T. (1979). *Quasi-experimentation*. Boston: Houghton Mifflin.

8

Evidence as "Proof" and Evidence as "Inkling"

Jennifer C. Greene

This chapter is premised on the understanding that evaluation is both influenced by the political, organizational, and sociocultural context in which it is conducted and, in turn, serves to reshape or reconstitute that context in particular ways (House, 1993). That is, evaluation is not a bystander or neutral player in the debates that often surround it, but rather an active contributor to those debates and to the institutions that house them. The vital question then becomes, what kind of contribution should evaluation make to contested spaces and issues?

To address this question, this chapter first outlines the political, organizational, and sociocultural assumptions and stances that comprise the current context of the demand for "evidence." Under these assumptions, evidence is championed as able to, at long last, make our social systems as "efficient and effective" as our physical and technological infrastructures. These assumptions and stances, while not monolithic, characteristically convey a particular perspective on the nature of human phenomena and the role and responsibilities of government in democratic societies. To engage in evaluation practices

AUTHOR'S NOTE: An earlier version of this chapter was presented at the Claremont Graduate University Stauffer Symposium, "What Constitutes Credible Evidence in Evaluation and Applied Research?" Claremont, CA, August 19, 2006.

that support this form of the demand for evidence thus is to substantiate the perspective—and the underlying assumptions and stances—that frame it. I will then argue for a different conceptualization of evidence, one that is framed by a different set of assumptions and stances about human phenomena and democratic institutions and one that thereby positions evaluation as an active contributor to open, inclusive, and democratizing conversations about important public issues. The discussion focuses on evaluation, but is intended to be equally relevant to applied social research.

Introduction

Who could seriously be against the use of evidence in decision making, especially the use of *credible* evidence in decisions about federal policy priorities for human and social needs, or decisions about improvements needed in an HIV/AIDS education program in rural Idaho, or decisions about how best to deter criminality by young African American men in northeastern urban centers, or decisions about how best to spend a local United Way budget? And, in particular, is there an *evaluator* anywhere in the known universe who opposes the idea of grounding important decisions about human affairs in empirical data about those affairs? Indeed, ever since Carol Weiss (1980) first alerted the then-fledgling evaluation community to the often minuscule influence of social science data in U.S. public policy decision making, evaluators have longed for a time when the fruits of their labors were seriously attended to. Our collective preoccupation with utilization bespeaks our continuing faith in the power and authority of empirical evidence. Generating credible evidence to enhance understanding and support decisions about important human affairs constitutes a shared center of the evaluation enterprise, even as we go about our craft in different ways with different commitments and different consequences of other kinds.

So what's the problem? Why is the current demand for "scientific evidence" to support policy decisions, especially in the public domain, so controversial? What is generating all the debate, including the various perspectives shared at the August gathering of evaluation scholars, the Claremont University Stauffer Symposium of 2006?

In this chapter, I will briefly first recount my understanding of the character of this contested issue. While my perspective on the issue is a widely shared one—and thus accessible in many scholarly and more popular venues—it is critical to remind ourselves of just what is at stake in this debate. I will then recount and illustrate some of my own ideas about what constitutes credible evidence in evaluation and applied research, arguing primarily for the importance of understanding the inherent *complexity* of human phenomena in contrast with evidence that both denies and simplifies the wondrous and diverse panorama of the human species.

An Analysis of the Current Demand for Credible Evidence in Social and Educational Inquiry

The controversy over the contemporary demand for scientific evidence in support of policy decisions is multifaceted and complex. My portrait of the current demand for credible evidence, which is widely shared but certainly not in every detail, includes two clusters of interconnected assumptions and ambitions: (a) assumptions about the nature of human phenomena and about the knowledge we can have about these phenomena, and (b) ambitions about politics and privilege, well disguised with code words like scientific and rigorous and, yes, evidence-based.

Underlying Assumptions about Human Phenomena and Social Knowledge

> The positivists can't believe their luck, they've lost all the arguments of the last 30 years and they've still won the war! (Stronach, Piper, & Piper, 2004, p. 144)

Indeed, the worldview underlying the current demand for evidence is, generously speaking, a form of conservative post-positivism but in many ways is more like a kind of neo-positivism. Many of us thought that we'd seen the last of this obsolete way of thinking about the causes and meanings of human activity, as it was a consensual casualty of the great quantitative-qualitative debate among applied social scientists in the latter part of the 20th century, having been declared moribund by philosophers some decades previously. Some of the major tenets of this worldview include the following:

- Human phenomena are just like natural phenomena, as they are all caused by forces and factors in the external environment. Educational researcher Bob Slavin (2002), in one of his arguments for "evidenced-based education policies," bemoans the absence in the field of education of the "progressive, systematic improvement over time that has characterized successful parts of our economy and society throughout the 20th century, in fields such as medicine, agriculture, transportation, and technology" (p. 16). In this worldview, the job of educational researchers and evaluators is to follow the lead in these other fields and discover the generalizable external factors, forces, and conditions that importantly influence teaching and learning.

- Legitimate or valid knowledge about human phenomena is scientific. It is objective and unbiased. It is untainted by personal values or political stances and free from moral-ethical considerations about human affairs. Science is the domain of empirical facts. Values, politics, and moral-ethical concerns are best left to the priests and the pundits.

The challenges to these assumptions are well-known, and I won't belabor them here (see, for example, Denzin & Lincoln, 2000; Schwandt, 2000, 2003).

Underlying Ambitions About Politics and Policies

Also underlying the infatuation with evidence about human affairs, especially among conservatives in government, are assumptions about methodology that signal political strategizing, overt or covert as it may be. That is, these assumptions or stances are not really about epistemology, defensible methodology, or warranted claims to know, even though framed as such. Instead, they represent political principles and tactics to attain them. Here are some examples of these assumptions and their accompanying political strategies.

- Ignoring the widespread acceptance of the plurality of legitimate epistemologies that characterize contemporary philosophy of science and social inquiry, the demand for evidence advances a "master epistemology," in the words of postmodern educational scholar Betty St. Pierre (2002). Speaking of the National Research Council (NRC) report about what constitutes *scientific* educational research (Shavelson & Towne, 2002), St. Pierre (2002) continues, "The very dangerous claim that is made here is that a single epistemology governs all science" (p. 26). Tom Schwandt (2007) talks about this as "'epistemological politics' in which some knowledge and knowers are privileged over others in making decisions about practices and policies in education, health care, and social services. . . . It is this epistemological politics, not the relative merits of experimental and quasi-experimental designs, that underlies federal directives on methodology choice."

- The push for scientific evidence in government decision making must further be seen as part of contemporary accountability politics, or at least as situated within extant accountability systems. Two instances of this positioning are offered. First, in focusing evaluation and applied research around particular ideas about scientific evidence, social inquiry becomes a tool for institutional control and policy argument (House, 1993, 2004; Schwandt, 2007). As a tool, social inquiry is used to advance policy in particular directions, for example, privatizing education in the United States or, in the United Kingdom, reconstructing education "as a fantasy of economic instrumentality and a creature of normative quantification at all levels (pupil outcomes, teacher performance, researcher productivity, school/system ranking, and so on)" (Stronach et al., 2004, p. 146). Second, the empirical information that social inquiry contributes to policy—that is, the "scientific evidence"—is assumed to carry great weight in a highly rational decision-making process. This assumption ignores the considerable literature on the rather modest role, at best, that social science plays in the policy arena. Even worse, assuming a direct influence of scientific evidence on policy making obscures the actual politics of policy decisions about accountability behind a parade of effect sizes, F-ratios, regression weights, and linear modeling. And we must remember that the stakes in our current accountability systems are very high.

- As we all know, accompanying the demand for evidence has been a privileging of a particular methodology viewed as best at generating the evidence desired, and that is the randomized experiment. Sometimes the term *evidence* and especially *scientific or rigorous evidence* is code for randomized controlled trials, or RCTs. Yet, in heavily promoting experimentation, proponents of this view reverse the logical and time-honored order of decisions when conducting social inquiry. First, one identifies the inquiry purposes and questions, and only then selects a methodology that fits these purposes and questions (Chelimsky, 2007). Method is always the servant of substance, never the master. Moreover—and this is the critical point here—questions about the causal effects of social interventions are characteristically those of policy and decision makers, while other stakeholders have other legitimate and important questions (Chelimsky, 2007). This privileging of the interests of the elite in evaluation and research is radically undemocratic.

In short, as so aptly summarized by Eleanor Chelimksy (2007) in an article focusing on the U.S. Department of Education's (ED) current policies on methodology, "In the end, the paradox of ED's priority to the experimental design is that it is non-experimental: it reflects the introduction of ideology into the heart of the empirical paradigm" (p. 24).

Interlude

Our work as evaluators is importantly influenced by the particular characteristics and contours of the contexts in which we work. And, in turn, our work serves to reshape, or not, those contexts in particular ways (House, 1993; House & Howe, 1999). Evaluation, and the institutions, politics, and cultures that characterize the contexts in which it is situated, are mutually constitutive. In particular, there are no viable sidelines in democratic political discourse and policy. The very activity of generating evaluative knowledge about social programs and policies helps to constitute the form and function of this discourse and the direction of the policies. An evaluative practice that divorces technical rationality from moral responsibility helps to shape democratic institutions and policies that do the same. Referring again to the NRC report on scientific research in education, educational researchers Fred Erickson and Kris Gutierrez (2002) commented, "By not challenging the reigning optimism about hard science as a royal road to improvement . . . the committee report could be read as supporting a discourse of scientism or the appearance of rigor in educational research rather than its actual substance" (p. 22).

I strongly believe that evaluators should resist and disrupt the scientific evidence-based-policy-and-practice ethos that currently reigns in government and other domains that are critical to our well being in the United States. This does *not* mean that evaluators should not conduct randomized experiments or other forms of experimentation. Experiments can provide valuable information about important causal questions, and they certainly have a vital place in the evaluation repertoire, as one among many viable approaches and methodologies. So, the argument is not about method. Rather, it is about the *politics* of method—the political underbelly of the current demand for evidence-based policies and practices.

In the remainder of this chapter, I would like to focus on one topic of resistance and disruption, and that is the wondrous complexity of human phenomena. Paralleling the discussion of the evidence argument above, I will first very briefly note the philosophical dimensions of this complexity, because this is relatively well-traveled territory. I will include in this discussion some of the practical dimensions of social inquiry under assumptions of complexity. Then I will turn to the politics of social inquiry that intentionally respects and honors the mysteries of being human.

An Argument for Social and Educational Inquiry That Meaningfully Honors Complexity

A skeptical attitude towards statistically correlated, evidence-based best practice is correct, but its attraction to politicians and administrators in democratic systems dominated by short-term agendas and timescales is obvious. (Stronach et al., 2004, p. 145)

Simplicity and certainty are what governments seek. Complexity and uncertainty are what we [qualitative evaluators] habitually deliver. . . . The government wants to know what works, and we have to tell them that nothing works every-where, and that their best bet is to fully understand why this is so. (Simons, 2004, pp. 410–411)

Considering Philosophy and Practice

The philosophical argument that human activity is very complex is rooted in an interpretivist or constructivist paradigm. Proponents of this view or mental model maintain that human action is *not* like activity in the physical world, but rather is most importantly guided by the meanings that people construct in particular times and places, in interaction with others in the set-ting and with the setting itself. So, what is important to know in social inquiry are these constructed meanings and the relational processes by which they come about. Thus, social knowledge is interpreted, contextual, dynamic or even transient, social or communal, and quite complicated. It also includes values and ideologies, as well as moral and ethical concerns. Stripping human experience of its beliefs, commitments, principles, and passions is to render it other than uniquely social, uniquely human.

In one of my favorite articles in this debate, educational researcher David Berliner (2002), who is a Regents Professor at Arizona State University and a strong post-positivist thinker, claims that educational research is "the hardest science of all" (p. 18). Permit me to quote a bit directly from this article.

The distinctions between hard and soft sciences are part of our culture. Physics, chemistry, geology, and so on are often contrasted with the social sciences in gen-eral and education in particular. Educational research is considered too soft, squishy, unreliable, and imprecise to rely on as a basis for practice in the same way that other sciences are involved in the design of bridges and electronic circuits, sending rockets to the moon, or developing new drugs. But the important dis-tinction is really not between the hard and soft sciences. Rather, it is between the hard and the easy sciences. Easy-to-do science is what those in physics, chemistry, geology, and some other fields do. Hard-to-do science is what the social scientists do and, in particular, it is what we educational researchers do. In my estimation, we have the hardest-to-do science of them all! We do our science under conditions that physical scientists find intolerable. We face particular problems and must deal with local conditions that limit generalizations and theory building—problems that are different from those faced by the easier-to-do sciences. (p. 18)

Berliner then discusses three examples of these problems:

1. *The power of contexts*

   In education, broad theories and ecological generalizations often fail because they cannot incorporate the enormous number or determine the power of the contexts within which human beings find themselves. . . . A science that must always be sure the myriad particulars are well understood is harder to build than a science that can focus on the regularities of nature across contexts. (p. 19)

2. *The ubiquity of interactions*

Context is of such importance in educational research because of the interactions that abound. The study of classroom teaching, for example, is always about understanding the 10th or 15th order interactions that occur in classrooms. Any teaching behavior interacts with a number of student characteristics. . . . Simultaneously, student behavior is interacting with teacher characteristics, such as the teacher's training in the subject taught [and] conceptions of learning. . . . But it doesn't end there because other variables interact with those just mentioned—the curriculum materials, the socioeconomic status of the community, peer effects in the school . . . and so forth. Moreover, we are not even sure in which directions the influences work, and many are surely reciprocal. (p. 19)

3. *Decade by findings interactions*

There is still another point about the uniqueness of educational science, the short half-life of our findings. For example, in the 1960s good social science research was done on the origins of achievement motivation among men and women. By the 1970s, as the feminist revolution worked its way through society, all data that described women were completely useless. . . . Solid scientific findings in one decade [sometimes] end up of little use in another decade because of changes in the social environment that invalidate the research or render it irrelevant. (p. 20)

On a side note, Berliner (2002) makes the point in his discussion that it is because of the need to understand the particularities of each local context that "qualitative inquiry has become so important in educational research" (p. 19). Similar points are made in more depth by qualitative inquirers Erickson and Gutierrez (2002). They argue that "an adequate causal analysis must identify the specific mechanisms that generate specific outcomes within particular structural circumstances . . . specifications made possible by direct observation within the local situation of complexity and contingency" (p. 23). Educational evaluator Helen Simons (2004) makes a similar point, again with some depth, arguing in particular for the vital importance of narratives of lived experience for inquiry intending to enhance professional practice.

But this discussion is not about method. So, let me now turn to some of the political dimensions of this commitment to complexity of human action and understanding.

Considering Politics

The first order of the politics of complexity is to resist what Ernie House (2004) calls the "methodological fundamentalism" of the current (as of this writing) U.S. administration. (House's rationale here is simple. All opportunities to resist this administration's policies, both domestic and international, must be seized and exploited to their fullest potential.) House portrays federal evaluation policy as resting on the same simplistic dualisms as those that underlie many fundamentalist religions—it's true or it's false, it's right or it's wrong, you're either with me or against me, you're either a believer or damned for eternity. Moreover, true believers only "associate with other true believers and avoid non-believers, thus closing the circle of belief and increasing certainty" (p. 3). True believers also believe they have the moral right to coerce others to follow the one true path. With respect to the "methodological fundamentalism" for evaluation espoused by the current administration, House observes,

> Some government agencies demand that all evaluations must be randomized experiments. Other ways of producing evidence are not scientific and not acceptable. There is one method for discovering the truth and one method only—the randomized experiment. If we employ randomized experiments, they will lead us to a Golden Age in education and social services. Such is the revelatory vision. There are sacred figures from the past and sacred texts. Core believers are absolutely certain they are right, that randomized experiments reveal the truth. They do not listen to critics, and they do not comprehend the arguments against the method. A mandate for randomized trials has been written into legislation without discussion with professional communities. Avoiding contrary ideas is part of the orientation, and of course, the policy is enforced by government edict. (p. 4)

Methodological fundamentalism offers just one source of truth. That is, it denies and ignores—or perhaps even aspires to eliminate—the cultural and sociopolitical pluralism and dynamic resourcefulness that vitally characterize our society today. Methodological fundamentalism as government control and manipulation of information—a.k.a. scientific evidence—threatens not only evaluation but also our pluralistic democracy itself (House, 2004, p. 6).

My second point constitutes more of an affirmative reason for promoting the idea that the activities and practices of people are profoundly complex. This point is that complexity is deeply contextual—as so well argued by David Berliner—and, as such, embraces the magnificent multiplicity of ways of thinking, acting, and being that abound in our society and the world more broadly. Complexity honors and respects the wondrous diversity of the human species.

By diversity I mean both the historical markers of "disadvantage" in our contemporary society—notably, race, ethnicity, class, gender, sexual orientation, able-bodiedness, and cultural traditions—*and* the infinitely astonishing other ways in which human beings are different from one another. In this conceptualization of diversity, traditional social categories are both respected— because to do otherwise is to ignore past injustices and risk perpetuating them—and also troubled social constructions. Troubling traditional markers of diversity opens spaces for getting beyond them to other more personalized and meaningful dimensions of the human character and spirit.

As I have said elsewhere (Greene, 2005; Greene, Millet, & Hopson, 2004), there is no more urgent national or global priority than to engage with this diversity, to learn how to live with, appreciate, and accept our differences. Too many of the world's societies remain seriously fractured and even ruptured by differences in race, class, religion, culture, disability status, and other demographic markers of diversity. Radical inequities and injustices of access and opportunity persist, based on nothing more substantial than historical legacies of discrimination and continuing prejudices. As social inquirers, I believe we have a responsibility to conduct our work with a deliberate intention to locate and meaningfully engage with the differences that manifest in a given context. One important way to do this is to privilege and honor complexity.

Third, the inherently contextual character of complexity evokes not just personal and social characteristics, as I just discussed, but also structural, economic, and political features of the spaces and places people inhabit. Our contexts are molded as much or more by these macro influences as by individual and interpersonal characteristics. Take a front page example. Teaching in a public high school in a severely underresourced urban community that is also beleaguered by higher-than-average incidences of crime and drug use, is quite a different challenge from teaching in a well-resourced high school in a community that is safer and cleaner than average. These challenges have more to do with the structural features of these different communities—features constructed over decades, mostly by people who don't live there—than they do with the people who actually live there (see Hopson, Greene, Bledsoe, Villegas, & Brown, in press).

It is therefore vitally important that our social research and evaluation prominently attend to the structural dimensions that influence human action, and this is more likely to happen with a vision of human action as fully contextual and thereby complex, as compared to a vision in which contextual characteristics are something to be controlled—statistically *and* politically.

Finally, and admittedly redundantly, a research or evaluation practice that envisions and endeavors to understand the full complexity of human action—in all of its contextual diversity—is a practice that legitimizes the multiple perspectives and experiences of all of the people being studied. It is a practice that gives voice to these myriad perspectives and experiences. It is a practice that is thereby in form and function democratic and potentially democratizing.

Illustrations

In this final section, I offer two illustrations of "evidence-based evaluation"— evaluation conducted to gather evidence that is philosophically archaic and politically elitist. These examples are crafted to illuminate the many strands of complexity, contextual particularity, and stakeholder voice that are missing from an evaluation practice devoted to gathering "evidence" as (mis)construed by evidence advocates in the contemporary debate.

Evaluating an After-School Tutoring Program

Facing threats of financial sanctions and eventual closure if student test scores do not rise (under the federal No Child Left Behind Act of 2001), many U.S. public schools today have implemented programs designed to provide supplementary academic instruction to students, often targeting those scoring just below the cut-score that represents satisfactory performance. Orange Grove Middle School, located in a southeastern urban area, recently implemented an after-school tutoring program of this kind. In this program, retired teachers volunteer to provide individual and small-group tutoring in language arts and mathematics to participating students. For students, the program is voluntary, although it takes place within the same structure as the long-standing Orange Grove after-school program, which is designed to provide safe, supervised recreational activities for students with working parents. Moreover, parents pay a fee (on a sliding scale) for the traditional after-school program, while the tutoring program is free.

An evidence-based evaluation of this after-school tutoring program would seek to answer a question like, "To what extent does student participation in this kind of after-school tutoring program lead to increased student test performance?" This is a defensible evaluation question that likely calls for a comparative design, comparing the test performance of participating students with the test performance of a comparable group of students who did not participate in the program.

But what would be missing, misrepresented, or even silenced in such an evaluation? Many things, including the following.

- Test performance itself is but a tiny window on the dynamic conversational and contextual exchange that constitutes meaningful teaching and learning. All these other strands of learning would be absent.
- The particular characteristics, history, demography, culture, vitality, and conflicts of the Orange Grove school community would not be acknowledged as important to the learning of students in the program.
- The fairness of the processes by which students come to participate in the program would not be examined or critiqued.
- The students' own educational experiences in the tutoring program would be ignored.
- The experiences of the tutors, the retired teachers who volunteered to tutor the students, would likewise be ignored.
- The perceptions and understandings of participating students' parents would not be valued.
- Variations *within* the group of participating students, and their families, would not be attended to as meaningful influences on students' educational challenges and accomplishments.
- Concerns about the economics of participation would be ignored.
- Concerns about the developmental needs of children—beyond academic success—would not be engaged.
- Questions about school, district, and governmental responsibilities for these children's educational success would not be addressed, as the focus is on the responsibilities of the student.

Evaluating a "Drug Court" Program

In recent years, some municipalities have adopted a "Drug Court" program as an alternative to the traditional penal code and punishment for arrestees convicted of drug abuse. The program theory underlying Drug Court is that drug users are not criminals but rather misdirected and potentially "law-abiding" citizens, in some senses victims themselves. With a firm set of guidelines and clear criminal consequences for violating these guidelines, many drug users can be rehabilitated outside of the criminal justice system. In lieu of incarceration, Drug Court participants undergo a 6- to 10-month program of regular counseling and regular tests for drug use. Failure in Drug Court means a criminal sentence and record. Success means return to the society at large without a criminal record or time spent behind bars.

An evidence-based evaluation of a Drug Court program implemented in a small Midwestern city would likely ask a question like, "To what extent does participation in the Drug Court reduce drug use offense and recidivism in the criminal justice system?" Again, this is a defensible evaluation question that likely calls for a comparative design, comparing the drug use and arrest records of participants with the same records for a comparable group of drug offenders who did not participate in the program. This context may even be well-suited to a randomized experimental design.

But what would be missing, misrepresented, or even silenced in such an evaluation? Here are some examples.

- Focusing only on drug use and arrest records would miss the complex constellations of factors and circumstances that accompany drug abuse for program participants.
- The disproportionate representation of certain demographic groups in the local population of drug offenders—*and* the structural factors that contribute to this disproportionality—would not be addressed.
- The life trajectories of program participants following program completion—be it success or failure—would not be studied.
- The experiences of participants in the program, and of possible control group participants in prison, would not be attended to.
- The character and extent of the drug problem in the local community would be ignored: Who sells drugs and who buys them? Where do the drugs come from? What are law enforcement efforts to combat the drug trade? In what ways are the local mental health institutions involved in helping people with drug abuse problems?
- The perceptions of the program staff, including the local judicial system, would not be garnered for their insights and understandings.

In short, evidence-based evaluation concentrates evaluation resources around one small question—"Does the program work?"—and uses but one evaluation methodology, despite a considerable richness of options. The result is but one small answer.

Conclusion: So What Counts as Credible Evidence?

All evaluators and applied researchers value evidence that is warranted and that meaningfully contributes to decision making in service of the public good. Evidence is central to the aspirations of the applied social science community. But within the pluralism of contemporary social science, the meanings and possible uses of evidence are contested. As argued in this chapter, what constitutes warranted evidence depends on underlying assumptions about human phenomena and especially on the political agenda prompting the call for evidence. A call for evidence as the arbitrator of policy disputes undervalues the radical complexity of human affairs and suggests that different policy stances can be easily and legitimately reconciled through "evidence about what works." In some ways, this stance displaces individual responsibility for policy decisions onto evidence—a responsibility evidence cannot legitimately shoulder. Rather, evidence about social phenomena—like the phenomena themselves—is quirky, not definitive; is particular, not general; and is ephemeral, not generalizable. Moreover, evidence is best positioned as an invitation to dialogue rather than an answer to an unanswerable question.

So what kind of evidence is needed from applied social research and evaluation today? Not evidence that claims purchase on the truth with but a small answer to a small question, neat and tidy as it may be, but rather, evidence that provides a window into the messy complexity of human experience; evidence that accounts for history, culture, and context; evidence that respects difference in perspective and values; evidence about experiences in addition to consequences; evidence about the responsibilities of government, not just the responsibilities of its citizens; evidence with the potential for democratic inclusion and legitimization of multiple voices—evidence not as proof but as inkling.

References

Berliner, D.C. (2002). Educational research: The hardest science of all. *Educational Researcher, 31*(8), 18–20.

Chelimsky, E. (2007). Factors influencing the choice of methods in federal evaluation practice. In G. Julnes & D. Rog (Eds.), *Informing federal policies on evaluation methodology: Building the evidence base for method choice in government sponsored evaluation* (pp. 13–33). (Vol. 113 of *New Directions for Evaluation* series). San Francisco: Jossey-Bass.

Denzin, N. L., & Lincoln, Y. S. (2000). Introduction: The discipline and practice of qualitative research. In N. L. Denzin & Y. S. Lincoln (Eds.), *Handbook of qualitative research* (2nd ed., pp. 1–29). Thousand Oaks, CA: Sage Publications.

Erickson, F., & Gutierrez, K. (2002). Culture, rigor, and science in educational research. *Educational Researcher, 31*(8), 21–24.

Greene, J. C. (2005). Evaluators as stewards of the public good. In S. Hood, R. K. Hopson, & H. T. Frierson (Eds.), *The role of culture and cultural context: A mandate for inclusion, truth, and understanding in evaluation theory and practice* (pp. 7–20). (*Evaluation and Society* series). Greenwich, CT: Information Age Publishing.

Greene, J. C., Millet, R. C., & Hopson, R. K. (2004). Evaluation as a democratizing practice. In M. T. Braverman, N. A. Constantine, & J. K. Slater (Eds.), *Foundations and evaluation: Contexts and practices for effective philanthropy* (pp. 96–118). San Francisco: Jossey-Bass.

Hopson, R. K., Greene, J. C., Bledsoe, K. L., Villegas, T. M., & Brown, T. A. (in press). A vision of urban educational evaluation. In W. T. Pink & G. W. Noblit (Eds.), *International handbook of urban education*. Dordrecht, the Netherlands: Springer.

House, E. R. (1993). *Professional evaluation.* Thousand Oaks, CA: Sage Publications.

House, E. R. (2004, October). *Democracy and evaluation.* Keynote address presented to the European Evaluation Society, Berlin.

House, E. R., & Howe, K. R. (1999). *Values in evaluation and social research.* Thousand Oaks, CA: Sage Publications.

Schwandt, T. A. (2000). Three epistemological stances for qualitative inquiry: Interpretivism, hermeneutics, and social constructionism. In N. L. Denzin & Y. S. Lincoln (Eds.), *Handbook of qualitative research* (2nd ed., pp. 189–214). Thousand Oaks, CA: Sage Publications.

Schwandt, T. A. (2003). *Qualitative inquiry: A dictionary of terms* (2nd ed.). Thousand Oaks, CA: Sage Publications.

Schwandt, T. A. (2007). Thoughts on using the notion of "evidence" in the controversy over methods choice. In G. Julnes & D. Rog (Eds.), *Informing federal policies on evaluation methodology: Building the evidence base for method choice in government sponsored evaluation* (pp. 111–127). (Vol. 113 of *New Directions for Evaluation* series). San Francisco: Jossey-Bass.

Shavelson, R. J., & Towne, L. (Eds.). (2002). *Scientific research in education.* Washington, DC: National Research Council, National Academy Press.

Simons, H. (2004). Utilizing evidence to enhance professional practice. *Evaluation, 10*(4), 410–429.

Slavin, R. E. (2002). Evidence-based education policies: Transforming educational practice and research. *Educational Researcher, 31*(7), 15–21.

St. Pierre, E. A. (2002). "Science" rejects postmodernism. *Educational Researcher, 31*(8), 25–27.

Stronach, I., Piper, H., & Piper, J. (2004). Re-performing crises of representation. In H. Piper & I. Stronach (Eds.), *Educational research: Difference and diversity* (pp. 129–154). Aldershot, UK: Ashgate.

Weiss, C. H. (with Bucuvalas, M. J.). (1980). *Social science research and decision making.* New York: Columbia University Press.

9

Reasoning With Rigor and Probity

Ethical Premises for Credible Evidence

Sharon F. Rallis

My Story

I begin my consideration of credible evidence in organizational and program evaluation with the assumption that social and behavioral programs are designed to improve the lives and work of people. Second, I accept the definition of evaluation as "systematic assessment of the operation and/or outcomes of a program, compared to a set of explicit or implicit standards, as a means of contributing to the improvement of that program or service" (Weiss, 1998, p. 4). Weiss also says, "With the information and insight that evaluation brings, organizations and societies will be better able to improve policy and programming for the well-being of all" (p. ix). The application of precise and exacting standards in the conduct of evaluation comprises the rigor required for evaluation to be scientific inquiry that produces credible evidence. However, being that the ultimate goal of evaluation is to improve human lives and work, then just as important as rigor is *probity*, that is,

AUTHOR'S NOTE: I thank Jana Kay Slater for her collegiality over the years, sharing reflections on work, allowing me to use her data, and editing my words.

goodness or absolute moral correctness, in determining what constitutes credible evidence in evaluation and applied research.

My early experiences with formal evaluation research, however, belied this purpose of informing improvement for the well-being of all. The story of one of those evaluations illustrates the contradiction. Many years ago, I was teaching in a federally funded summer program, Project Realization, for emotionally troubled early adolescents who were performing poorly in school. These youngsters were considered to have low self-esteem, which was inhibiting their academic achievement. The project provided challenging and engaging physical tasks, with sufficient guidance so the participants could complete the tasks with success and with counseling to help them make sense of their successes. We believed that success in these areas would bolster their self-confidence and would eventually transfer to their school-work. The physical challenges were those commonly used in Outward Bound programs. We scaled rock walls, repelled off cliffs, and climbed and camped in New Hampshire's White Mountains.

Naturally, the federal funding source required an evaluation, so the project contracted a prestigious evaluation firm that presented us with their plan to split the group randomly into two halves, with one participating in the physical activities and counseling and the other getting only the counseling. They would administer pre and post standardized norm-referenced achievement tests to determine the effect of the interventions. Then they would ask a cause-and-effect question: did the project intervention raise the students' scores? We demurred on both parts of the plan. First, we did not think it fair to deprive half of the kids of the physical activities, and second, we doubted that the tests would reveal what impact the program actually had on either group—we recognized that the link between their achievement of the physical tasks and their achievement in school was not direct.

The evaluators held to their plan to determine a single outcome—after all, they pointed out, if our goal was to increase achievement, the tests were the appropriate standard for measurement. They assured us that the only valid evaluation method was the quasi-experiment they had designed. We felt we had no choice. The result was that the group we called the *Bounders* scored lower on the posttest (an implementation dip?)—several refused even to take the posttest—while the control group remained the same. We lost our funding. The evaluation helped neither the program nor the lives of these young people.

I decided I did not value evaluators and their scientific validity. I asked, "How credible was their interpretation of the evidence that the program was a failure?" As the designers and implementers of the program, we interpreted their "evidence," the decrease in test scores, differently; we saw it as evidence that the *Bounders* had gained enough self-esteem to reject the test. In fact, the questions we asked in evaluating our program were different from those of the evaluators we had hired. They were solely interested in externally defined outcome measures, whereas we wanted to know what participation meant to the teenagers.

Still, what evidence could we offer to support our belief that our intervention had improved the well-being of these youngsters? What were our criteria and indicators? We had their stories of their experiences, something the evaluators had overlooked entirely. Would their story provide credible "evidence"? Our evaluators claimed their study was scientific and had rigor, but something was missing. Based on my subsequent learning about evaluation, I suggest that something is probity—goodness and moral soundness.

In search of that missing piece, I began to study evaluation (Carol Weiss became one of my teachers), and, in part to combat my distaste for evaluations I had been subjected to, I became an evaluator. What drove my actions was commitment to make my evaluations useful for the program personnel and participants. For me, the issue became less method than purpose. If I wanted to help people learn about and improve their programs and services, I first needed to ask, "What do we need to know about the programs and services, and then how can we learn?" I came to understand scientific inquiry and credible evidence in a different light. And I found and used strategies— such as intensive ethnographic or phenomenologic interviewing—to collect my evidence with probity, and in line with my teacher's claim that an evaluation's purpose is to improve programming for the betterment of all.

Scientific Inquiry Defined

So, what *is* scientific inquiry? Definitions abound. While the U.S. Department of Education and the current No Child Left Behind Act labels randomized controlled trials (RCT) as the "gold standard" for determining causality, other groups suggest broader understandings of science. As a science educator who reviewed my qualitative methods book (Rossman & Rallis, 2003) wrote, "Science isn't what you think it is—there is more art in science than you recognize." James Watson agrees; he describes in *The Double Helix* (1968) how the discovery of the structure of DNA required rigorous reasoning, but it also involved creativity, politics, mystery, and love. "Science seldom proceeds in the straightforward logical manner imagined by outsiders. Instead, its steps forward (and sometimes backwards) are very often very human events in which personalities and cultural traditions play major roles" (p. ix). Thomas Kuhn (1970) reminds us that we accept something as truth until the scientific community accumulates enough evidence that another truth exists. And my father (who led the team that developed the plastic that telephones are made of) always pointed out to me that "You cannot control what happens in a Petri dish; all you can do is observe and question."

More recently, the Committee on Scientific Principles for Education Research (2002) has defined scientific inquiry as

> A continual process of rigorous reasoning supported by a dynamic interplay among methods, theories, and findings. It builds understandings in the form of models or theories that can be tested. Advances in scientific knowledge are achieved by the self-regulating norms of the scientific community over time, not, as sometimes believed, by the mechanistic application of a particular method to a static set of questions. (p. 2)

What strikes me is the declaration of what scientific inquiry is *not*: the mechanistic application of a particular method to a static set of questions. The committee members recognize the role of the scientific community of discourse, and they imply that scientific research involves human judgment.

The scientific community, then, holds the key to credibility. My point is that scientific knowledge is a social construct, so credible evidence is what the relevant communities of discourse and practice accept as valid, reliable, or trustworthy. Judgments about the quality of inquiry represent "the social construction of knowledge . . . [T]he key issue becomes whether the relevant community of scientists evaluates reported findings as sufficiently trustworthy to rely on them for their own work" (Mishler, 2000, p. 120).

I have come to see a true scientist, then, as one who puts forward her findings and the reasoning that led her to those findings for others to contest, modify, accept, or reject.

Still, we are speaking of evaluation, not science, so we might question whether evaluators are scientists. While evaluation uses scientific methods to produce knowledge, evaluators might be more closely related to policy analysts. According to Weiss's definition, the products of evaluation inform policy and programming, not science. Scientists generally determine what theories, laws, or hypotheses are true or probably true, whereas policy makers and analysts focus on courses of action that are likely to address a social need (Phillips, 2007). The information needs of scientists and policy analysts/evaluators are different, so each group uses evidence differently. In evaluation and policy uses, politics and values come into play. As #11 of Cronbach's *Ninety-Five Theses* for evaluation claims, evaluation is as much about political interaction as about determining facts (Cronbach & Associates, 1980, p. 3). Thus, the evidence is less important than the ethical premises:

A policymaker no doubt will consult the empirical data, but rightly will be swayed by ethical premises and by notions of what constitutes a good and caring society, and by his or her conceptions of the rights that all individuals possess. (Phillips, 2007, p. 383)

Each policy maker will weigh the factors differently, deciding for him- or herself what course of action to take, according to his or her read of the evidence.

As an evaluator—that is, a social scientist who informs policy making—I reject reasoning based solely on one indicator or one dimension as narrow and limiting. Such reasoning is not rigorous. Therefore, I reject the findings of the Project Realization evaluators because they looked at only one indicator. They captured only one slice of the kids in the program—and even that slice could be interpreted in many ways. I also reject the findings on the basis of the ethical premises of the study. The findings lack wholeness, integrity, and a moral soundness; that is, they lacked probity.

Probity and Moral Reasoning

So, what *is* probity? Why is probity important? First, probity implies wholeness and integrity. Evidence with probity is credible because it acknowledges that "truth" is more than meets the eye and that it demands multiple avenues toward understanding the phenomenon. For probity I need to see and hear, and sometimes to feel or experience, for myself. Moreover, I believe that probity implies rigorous reasoning to meet the definition of moral soundness.

Moral soundness requires reasoning through moral principles. "The point of moral principles is to regulate interactions among human beings" (Strike, Haller, & Soltis, 1998, p. 41)—and what is social science research but an interaction among human beings? Organization and program evaluation, as social science research, is inextricably and unavoidably historically, politically, and contextually bound. Because it is an applied inquiry, it involves people: participants, funders, providers, taxpayers—all the various stakeholders. Evaluation is about people who have agendas, is funded by people who have their own interests, and is conducted by people who have their own perspectives. A rigorous evaluation must ask, "What moral principles guide the evaluators' interactions with participants and guide the methods used to collect data about the interactions in the organizations and programs?"

Moral principles form the basis of ethics—that is, standards for conduct. However, not everyone agrees upon or acts on a common ethic. Ethical theories can be grouped into two broad categories: consequentialist and nonconsequentialist. The moral principles from which *consequentialist* ethical theories derive focus on the results of actions in order to determine their rightness or wrongness. Any particular action is neither intrinsically good nor bad; rather, it is good or bad *because of its results in a particular context*—its consequences. Consequentialist ethical theories care not about the means or motive, only the end result. Evaluators who rely on experimentation to understand the outcome of interventions are consequentialists. The best-known example of this thinking is *utilitarianism*—the greatest good for the greatest number. An illustration comes from high-stakes testing. The reasoning behind this policy may well be that the high expectations set by a standardized test for high school graduation benefit the greatest number of students. Individual students may suffer for a variety of reasons (disabilities, cultural differences, testing phobia, to name a few), but their sacrifice is seen as worth the beneficial consequence of bringing the whole to meet a common standard.

An alternative reasoning is guided by *nonconsequentialist* ethics. The ethical premise behind this category of theories derives from the moral principle that universal standards guide all behavior, regardless of the consequences in a specific context. These theories consider the means over the ends. One nonconsequentialist ethic follows the principle of *individual rights and responsibilities*. Evaluators practicing with this ethic judge by the degree to which organization or program actions uphold the unconditional worth and respect of participants. These evaluators attend to the means and context more than to the outcome of a program. They ask, "What does the experience mean to the individual?"

A related premise is grounded in the principle of *justice*. Evaluators operating with this ethic use fairness and equity as the measures for judging the merit of programmatic actions. How are services distributed and benefits allocated? The needs and experiences of the weakest and most vulnerable, the few, are valued as much as if not more than those of the strong or the many (see Rawls, 1971). This principle maintains that serving and strengthening the least advantaged builds society as a whole, with all members more fully contributing, and it guides evaluators to capture silenced and ignored voices.

Another nonconsequentialist perspective considers the moral aspects of interactions and relationships above principles. The *ethic of caring* (Noddings, 1995) recognizes the moral interdependence of people over their individual moral agency: "Our goodness and growth are inextricably bound to others we encounter" (p. 196). *Caring* evaluators honor the connections between organization and program participants; an organization or program is a network of those doing the caring and the cared-for: "What does he or she need? Will filling this need harm others in the network of care?

Am I competent to fill this need? Will I sacrifice too much of myself? Is the expressed need really in the best interests of the cared-for?" (p. 187).

Caring evaluators respect the connections among the participants, the program, and ourselves. We want to understand the interactions and the relationships themselves, the interdependencies: how does one person's meaning-making interact with and influence another's? A *caring ethic* considers respect to be dynamic, symmetrical, and connective; we give respect, and we are respected (Lawrence-Lightfoot, 2000). We respect the participants and their relationships within their settings. At the same time, we work to create conditions that allow the participants to respect our need to discover and understand their experience.

To the evaluator falls the task of reasoning out the ethic to apply in each case. A given study might call for an evaluator to draw on more than one moral principle or from both ethical perspectives. For example, influential stakeholders or clients might demand consideration of outcomes over process in the program, so the evaluator whose reasoning points toward a nonconsequentialist perspective in choosing an approach for the study will be challenged to blend approaches to address both ethics—as long as the moral principles involved do not contradict each other.

Research Ethics, Tools, and Evidence

My evaluation approach is grounded in nonconsequentialist theories. These shape research ethics that turn away from the experimental type of studies that seek to know outcomes and turn toward the qualitative approaches that inform process and meanings. The evidence produced is much more interpretive and tentative than facts or figures to support certain conclusions. The moral reasoning behind the nonconsequentialist ethics leads to the use of tools that are interactive, aiming to capture the multiple and multifaceted experiences of participants. We want to know what the events and activities in the context mean to the participants. We want to hear their voices: we interview, we observe, we analyze their discourse. We leave to others to do the surveys that yield broad information and generalizations and well-done experiments that can reveal causal relationships—we recognize that both are important. Their surveys and experiments deal in consequences; they do not tell details within the story of the organization or program.

The evidence we collect to tell a story looks quite different from that of our colleagues who measure outcomes. Our aim is not to cast judgment as did the evaluators of Project Realization, but to discover what happened and what the experience meant to the program participants. We hope that our discoveries can lead to improving the program and thus, the well-being of the participants (as Weiss posits in her definition). To do so, we need to add individual voices—their interpretations of the phenomenon or experience. The actual words of participants in a variety of social service and educational programs reveal the diverse perspectives and unique stories that construct alternative realities for those programs.

Capturing these words and voices requires intensive and interactive interviews that produce thick descriptions. Such descriptions honor the idiosyncratic and contextual nature of human experience and allow complex and dynamic interpretations of that experience. We borrow tools from *ethnography, phenomenology,* and *sociolinguistics/semiotics*—in other words, tools to understand interactions and relationships; tools to understand lived experience; and tools to understand how people communicate their meanings for activities, events, objects, and people.

To illustrate credible evidence that focuses on experience, not outcomes, the quotes that follow are taken from the evaluation and needs assessment of the Sacramento County HIV/AIDS Education and Prevention Program conducted by the Public Health Institute. This case provides a dramatic example of how participants' voices offer otherwise missing insights. In the fall of 2002, the Sacramento County HIV/AIDS Education and Prevention Program contracted with the Public Health Institute to collect information from HIV-positive persons regarding their need for and interest in education and prevention services. Because the evaluators, Slater and Constantine, were not interested in outcomes, they conducted multiple interviews with program participants and HIV-positive community members. The report, entitled *What HIV+ Persons Tell Us About Prevention for Positives,* offered 10 recommendations that were ultimately used by the county's Financial Allocations Steering Committee to drive decisions about funding priorities for the 2003–2004 fiscal year.

The evaluators used an exploratory approach to determine needs and interests:

> Participants were asked to write a true "story" about themselves and were provided a series of writing prompts to steer their stories. Prompts were specifically designed to elicit information about personal needs that could potentially be served through the County's Prevention for Positives activities. Each participant was asked to spend one hour writing, and was encouraged to "write from your heart."
>
> The call for stories was distributed via email and personal contact. Invitations to participate were sent via email to key informants (HIV+ individuals who were active in the Sacramento HIV community); these key informants then further distributed the invitations electronically to individuals throughout the

Sacramento County HIV+ community. As a result, some participants received the invitation to write via email. In other cases, service providers printed the invitations from their computers and distributed them to clients. To reach the street population, an outreach worker distributed the call for stories during the course of his normal work. Combined, these approaches worked well—reaching a broad spectrum of the HIV+ population—and resulting in a larger pool of HIV+ participants than had been projected as needed for the study.

A total of 31 written stories were returned to the evaluator via email (about 25 percent) and mail (another 25 percent); the remainder (nearly half) were delivered in-person by [the outreach worker]. (Slater & Constantine, 2003, pp. 11–12)

In the participants' words, Slater and Constantine heard concerns about diagnosis and about hope. Here are the voices of HIV-positive people about diagnosis:

[The nurse] came up to me and I noticed that she had a strange, almost blank, look on her face. She said that the results of [the] gonorrhea test came back negative, hesitated for a second, and then said, "but your HIV test came back positive." To this day, I have no idea or recollection of what the nurse said to me after giving me the results.

When you are first diagnosed, you just want to use more and more drugs. I was strung out, homeless, depressed and pregnant. I couldn't go two hours without putting a needle in my arm. I was scared, very angry and very lonely, isolated.

I was so disgusted and sickened by my diagnosis. When I was in recovery, I was taking seven showers a day. I couldn't get that dirty word [HIV] off me.

It almost made me take my life.

These powerful statements reveal the uniqueness of each person's experience with diagnosis—the evidence is in the words: "no idea or recollection"; "scared, very angry and very lonely, isolated"; "couldn't get that dirty word off me"; "take my life." Further interpretation is not necessary; summarizing diminishes the emotion.

Next, here are some of their words about hopefulness:

I got over the initial shock and learned I could live and I didn't have to die. I was at peace. . . . I've become clean and sober. I no longer live in and off the streets to survive.

I used to inject drugs 3x's a day, run with a rough crowd, had sex addictions. Becoming HIV positive saved my life. I gave birth to a child with AIDS, she was adopted. Those 2 circumstances caused me to enter into recovery. I've turned my life around. I no longer want to die, I want to live.

I was angry, humiliated, consumed by self-pity, and trying to feel well enough to get up each day. Ironically, my body kept getting better, gradually. I got financial help everywhere I could find it and became pretty adept at being a "charity/welfare" entrepreneur.

At first I was devastated in a negative way, since then I have been a member of the Sacramento HIV planning council, an advisor to the state office of AIDS, and a positive speaker. . . . I instituted the "buddy" program, served as a care-giver, tried to help improve the quality of life.

In the voices, we hear the nuances in each participant's reactions and actions, the subtle shades of feeling.

Slater and Constantine (2003) also heard participants describe what is hardest about living with HIV/AIDS.

- Medication

  The mere fact that my own being is compromised in so many ways. I have allowed myself to become medically regimented and dependent on chemicals that seem to have taken over the "me" I remember having been.

- Lost opportunities

  Thinking that I'll never be able to own a home or get a new car, or go on a nice vacation.

- Fear of death

  One of the hardest things for me to deal with was not being able to picture myself alive after the age of 30.

- Parenthood

  Losing my 2 youngest to adoption due to my HIV status. When in court, the judge said the adoptive parents would be better because I have a "life-threatening disease."

- Work

  I've learned that you can't be honest and HIV positive. On a job application, how can I say I've been sick for 11 years? No one wants to tell employers or co-workers that they are positive.

Slater and Constantine (2003) brought these words to the county department of health. Health department personnel had expected that the primary need of people diagnosed with HIV/AIDS would be help in employment and everyday issues like finding homes. Instead, emotional isolation implicit in the quotes revealed that the people felt profoundly alone and needed services that would address their need for connection. They wanted support groups and opportunities to come together.

The voices were crafted into a report that presented participants' words. The report was then used in developing requests for proposals (RFP) for community-based organizations' (CBO) services that would specify ways to meet these emotional needs. The report also initiated conversations among funding sources and policy makers and informed HIV prevention programs.

Credibility

I put forward the evidence from these interviews and others to the research community and ask, "Do these words constitute credible evaluation evidence?" The transparency of the reasoning (both moral and method-ological) should allow judgments about rigor and probity from relevant communities of discourse and practice. I assert it is rigorous because it is grounded in theory and previous research and in moral principles of justice and caring. I am not implying that these data are all we need to understand the experiences of people with HIV/AIDS, nor am I saying that simply inter-viewing more people with more questions will tell us all. The findings contribute an important piece to a larger picture.

I recognize the multiple dimensions of evaluation research—that any one approach and its findings are incomplete, partial, and contestable. I believe the words from these participants with HIV/AIDS can enhance our under-standing of the problem and how people cope with the problem. The reported voices are the product of rigorous reasoning, and they embody pro-bity. This credible form of evidence offers insights that can help us improve policy and programming and better serve the people involved. I argue that this is the real basis of scientific inquiry.

Conclusion: So What Counts as Credible Evidence?

The title of this book asks, What counts as credible evidence in applied research and contemporary evaluation practice? Defining evaluation and applied research as a form of systematic inquiry that seeks to improve policy and programming and thus better human lives and work is a good place to begin. When, however, evaluators limit themselves to evidence obtained only through mechanical and replicable experimentation, their reasoning may miss an important aspect of rigor—probity or moral soundness. I suggest that credible evidence is cultivated through open explication of the moral premises on which the methods are grounded. The evaluation community can then determine the credibility of the evidence.

Evaluations may seek to determine outcomes or, alternatively, explore meaning and experience—the hows and whys. Both require systematic inquiry and rigorous reasoning, but the underlying ethical premises and the forms of evidence differ. Outcome evaluation is driven by *consequentialist moral principles*—a program or organization's practices are judged by the results. Using this ethical theory, the criterion for program success could be that services reached large numbers deemed needy. Or, indicators of an intervention's effects on various groups could be documented and analyzed. Evidence, in these cases, takes form as results and tends to be quantitative. *Nonconsequentialist moral principles* guide evaluations that explore processes within programs and organizations. These ethics ask what happens in the program or organization and what it means to participants and stakeholders. Evidence takes qualitative forms, such as stories, anecdotes, pictures, interview responses, and descriptions from observations. Understanding and making transparent the ethical theories on which the evaluation purposes rest allow evaluators to make moral choices about methods and to produce credible evidence.

Due to my experience both as a program practitioner and as a practicing evaluator, I am less interested in outcomes and more interested in the experiences of individuals, in the relationships embedded in program activities or service delivery, and in the perceived fairness of activities or service delivery. Thus, I use methods that follow the *nonconsequentialist* ethical theories. In this chapter, I have made transparent my reasoning and provided illustration for why systematically collected and analyzed words and phrases from ethnographic or phenomenologic interviews and observations make credible evidence.

References

Committee on Scientific Principles for Education Research (Author), Shavelson, R. J., & Towne, L. (Eds.). (2002). *Scientific research in education.* Washington, DC: National Research Council/National Academies Press.

Cronbach, L. J., & Associates (1980). *Toward reform of program evaluation.* San Francisco: Jossey-Bass.

Kuhn, T. (1970). *The structure of scientific revolutions* (2nd ed.). Chicago: University of Chicago Press.

Lawrence-Lightfoot, S. (2000). *Respect.* Cambridge, MA: Perseus Books.

Mishler, E. G. (2000). Validation in inquiry-guided research: The role of exemplars in narrative studies. In B. M. Brizuela, J. P. Stewart, R. G. Carillo, & J. G. Berger (Eds.), *Acts of inquiry in qualitative research* (pp. 119–145). Cambridge, MA: Harvard Educational Review.

Noddings, N. (1995). *Philosophy of education.* Boulder, CO: Westview.

Phillips, D. C. (2007). Adding complexity: Philosophical perspectives on the relationship between evidence and policy. In P. A. Moss (Ed.), *Evidence and decision making: The 106th Yearbook for the National Society for the Study of Education* (pp. 376–402). Malden, MA: Blackwell.

Rawls, J. (1971). *A theory of justice.* Cambridge, MA: Harvard University Press.

Rossman, G. B., & Rallis, S. F. (2003). *Learning in the field.* Thousand Oaks, CA: Sage Publications.

Slater, J. K., & Constantine, N. (2003, September). *Sacramento County HIV/AIDS Prevention and Education Program needs assessment: What HIV+ persons tell us about prevention for positives.* Sacramento, CA: Center for Research on Adolescent Health and Development, Public Health Institute.

Strike, K., Haller, E., & Soltis, J. (1998). *The ethics of school administration.* New York: Teachers College Press.

Watson, J. D. (1968). *The double helix: A personal account of the discovery of the structure of DNA.* New York: New American Library.

Weiss, C. H. (1998). *Evaluation* (2nd ed.). Upper Saddle River, NJ: Prentice Hall.

10

Seeing Is Believing

The Credibility of Image-Based Research and Evaluation

Sandra Mathison

As for a picture, if it isn't worth a thousand words, to hell with it.

—Ad Rheinhardt, minimalist American painter

This chapter explores the credibility of image-based research and evaluation, one form of evidence used to establish and represent truth and value. While there are unique features of images and image-based inquiry, their credibility exists within a larger framework for establishing the believability of facts and values.

The credibility of evidence, the knowledge it generates, is contingent on experience, perception, and social conventions. As such, it can and does change over time (consider that Pluto once existed as a planet, and now it doesn't) and can and should be arrived at through many means, eschewing the dominance of any one method. The credibility of evidence and the generation of knowledge is enhanced by embracing Feyerabend's (1975) notion of an anarchist epistemology, the notion that every idea or strategy, however new or old or absurd, may improve our knowledge of the social world.

Credible evidence cannot therefore be the province of only certain methods (such as observations or experiments) and cannot be expressed in only one way (such as statistical averages or vignettes). To extend Feyerabend's notion, credible evidence should be humanitarian, and include embracing political ideology as a source of credibility since such ideologies may be important in overcoming the chauvinism of particular perspectives, especially ones that maintain the status quo.

At any given time, our knowledge is the best it can be and so a common-sense realism prevails—we are reasonably certain at a given time that this or that is true, and we can act on that knowledge with relatively high degrees of confidence. In some senses, certainty is based on cultural norms, or intersubjective meanings, those things we collectively know and act on even if that knowledge is tacit. But because knowledge is contingent, there are limits to its certainty, and what we know will inevitably change. In general, the issue of certainty turns on sustaining a Cartesian dualism of a mind and a separate real world—rejecting this dualism refocuses the issue of certainty, away from mapping mind onto a physical reality and toward usable and sensible knowledge.

Qualities of good evidence include relevance, coherence, verisimilitude, justifiability, and contextuality. Contextuality is important in two respects. First is the contextuality of the evidence itself, as the charge that something is taken out of context is always a serious challenge to the credibility of evidence. So, context is paramount in establishing the credibility of evidence. Knowing the point of view (for example, economic, aesthetic, or political), who generates evidence, and how, are critical aspects of credibility. The more context provided for evidence, the more credible it is. Context is important in a second sense of providing specific criteria for judging the credibility of evidence. The most obvious example of this is culturally different criteria for establishing credibility—one might contrast Western scientific notions of credibility with aboriginal notions of what makes evidence credible. Adopting the anarchist position offered by Feyerabend allows for open-ended possibilities for what can count as credible evidence and therefore knowledge of the social world.

Seeing Is Believing, or Is It?

Images are all around us; we are all image makers and image readers. Images are a rich source of data for understanding the social world and for representing our knowledge of that social world. Image-based research has a long history in cultural anthropology and sociology as well as the natural sciences, but is nonetheless still relatively uncommon (Collier & Collier, 1986). Images should not be romanticized, but neither should their value as data and knowledge be ridiculed or avoided. Especially in Western industrialized cultures, images are often associated with artistic expression, entertainment, and persuasion. Images are seen as intuitive, representing implicit and subjective knowledge, while numeric, text, and verbal data are more associated with fact, reason, and objective knowledge. Images, in fact, are no more suspect than any other sort of data, such as numbers or text. Images, like any data, can be used to lie, to question, to imagine, to critique, to theorize, to mislead, to flatter, to hurt, to unite, to narrate, to explain, to teach, to represent. This chapter will discuss what image-based research is what it can contribute to social research, and more particularly discuss its credibility.

We do not necessarily need to see to believe, and indeed we believe many things we cannot or do not see directly. The Humean skepticism about the knowability of causation is a key example of knowing something without being able to see it. The classic billiard ball example illustrates this skepticism—in the Humean perspective we cannot see causation but we infer it from seeing one billiard ball moving across the table, hitting another, and causing that second to move. Even when what we know is not something we directly see, it is based on seeing, what is referred to in scientific parlance as observation. Seeing is intricately connected with believing, and thus knowing at the individual, cultural, or global levels of knowledge. Indeed there is biological evidence that seeing, at least in the context of space, is more reliable than other sources of data, and that the central nervous system summarizes visual information in a statistically optimal way (Witten & Knudsen, 2005).

What Is Image-Based Research and Evaluation?

Image-based research includes found and researcher- or participant-produced videos, photographs, drawings, cartoons, and other visual forms of expression and representation. In anthropology, sociology, and psychology, images have been used for some time as data and as an alternative approach to representing research results because they offer a different form for researchers and participants to express their experience and present themselves and their knowledge.

> Images are essential to human sense-making. We see and think and communicate using images. Like words, images can be used, construed, and read in different ways and can serve multiple functions. . . . Like words, images are part of who

we are, who we think we are, and who we become—they are integral to questions of identity and purpose. Like other aspects of sense-making, how images create meaning is a dynamic process involving dialectical negotiation or interaction between the social and the personal aspects in any give culture. (Weber, n.d.)

Image-based research involves those things that are intrinsically visual (like place, clothing, art) but also includes the visual, both real and metaphoric, in all contexts. Examples of images are photographs, video/film, drawings, cartoons, graphs and charts, typography, graphic art, graffiti, computer graphics, television, architecture, signs, as well as what is seen in the mind's eye. This last sort of image may not be recognized as truly visual, but indeed we give meaning to and judge the adequacy of people, events, and products by the images we hold only in our mind. Images of failing schools, successful classrooms, urban blight, and rural communities reside in our mind even if we have never been to those places.

Images are used in three ways: (1) as data or evidence, (2) as an elicitation device to collect other data, and (3) as a representation of knowledge. In the first case, the images are themselves the data or evidence in an evaluation or research study. The classic example is Margaret Mead and Gregory Bateson's photographic study of Balinese life (Mead & Bateson, 1942). This book includes 759 still photographs with captions including the context of the photos, complemented by theoretical discussion. Mead and Bateson were motivated to move beyond what Mead described as "ordinary English words" because of their inadequacy for capturing and communicating the emotions of the South Sea Islanders; photography and film became their alternate grammar. Children's drawings are another example of images as data. In my investigations of high-stakes testing in schools, children's experiences of testing have been captured in drawings of themselves, the testing context, and their relationships with their teacher and classmates. Figure 10.1 shows a cartoon and Figure 10.2 a self-portrait by a fourth grader taking the state-mandated English Language Arts test.

Using images to elicit other data, like cultural or personal meaning, is perhaps the most common form of image-based research (Harper, 2002). Auto-driven photography is a good example (see, for example, Clark, 1999). Evaluation or research study participants are given the opportunity to take photographs related to the inquiry questions at hand. The specific subject matter is left to participants, and as such the photographs become the physical manifestation of what participants pay attention to, perhaps what they value. The photographs are not the end goal, however. The meaning the photographer-participants make of the photographs, expressed in interviews, is the key data being collected. In an assessment of customer satisfaction with a hotel, Pullman and Robson (2007) asked guests to take photographs of things

Figure 10.1   Cartoon Drawing as Data

SOURCE: Freeman and Mathison (2005).

that influenced their opinions of the hotel. The photographs became the basis for discussions with guests about what they did and did not like.

This same strategy is used with photographs or video not generated by participants. Researchers who bring a theoretical framework to the research may take photographs or videos that focus the elicitation on specific research

Josef (Hispanic urban fourth grader): "[I was] worried 'cause if I don't, if I fail again 'cause I did third grade, 'cause in third grade . . . my teacher said 'some of you going to pass into fourth grade,' and I didn't . . . 'cause if I fail then I have to go to summer school. And I don't want to go to summer school again."

Figure 10.2   Joseph's Self-Portrait as Data

SOURCE: Freeman and Mathison (2005).

questions. For example, in a study of a therapeutic camp for children with cancer, the researchers hypothesized that the nature of physical space was a critical dimension of the camp's therapeutic quality. The photos of places and spaces at the camp were taken by the researchers and used in the interview with campgoers to explore this hypothesis (Epstein, Stevens, McKeever, & Baruchel, 2006). Regardless of who makes the images, photographs, or video recordings, they are used to elicit participants' thoughts, decisions, reasoning, and reactions in situ (see, for example, Meijer, Zanting, & Verloop, 2002).

Visual images, much like verbatim quotes, figures, graphs, and tables, can be used to illustrate the interpretive text—a legitimate, but particular use of images. The third use of images is as the representation of knowledge generated by a research study or evaluation. In other words, the image is the result of the research and is the communicative device for reporting findings. This use of images in research and evaluation challenges a taken-for-granted assumption that legitimate knowledge of what is or is not valued is best expressed in words, whether spoken or written. And the dominance of print media in academia reinforces this assumption. However, media other than text has become increasingly accessible and communicable with increased access to the World Wide Web. Large databases of images are now easily accessible, such as in the Landscapes of Capital Project (http://it.stlawu.edu/~global), an analysis of the role of corporate television commercials in shaping and defining global capitalism, and in Kaplan and Howes's (2004) Web-based compilation of photographs taken by students and staff in a secondary school.

The Kids With Cameras projects are another example of photographs as representation, made popular by the movie *Born Into Brothels*. While this project promotes photography as an empowering skill that will benefit these children, their photographs stand as representations of their life, a representation that needs no further interpretation or embellishment. The idea is that participant photography is a research strategy that permits participants to speak directly, and thus be empowered to influence their community, as well as decision and policy makers. The generic strategy is called "photovoice" (Wang, 1999; Wang & Burris, 1997). Photo essays are another example of images as representation, such as the representation of growing up in Los Angeles in Lauren Greenfield's (n.d.) *Fast Forward*, a series of photographs with contextualizing text. Peter Menzel's (1995) *Material World: A Global Family Portrait* (photographs taken by the photographer) and Jim Hubbard's (n.d.) *Shooting Back* (photographs taken by homeless children) are other excellent examples of image as knowledge.

Many graphs and charts are images, often communicating large data sets in simple or intuitive ways—Edward Tufte's work is the most significant in this area. Combining an aesthetic sensibility with a goal to communicate information, Tufte illustrates how descriptive information can be visualized to tell stories of multidimensional relationships. Tufte (1990) describes this as envisioning information, work he suggests is at "the intersection of image, word, number, art" (p. 9).

Credibility of Image-Based Research and Evaluation

All data are susceptible to manipulation, distortion, or misuse, but images no more so than any other kind of data. Just as statistics can be used in ways that distort meaning, so too can images distort meaning. "Photoshopped" has become a verb indicating an image has been digitally changed to deliberately distort meaning, for example, and has been extended to other uses such as when the media focuses on celebrity breakups rather than the victims of Katrina or when history textbooks do not include embarrassing moments of racism or sexism. The more technical term for photographic manipulation is "scitexing" (named for the company that developed the technology) and can include overlaying multiple negatives, airbrushing, image quilting, and so on. There is a long history of the manipulation of images for whimsical, commercial, and political purposes, and credibility in image-based research must necessarily consider such possibilities (see Loizos, 2000, and the website *Is Seeing Believing?* at www.frankwbaker.com/isb.htm for more on the manipulation of images). But, researchers and evaluators are no more likely to manipulate image data than they are to manipulate statistical data.

Four considerations for establishing the credibility of image-based research are discussed below: (1) quality of the research design, (2) attention to context, (3) adequacy of the image from multiple perspectives, and (4) the contribution images make to new knowledge.

Research Design Provides the Framework for Credibility

In part, the credibility of any data can be judged by reference to the design of the evaluation or research project (Wagner, 2004). There is a tremendous debate about what constitutes the best research design, marked by a recent advocacy for randomized clinical trials (and indeed, that is part of the motivation for this book). There is not, however, unanimity about what is best, in part because best for what and in what context is an important part of the equation. Without indulging in a discussion of the very different perspectives about what constitutes an adequate research design, the credibility of images can be established within the context of whatever research design is used.

Image-based research can operate within a neopositivist framework where image data are like any other kind of data. The credibility of the evidence, and the threats to credibility, are established procedurally. Research and evaluation studies intend to answer questions or test hypotheses. Whether the evidence collected provides credible answers or conclusions depends on such strategies as establishing the validity of the measures (i.e., are the images actually what is of interest), the reliability of images (i.e., do individuals or researchers agree on images), the sampling of images from a knowable population of images in an explicit and defensible way, and whether the analysis follows understood conventions.

An interpretivist or critical research or evaluation study that employs images as evidence will also make reference to procedures to establish credibility. For example, it is likely that participant-generated images would be favored over researcher-generated images, to be coherent with the intention to understand the meaningfulness of a construct, experience, program, and so on from the participants' point of view. Another example would be a clear and transparent justification for the selection of images to use in elicitation strategies. Yet another example would be a description of how analytic categories are generated and used in the analysis and conclusions. In addition, other conventions such as prolonged engagement (images collected over time, in multiple contexts) and responsiveness (the use of images reflects a respectful interaction between researcher/evaluator and participants) might be the focus.

An especially unique attribute of an interpretivist research design is the inclusion of a personal account of how and why the study was done. Personal accounts may be included in appendices, forewords, or afterwords, and outline the positionality of the study author, making explicit that persons and not merely technique shape the inquiry.

Regardless of the underlying epistemologies, the credibility of image-based research can be judged by the defensibility of the study design. Truth or credibility is, at least in part, established through conventions. While different camps of inquiry accept different conventions for establishing truth, there is a set of conventions to which a particular image-based evaluation or research study or image-based evidence can be compared. Image-based evaluation and research, like any, can therefore be established by reference to procedures that by agreement of a community of inquirers have come to be acceptable.

Credibility of Images as Evidence Requires Attention to Context

When they photographed social life in Bali, Bateson took pictures while Mead noted when, where, and under what circumstances the photograph was taken (Mead & Bateson, 1942). In presenting the images in their book, careful attention was paid to sequencing the photographs in the order they were taken. This was done in some cases because the photographs illustrate an event that has a temporal quality (a dance, a ceremony, preparation of a meal), but in a larger sense Mead and Bateson were providing a context within which they and the viewer/reader could understand Balinese social life.

Visual sociology and other image-based research often use and make images that resemble other uses of images, such as photojournalism or art.

> Visual sociology, documentary photography, and photojournalism, then, are whatever they have come to mean, or been made to mean, in their daily use in worlds of photographic work. They are social constructions, pure and simple. In this they resemble all the other ways of reporting what we know, or think we have found out, about the societies we live in, such ways as ethnographic reports, statistical summaries, maps, and so on. (Becker, 1998)

In his analysis, Becker (1998) illustrates that knowing who is creating and using images is a critical aspect of establishing their credibility. He asserts that images, like all cultural objects, get meaning from their context. A common means for providing context is the combination of images with text. Using Mead and Bateson's (1942) book on Balinese life as an example, when opened the pages facing each other provide a complement of image and accompanying contextualizing text: photographs appear on one page and two kinds of text on the other—a few paragraphs of interpretation and captions indicating when, where, and by whom the photograph was taken and what was going on at the time, as well as interpretive text suggesting the generalizable or theoretical meaning of the photographic evidence. Detail, then, is one way to provide context: "[I]n visual reasoning, art, typography, cartography, even sculpture, the quantity of detail is an issue completely separate from the difficulty of reading. Indeed, at times, the more intense the detail, the greater the clarity and understanding—because meaning and reasoning are contextual" (Tufte, 2003, p. 12). While talking about data displays in general, Tufte's (2006) emphasis on detailed documentation as the key to credibility applies to images of all types (p. 132).

Mead and Bateson's (1942) work exemplifies explicit, detailed contextualizing of images, but credible image-based research may also imply the context. "Because the images themselves, sequenced, repetitive, variations on a set of themes, provide their own context, they teach viewers what they need to know in order to arrive, by their own reasoning, at some conclusions about what they are looking at" (Becker, 1998, p. 14). The credibility of images is enhanced by providing or implying context (whether through text, narration, or other images) and by using complex and detailed images.

Adequacy of the Interpretation of the Image

The adequacy of the interpretation of images as data is the third aspect of credibility, and can be understood in terms of the focus on the subject matter, focus on the creation, or focus on the audience or viewers of the images (Werner, 2006). One or the other of these foci may be more relevant in establishing the credibility in any particular study, but regardless of the foci, at the heart of the adequacy of the interpretation is a sense of authenticity. Table 10.1 summarizes these foci, including key questions one might ask to establish the credibility of an image or an image-based study.

In assessing the adequacy of the interpretations in image-based studies, one can look first at the subject matter or content of the image. In other words, what sense is made of the image? The content of the images can be read in ways that range from relatively low inference (like describing what

Table 10.1   Features of the Interpretation of Images

	Readings of Images		Questions to Establish Credibility of Images
Focus on subject matter	• Literal reading	Low Inference ↓ High	• What are the physical features of the image? Who or what is portrayed? What is the setting?
	• Biographical reading		• What is the relationship of the image to current practices? To identities? How is the image socially situated?
	• Empathetic reading		• What common experiences are invoked?
	• Iconic reading		• How does the image relate to bigger ideas, values, events, cultural constructions?
	• Psychological reading		• What are the intended states of mind and being?
Focus on image creation	• Technical reading		• What are the design features? Are images scaled or mapped?
	• Editorial reading		• What values, knowledge are communicated by the author or creator?
	• Indexical reading		• How does the image related to values of the time and place?
	• Spectatorship reading		• Where is the viewer situated in relation to the image?
Focus on audience/viewers	• Reading of effects		• What impact does the image have on viewers?
	• Reflexive reading		• How do viewers see themselves within the interpretation? How does the image interact with biography?

is in the image) to much higher inference (such as imputing particular states of mind to people in images). The key overall concern is the degree to which the interpretation is supported by evidence from the images themselves. Table 10.1 lists four kinds of readings that may be part of the interpretation and accompanying questions to test the credibility of those interpretations. Take, for example, the common image of a map. The content of the map can be interpreted in a relatively straightforward, literal way—such as what place is portrayed, and what features of the place are included. But the map also lends itself to higher inference interpretations such as what kinds of places or things are valued, perhaps by being given prominence (museums, personal events), and what is devalued by its absence. Specifically, if one looks at the common iconic map of the London Underground, the image portrays a sense of places in relation to one another, communicates how far apart places are, and evokes a sense of neatness and symmetry to the city. If one then compares this iconic map to the less common but geographically correct map of the London Underground, a different sense of place is communicated.

In my research about the meaning children make of the high-stakes testing experience in schools, we solicited drawings of kids in their classrooms. We found that when fourth-grade students were asked to draw pictures of their test-preparation activities, the urban students drew themselves with a teacher standing near them saying things like "good job" (see Figure 10.3), thus portraying a particular relationship between teacher and students in this context.

But images are not just of something, someone, or someplace. They are created, and in image-based research they can be created by the researcher/evaluator, by the participants, or by a collaborative endeavor. Judging the credibility of the image and the study may also require attention to the creator. At one level, the credibility of the image can be judged by its technical qualities. If appropriate, does the image include elements of scale that provide adequate context for its interpretation? How is the image set up with regard to perspective? No image is a transparent window, and the creator's choices in its creation provide a point of view from which to understand the context. This point of view includes not only the technical decisions (black and white or color, line drawing or oil painting, distant or

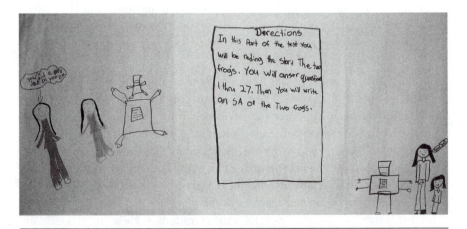

Figure 10.3   Urban Fourth Grader's Drawing of Relationship Between Herself and Her Teacher

close up, front or back images) but also reflects the creator's cultural context and values in a particular time and place. In Table 10.1, these are referred to as editorial and indexical readings. The last sort of reading is one that considers the interpretation of the image in relation to the viewer: where does the image situate the viewer, the reader of the image?

Look again at Figure 10.2, Joseph's self portrait while taking the English Language Arts test. In this case, the creator of the image is known, which is not always the case, especially if images are found rather than created in the study context. Joseph can tell us things about what the image means, and he does in the interview excerpt included with his portrait. There are things about the drawing that Joseph may not be able to tell us, but that may be meaningful, such as the significance of the colors he chose, and the fact that Joseph looks directly at us out of his portrait.

Images imply a viewer, and image-based studies specifically define the viewer as the researcher/evaluator or the study consumer. Thus the credibility of the use and interpretations of images requires attention to audience. What impact do the images have on viewers? Are the researcher's interpretations coherent with the viewer's interpretations? How do the images and the interpretations of them interact with the biographies of consumers? Take Joseph's self portrait again as an example. We might ask, how do we see Joseph in the testing situation? and how do others understand Joseph's experience? I have a large matted version of this drawing, along with several others, on my office wall. They are pictures that draw people in, and inevitably visitors want to talk about them. Seeing these pictures, people ask me questions— about the kids, about the research, about why I used drawing. But they are also compelled to speculate about what they mean, to show empathy by feeling sad for kids like Joseph, to share in the satire inherent in some drawings, to be happy for the drawings that show pride in doing well on the test, and to tell stories of their own experiences with assessment in schools.

Credibility Is Dependent on the Extent to Which the Image-Based Study Contributes to New Knowledge

It is a truism to suggest that research and evaluation should result in new knowledge, new understandings of the focus of the study. In a traditional social science framework, a relatively small, particular, and focused audience is implied. Study results are reported in peer-reviewed journals and books that speak to others with similar interests to those of the study authors. New knowledge in this context is new to a group of colleagues working hard on inquiry about the same phenomena, and the study is indexed to an existing body of literature. This test of credibility may apply to image-based studies.

Attention is paid to whether the claims follow from the evidence, and whether the arguments are well-founded, defensible, and coherent.

The ubiquity and accessibility of images may suggest new contexts in which the credibility of the study to contribute to new knowledge might be judged. Because images have a populist character, image-based studies may be more accessible to study participants (and people like them), the public, and even policy makers, and therefore potentially broader contexts for knowledge generation may be important in considering the credibility of the study. Credibility in this more populist context might also involve questions about the image-based study's verisimilitude, authenticity, and usefulness as a catalyst for change. Instead of a rhetoric of scientific proceduralism, the rhetoric is one of believability, often a call to join the study author and participants on a journey to understanding and knowing (Wagner, 2004, p. 1500). In this context, the balance of interpretation to evidence will tip toward evidence, in contrast with the social science reports where interpretation is illustrated by evidence. This difference may contribute to the ambiguity of image-based studies, but also emphasizes the profoundly empirical nature of such inquiry.

This populist context of credibility does not seek legitimation within a body of literature created by a relatively small community of scholars, but rather seeks legitimation in its ability to communicate with diverse consumers. Evaluation studies are first and foremost about understanding the value and merit of something within a particular context, often with an eye to making things better. While image-based approaches are not a singular answer to how to do this well, it is the case that they may have certain advantages given this intent. Wagner (2004) suggests that inquiry should be multifaceted: "Being smart about that requires that we learn what we can from not only social scientists but also documentary photographers and filmmakers, at least some of whom celebrate both art and empiricism and aim for both telling images and telling truths" (p. 1505).

Conclusion: So What Counts as Credible Evidence?

It is too simplistic to assert that seeing is believing, but the fact that our eyes sometimes deceive does not obviate the credible knowing from doing and viewing image-based research and evaluation. This chapter has focused on how we establish the credibility of images and image-based research and evaluation, not because images are better or more compelling evidence but because this detailed examination illustrates that any evidence may be credible and truthful. As suggested in the introduction to this chapter, the credibility of any evidence ought not to be established solely or even primarily by the methods by which it is generated. Whether one is doing ethnography or randomized experiments or survey research is not the key feature in establishing the credibility of the evidence generated. What counts as credible evidence is defined within inquiry traditions, within epistemological traditions. There are fundamental differences among these traditions, so the credibility of evidence or data within any particular tradition is first established within that particular tradition.

As we investigate and evaluate social phenomena, the larger context that eschews a hegemony of any particular tradition and any particular kind of evidence increases our potential knowledge of and methods of valuing those social phenomena. Images, correlations, effects sizes, vignettes—indeed, any and all evidence—must be taken seriously and examined in ways that reject the search for a single truth. Considering any and all evidence moves us to thinking about the usability and sensibility of evidence within the larger social context.

References

Becker, H. S. (1998). Visual sociology, documentary photography, and photojournalism: It's (almost) all a matter of context. In J. Prosser (Ed.), *Image-based research: A sourcebook for qualitative researchers*. London: Falmer.

Clark, C. D. (1999). The auto-driven interview: A photographic viewfinder into children's experiences. *Visual Sociology, 14,* 39–50.

Collier, J., Jr., & Collier, M. (1986). *Visual anthropology: Photography as a research method*. Albuquerque: University of New Mexico Press.

Epstein, I., Stevens, B., McKeever, P., & Baruchel, S. (2006). Photo elicitation interview (PEI): Using photos to elicit children's perspectives. *International Journal of Qualitative Methods, 5*(3), Article 1. Retrieved January 3, 2007, from http://www.ualberta.ca/~ijqm/backissues/5_3/pdf/epstein.pdf.

Feyerabend, P. (1975) *Against method*. New York: Humanities Press.

Freeman, M., & Mathison, S. (2005). *Urban and suburban students' reported experiences with high-stakes testing in New York State*. Paper presented at the Annual Meeting of the American Educational Research Association, Montreal, Quebec, Canada.

Greenfield, L. (n.d.). *Fast forward*. Retrieved January, 8, 2007, from http://zonezero.com/exposiciones/fotografos/lauren2/portada.html.

Harper, D. (2002). Talking about pictures: A case for photo elicitation. *Visual Studies, 17,* 13–26.

Hubbard, J. (n.d.). *Shooting back*. Retrieved February 6, 2007, from http://www.shootingback.org.

Kaplan, I., & Howes, A. (2004). Seeing through different eyes: Exploring the value of participative research using images in schools. *Cambridge Journal of Education, 34*(2), 143–155.

Loizos, P. (2000). Video, film, and photographs as research documents. In M. W. Bauer & G. Gaskell (Eds.), *Qualitative researching with text, image, and sound.* Thousand Oaks, CA: Sage Publications.

Mead, M., & Bateson, G. (1942). *Balinese character: A photographic analysis.* New York: New York Academy of Sciences.

Meijer, P. C., Zanting, A., & Verloop, N. (2002). How can student teachers elicit experienced teachers' practical knowledge? Tools, suggestions, and significance. *Journal of Teacher Education, 53*(5), 406–419.

Menzel, P. (1995). *Material world: A global family portrait.* San Francisco: Sierra Club Books.

Pullman, M., & Robson, S. (2007). A picture is worth a thousand words: Using photo-elicitation to solicit hotel guest feedback. *Cornell Hotel and Restaurant Administration Quarterly, 48*(2), 121–144.

Tufte, E. R. (1990). *Envisioning information.* Cheshire, CT: Graphics Press.

Tufte, E. R. (2003). *The cognitive style of PowerPoint.* Cheshire, CT: Graphics Press.

Tufte, E. R. (2006). *Beautiful evidence.* Cheshire, CT: Graphics Press.

Wagner, J. (2004). Constructing credible images: Documentary studies, social research, and visual studies. *American Behavioral Scientist, 47*(12), 1477–1506.

Wang, C. (1999). Photovoice: A participatory action research strategy applied to women's health. *Journal of Women's Health, 8*(2), 85–192.

Wang, C., & Burris, M. (1997). Photovoice: Concept, methodology, and use for participatory needs assessment. *Health Education and Behavior, 24*(3), 369–387.

Weber, S. (n.d.). *Concerning images.* Retrieved January 2, 2007, from http://iirc.mcgill.ca/

Werner, W. (2006). Reading pictures of people. In E. W. Ross (Ed.), *The social studies curriculum: Purposes, problems, and possibilities.* Albany: SUNY Press.

Witten, I. B., & Knudsen, E. I. (2005). Why seeing is believing: Merging auditory and visual worlds. *Neuron, 48*(3), 489–496.

11

Toward a Practical Theory of Evidence for Evaluation

Thomas A. Schwandt

Science is organized knowledge. Wisdom is organized life.

—Immanuel Kant

The field of evaluation remains captivated by the qualitative versus quantitative debate that engrossed it in the late 1970s and early 1980s. The latest manifestation of the debate is the controversy surrounding the nature and use of evidence in making decisions about the value (merit, worth, significance) of various evaluands. In this debate, defenders of experimental (read "quantitative") designs are squaring off against apologists for non-experimental (read "qualitative") designs in an argument about which is better capable of producing credible evidence. The original debate often generated more heat than light because it too frequently focused on quarrels about differences in methods rather than attending to more complex underlying issues at the intersection of the epistemology and social and political theory of evaluation. In much the same way, the present iteration of the debate is misguided because, once again, it centers on questions of method while ignoring more primary matters concerning what constitutes evidence and its responsible use.

A moment's reflection on everyday life reveals that navigating our way through—and judging the value, significance, and consequences of—events and relationships demands knowledge of the patterns as well as the peculiarities of human behavior; understandings of the common as well as the idiosyncratic meanings we attach to actions and language; wisdom to respond appropriately and effectively to complex circumstances in situations lacking rules for conduct; and a dependable grasp of the contributory, if not causal, relationship between human actions and their effects. To put it a bit more plainly, to be ordinary, conscious, aware, attentive, and responsive evaluators, citizens, parents, friends, teachers, administrators, health care workers, and the like is to employ a very catholic epistemology that seeks reliable evidence bearing on three broad, important questions—What happened here? What does that mean? Why did that happen? We routinely make use of a variety of empirical means to generate this evidence. As a result, we know different things about ourselves and our actions and we know them in different ways. Taken collectively, these different understandings, and different ways of reaching those understandings, help us form a comprehensive picture of what we are up to, why and how, what it means, and whether we are doing the right thing and doing it well. Thus, there is little genuine merit in debating whether any particular method of investigation is superior for producing credible evidence in and for evaluation. Evaluating the merit, worth, or significance of our judgments, actions, policies, programs, and so on requires a variety of evidence generated via both experimental and nonexperimental methods.

Likewise, there is little value for the field of evaluation as a whole in debating the proposition that randomized controlled trials (RCTs) are some sort of gold standard for generating evidence. RCTs are valuable tools of investigation. Experiments with randomized control groups are ideally suited for producing unbiased conclusions about the average numerical effects of an intervention or treatment. Considerable difficulty, however, results when applying global evidence (i.e., average effects) to local problems (i.e., the problem of treatment-effect heterogeneity, or the efficacy versus effectiveness argument) (Kravitz, Duan, & Braslow, 2004). Furthermore, RCTs are not always the best choice of study design and in some situations do not give remarkably better evidence than nonrandomized study designs (e.g., Grossman & MacKenzie, 2005; Petticrew & Roberts, 2003; Worrall, 2002). In other words, observational studies often provide excellent evidence as well. Finally, a great deal of what we know and accept about the natural world, particularly from the field of physics, is based on evidence of single experiments that involves neither statistics nor randomization (Cartwright, 1989). Similarly, we are confident in acting on all kinds of understandings of the social world absent their experimental empirical verification.

It is important for the reputation of the practice of evaluation—in the public at large and in the academy—to avoid the scientism suggested by the idea of setting up any given method as a gold standard for producing evidence. This is not new advice. More than 30 years ago, the renowned sociologist Martin Trow (1970) encouraged discussion and debate regarding the relative usefulness of methods of participant observation and interviewing for the study of specific social problems but cautioned that such appraisal "is very different from asserting the general and inherent superiority of one method over another on the basis of some intrinsic qualities it presumably possesses" (p. 149).

Clearing out the underbrush of the quantitative-qualitative debate and the thicket of scientism makes it possible to frame the discussion of what constitutes credible evidence in evaluation in potentially more educative and enlightening ways. This chapter suggests one such way. It discusses some requirements of a potential theory of evidence for evaluation that attends to questions of the credibility, relevance, and probative value of evidence while embracing a range of methods. At minimum, an adequate theory of evidence includes analyses of several kinds—the character of evidence, the ethics of evidence, the contexts of the application of evidence, and the nature of rationality and argumentation (including the notion of an evidence "base" for decision making). This particular examination of such a theory draws heavily on the literature in clinical medicine. This is a conscious choice since that practice and its ways of thinking about evidence are often evoked as a guiding light for what mere mortals in the social and behavioral sciences ought to regard as evidence.

The Character of Evidence

By evidence, we generally mean information helpful in forming a conclusion or judgment. Framed in a more rigorous epistemological perspective, evidence means information bearing on whether a belief or proposition is true or false, valid or invalid, warranted or unsupported. At present, we face some difficulty and confusion with understanding the term *evidence* in evaluation because it is often taken to be synonymous with the term *evidence-based*. The latter notion, however, has two shortcomings. First, it is narrowly interpreted to mean that only a specific kind of scientific finding—that is, evidence of causal efficacy—counts as evidence. Second, the idea of an evidence *base* (at least in its original formulation in evidence-based medicine) suggests that evidence is the literal *foundation* for action because it provides secure knowledge (Upshur, 2002).

For a theory of evidence to be adequate and useful in evaluation, it cannot be so circumscribed. We would be well served by considering more broadly how the notion of evidence is used in a variety of disciplines and fields as well as in our everyday ways of getting on with one another. Unfortunately, as Twining (2005) notes, the narrow usage of the term *evidence* in evidence-based practice

> excludes most of what counts as evidence in law, history, and most other disciplines, especially in the humanities. . . . Furthermore, in law or medical diagnosis or historical inquiry, in considering a particular case calling for judgment about a particular event or situation, insofar as the issue is susceptible to rational argument, the main distinction is not between scientific and intuitive (or subjective) judgment. Rather, it is between different kinds of generalization (scientific, common sense, case-specific) and particular items of information all of which have evidential functions in the context of an argument and all of which are subject to critical appraisal in respect of their evidentiary credentials [namely] relevance, credibility, and probative force. (p. 7)

For example, in the field of policy analysis, evidence drawn from analysis of speeches, internal memoranda, and interviews has been used to argue that the Bush administration expresses strong disdain for international law (Urquhart, 2006); in sociology, evidence drawn from extensive participant observation, interviews, and analysis of government documents is offered in support of the hypothesis that the Chinese Communist Party's rule has been a disaster for rural people (Mirksy, 2006); and evidence gleaned from historical documents was used to make the case that slavery was central to the history of the New World, and its distinguishing feature was its appeal to racial doctrine to justify the persistence of slavery (Fredrickson, 2006). These examples illustrate that notions of what comprises credible, believable, convincing, and trustworthy evidence are not decided by method choice alone, and that experimental science hardly has the only grasp on what constitutes evidence. As the philosopher Susan Haack (2003) has noted,

> The core standards of good evidence and well-conducted inquiry are not internal to the sciences, but common to empirical inquiry of every kind. . . . Respect for evidence, care in weighing it, and persistence in seeking it out, so far from being scientific desiderata, are the standards by which we judge *all* inquirers, detectives, historians, investigative journalists, etc., as well as scientists. In short, the sciences are not epistemologically privileged. (p. 23)

Everyday life also presents us with many opportunities to reflect on the nature and use of evidence. My 82-year-old mother recently had hip replacement surgery and the absence this past month of what was, for the better part of the past year, pained expressions on her face and constant struggling to get up from a chair and move about in a usual way throughout the house, is evidence that her spirit has returned and her demeanor radically improved. Based on my appraisal of this evidence, I now interact with her differently from how I did before the surgery. Her surgeon's examination of the hip X-ray at two months post surgery is evidence of the physical healing that has taken place in that joint. Based on his reading of that evidence and the physical examination, he feels confident that she can resume most all activities.

Of course, evidence per se never fully determines the truth or falsity of a proposition. Evidence must always be interpreted. Assessment of the following properties or characteristics of evidence depends on the proposition in question, as well as on the circumstances and practice in which the evidence is being brought to bear:

- *Relevance*—Does the information bear directly on the hypothesis or claim in question?
- *Credibility*—Can we believe the information?
- *Probative (inferential) force*—How strongly does the information point toward the claim or hypothesis being considered?

Thus, we have different ways of appraising these characteristics in, for example, criminal as opposed to civil law. Another example can be drawn from medicine, as shown in Table 11.1. Here, it is directly apparent that what is regarded as relevant evidence depends on the kind of question we are asking. Judging whether the evidence gathered is credible will depend, in large part, on whether agreed-upon methodological rules for generating the evidence in each case were followed (and, of course, this is a matter of interpretation). Whether the evidence brought forth is sufficient, cogent, and of high enough probative value to validate a knowledge claim in each case will be a matter of argument or rational consensus, because it is widely accepted that there is no foundation of unquestionable evidence in terms of which the validity of knowledge claims can be adjudicated (Hammersley, 2000).

Moreover, evidence per se cannot be wrong or right in some absolute sense. Our interpretations of it, however, can be flawed. We may choose to ignore the evidence—recall, for example, the Bush administration's claims that there were weapons of mass destruction in Iraq. We may make an incorrect inference based on the evidence—as that sage columnist Ann Landers once said, "Don't accept your dog's admiration as conclusive evidence that you are wonderful." We may leap too quickly to a conclusion absent sufficient corroborating evidence. This is the worry addressed by such methodological

Table 11.1   Types of Research Questions and Actionable Evidence

Research Question	Research Methodology/ Study Design	Evidence
1. What is the importance of patient preferences in the choice of treatment for benign prostatic hyperplasia?	Open-ended, in-depth interview study	Identification and characterization of reactions of individual patients to their disease and their assessment of risks and benefits of alternative treatment
2. In men with benign prostatic hyperplasia, is laser prostatectomy superior to transurethral resection of the prostate in terms of symptom relief, blood loss, and length of hospital stay?	RCT	Efficacy of the two treatments compared on outcome variables
3. Are we providing effective care to patients with benign prostatic hyperplasia in our region, and are they appearing to benefit from it?	Nonexperimental cohort study	Longitudinal description of interventions patients receive, events and outcomes they experience

SOURCE: Based on Sackett and Wennberg (1997).

moves as data source triangulation and the use of multiple methods, and it is why a good clinician always integrates evidence from the clinical examination, the patient's history, pathophysiological rationale (reasoning from principles of physiology to presumed clinical effect), knowledge of previous cases, and results of empirical studies in reaching a diagnosis and recommended treatment.

There are at least two reasons why evidence cannot serve as a secure and infallible base or foundation for action. First, whether evidence is conclusive (so strong as to rule out *all* possibility for error) or inclusive is always a matter of interpretation. The long-standing tradition of epistemological skepticism reminds us that we lack conclusive evidence for most every topic we can think of. Second, evidence exists to become obsolete—that is, it is "provisional, and always capable of being overturned, modified, refuted or superseded by better evidence" (Upshur, 2002, p. 114). Upshur (2000), in discussing medical evidence, identifies characteristics shared by evidence as used across multiple fields and disciplines. It is (a) *provisional*—it rarely attains absolute certainty; (b) *defeasible*—revisable in the light of new information and new findings; (c) *emergent*—it is expected to change with time; (d) *incomplete*—some types of evidence we will never possess because of ethical standards governing the conduct of research; (e) *constrained*—economic resources restrict possibilities of generating evidence, and computational constraints limit what can be known (e.g., two different treatments or technologies can be used in two different sequences; five treatments or technologies yield the possibility of 120 different sequences); and (f) *collective*—it is located in particular communities of inquirers. As Upshur (2002) explains, evidence generation and use is not simply a matter of the actions of a single rational agent; evidence in medicine (and increasingly in the fields of education, social work, and mental and public health) is digested and reformulated into abstracts, practice guidelines, and so on, and this "raises important questions concerning who has the authority to create, interpret and judge evidence." These characteristics of evidence are consonant with our understanding of the fallibilistic, nonfoundational character of knowledge. Thus, the term *evidence base* must be interpreted with caution: To claim that evidence may figure importantly in our decisions to act is one thing; to claim it is foundation for our actions is another.

The Ethics of Evidence

An adequate theory of evidence for evaluation must also take up the question of ethics. Evaluation is unquestionably an aspect of policy making. Try as we may, it is not possible to eliminate matters of value, ethics, purpose, or politics from policy making, for, by its very nature, policy making "requires making choices that are not value free or reducible to technical issues over which there is little controversy" (Rodwin, 2001, p. 439). Scientific evidence of various kinds forthcoming from evaluation plays a part in policy decisions; because it does, a theory of evidence ought to attend specifically to ethical issues in matters of the production, interpretation, dissemination, and use of evidence. The physician and senior fellow at the Center for Bioethics and Human Dignity, Edmund Pellegrino (1999) claims, "Because evidence has the power to convince others, it has an inescapable moral dimension. It can lead or mislead, enhance or diminish the lives of individuals and communities" (p. 34). Evaluation clearly seeks to convince in this way—it aims to make a persuasive case for the value (or lack thereof) of a given program, policy, product, or project.

Drawing on Pellegrino's (1999) work, we identify several dimensions of the ethics of evidence. First, the *collection, production, and interpretation of evidence* obviously require that the evaluator knows how to competently evaluate evidence so as to avoid using evidence that is fraudulent, meaningless, or misleading. This is no small undertaking, for the question of what constitutes evidence that is sufficient as well as persuasive enough to warrant accepting a hypothesis or strong enough to compel action is not a matter of employing decision rules but of argumentation. This is readily apparent in legal proceedings as well as in the social and behavioral sciences where it is widely accepted that setting thresholds for statistical significance, effect sizes, confidence levels, or odds ratios is not equivalent to determining the practical significance of an experimental finding.

Second, ethical considerations entailed in the *dissemination of evidence* for any purpose depend on a number of facts, which may be taken singly or in various combinations—"the audience to which the evidence is being addressed, the particular use to which the evidence is being put, the complexity of the evidence, and the degree of certainty of the evidence presented with respect to the truth, as well as the logic used to arrive at the conclusion" (Pellegrino, 1999, p. 37). We are, for example, on reasonably solid ground in assuming that peers in the evaluation profession have the technical competence to evaluate evidence within their specific fields of expertise. However, with lay audiences or the general public, Pellegrino argues, there is a much greater obligation to reveal the limitations and weaknesses in data or methodology, the incompleteness or preliminary state of evidence, and so on. He claims that

> Culpability in presenting evidence or understanding its fallibilities varies with the context within which the information is presented. The greater the gap in expertise between the purveyor of the evidence and her or his audiences, the greater the complexity of the evidence itself, and the more general or serious the policy implication, the greater culpability. (p. 39)

Third, the *use of evidence* by those who are not the primary source of the evidence they use—for example, policy makers, physicians, patients, parents, teachers, administrators, and social workers—raises questions about the obligations of evaluators to assist the users of evaluations to reflect on the moral responsibilities for the quality of evidence they invoke for their decisions. In other words, evaluation utilization is not simply a matter of understanding legitimate types of use (e.g., instrumental, conceptual, and symbolic) but also involves questions of the consequences of illegitimate use of evidence by consumers or clients of evaluation, or what Cousins (2004) described as mistaken use (incompetence, uncritical acceptance), mischievous use (manipulation, coercion), or abuse (suppression of evidence).

Finally, the use of evidence (be it quantitative or qualitative) is always implicated in a normative discourse of policy options and individual decision making. Upshur (2001) specifically speaks to this matter in the context of health interventions:

> There is a need to recognize the mutual relationship between health outcomes, outcome measures and normative discourse. There is no denying that medical practitioners and the public respond to media descriptions of health research. Whether to reduce cholesterol intake, increase green tea consumption, have one's PSA checked, or get a bone densitometry are all influenced by perceptions of effectiveness. The important point to make is that health outcomes and risk factors are not simply statistical measures or quantitative objective facts. They are manifestations of valued or desired states of being. . . . [T]here are individual and policy implications to how evidence is created and interpreted. This dimension of evidence has hitherto received scant attention in medicine, though it is well recognized in the social sciences and humanities. (p. 572)

In other words, the kinds of discussions we associate with talk of evidence such as the attainment of program and policy objectives, or program and policy outcomes and their measures, cannot be neatly separated from discourse about the normative intent of programs and policies. Scientific evidence of effect or outcome is implicated in our understanding of valued states of being such as "being educated," "living a productive life," "becoming adjusted to society and community," "overcoming addiction," and so forth.

The Contexts of the Application of Evidence

This third requirement of a theory of evidence for evaluation invites us to consider types of evidence and how they are brought to bear in making decisions about the value of an evaluand. Evaluative evidence is never exclusively generated by a single methodology or type of data source. Consider, for example, Michael Scriven's Key Evaluation Checklist (www.wmich.edu/evalctr/checklists/kec_feb07.pdf), which presents an evaluator with the responsibility of conducting an evaluation of process, outcomes, costs, comparisons, and transferability in order to come to a reasonable, evidence-based synthesis about the merit, worth, and significance of an evaluand. A variety of data are required to generate evidence on these subevaluations. We might think of these data in terms of the model in Figure 11.1 (adapted from Upshur, VanDenKerkhof, & Goel, 2001).

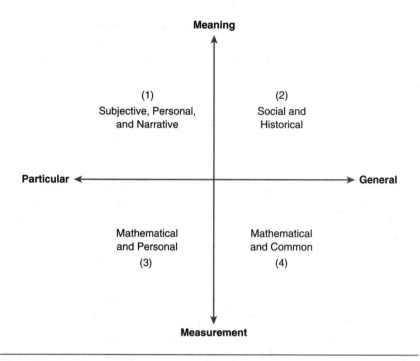

Figure 11.1   Conceptual Taxonomy of Evidence

SOURCE: Adapted from Upshur, VanDenKerkhof, and Goel (2001).

The vertical axis represents the range of methods used to generate evidence—that is, *meaning* is forthcoming from so-called qualitative methods and *measurement* from so-called quantitative methods. The horizontal axis represents the context of evidence—ranging from individual perspectives to population estimates. In the upper left-hand quadrant (1), evidence takes a narrative form often generated through case profiles, interviews, and focus groups. It consists of data on individual stakeholder and participant perceptions, beliefs, experiences, and so on. In the upper right-hand quadrant (2), evidence illustrates social views and preferences as documented in policy studies, case studies, and delphi group analyses. These studies often rely heavily on qualitative or narrative data. In the lower left-hand quadrant (3), evidence is primarily numerical and personal, focused on the measurement of attitudes, beliefs and preferences using psychometric and sociometric instruments. In the lower right-hand quadrant (4), evidence is numerical and focused on average effect or efficacy of an intervention. Evidence from the use of RCTs and quasi-experiments is to be found here.

Viewing evidence in this way makes it possible to recognize two important implications: First, evidence is the result of the search for useful knowledge (Banta, 2003). In evaluation, *useful* knowledge is that which bears on the question of the *value* of a given evaluand: (a) Value is not solely determined by causal efficacy; and (b) useful knowledge takes both numerical and non-numerical forms—experience as well as statistics produce information that can become evidence in decisions about value. In other words, there is a range of evidence that is not simply admissible, but required, for an evaluation judgment.

Second, it becomes clear that evidence is not ordered hierarchically, following the paradigm of epidemiology, in terms of research designs or methods (e.g., Hadorn, Baker, Hodges, & Hicks, 1996; Sackett, Strauss, Richardson, et al., 2000); rather, evidence is "a mediation between the context of its use and the method of its production" (Upshur et al., 2001, p. 93). The basis on which we substantiate the use of any method in evaluation is not a hierarchy of method—with RCTs at the highest level and expert opinion at the lowest level—but a judgment of the aptness of a given method to generate the kind of information needed to produce empirical evidence in support of a judgment of value of an evaluand.

The Nature of Rationality and Argumentation

Finally, an adequate theory of evidence for evaluation must take up the matter of the model of rationality or argumentation that is assumed in discussions of the use of evidence. A useful tool in this regard is work in informal logic (Upshur & Colak, 2003; Walton, 1998) that identifies different contexts for dialogue and argumentation. Four of these contexts that have particular relevance for the practice of evaluation are briefly described below. In the first three contexts, the evidential standard—that is, the extent to which scientific evidence is *required* as part of the argument—is variable. In the fourth context, evidence is absolutely required for the dialogue to take place.

1. *Persuasion*—In this context, there is a difference of opinion between the parties, and the goal of the dialogue is to resolve or clarify the issue and persuade the other party. Empirical evidence may be offered in support of a party's view, but values and preferences are equally involved. Evidence, in fact, may be neither necessary nor sufficient to persuade.

2. *Negotiation*—In this situation, trade-offs and bargaining rooted in the different interests of the parties dominates. Adjudicating the burden of evidence

may be subordinated to other needs, interests, goals, or beliefs of one of the parties involved.

3. *Deliberation*—The parties in this situation face a dilemma or practical choice of agreeing on the best course of action. Evidence may come (and probably ought) to bear on the deliberation, as for example House and Howe (1999) have argued. Other considerations are, however, equally likely to influence the course of the deliberation, such as professional/expert opinion, preferences and values of the parties, and so on.

4. *Inquiry*—The issue is burden of proof in this context, and the aim is to verify evidence and, consequently, support or reject a hypothesis. This is the context in which research evidence is absolutely necessary. The evidential standard is fixed, relatively speaking, within the rules of method adopted within a particular methodological or disciplinary practice.

Whether intended or not, many advocates of the idea of evidence-based practices appear to adopt the point of view (originating in the evidence-based medicine movement) that the kinds of evaluative decisions made in practices of clinical medicine, criminal justice, health care, education, social work, and the like are all best characterized as inquiry dialogues. What is assumed here—and reflected in hierarchies of evidence that practitioners are instructed to use as guides to decision making—is "a particularly robust kind of rational judgment: judgment that can be codified in rules or guidelines" (Thornton, 2006). It is well-known, however, that most of the decisions faced by practitioners (as well as by policy makers) about whether to adopt, implement, continue, revise, modify, or discontinue a policy, project, or program are matters of practical judgment that involve simultaneous consideration and integration of empirical evidence, expertise or professional opinion, and values and preferences (Chelimsky, 2007; Fischer, 2003). Practitioners and policy makers are embodied agents, and their practices are often best characterized as "dialectical, dynamic, pragmatic and context bound"; what is plausible and reasonable for them to do in a given situation is determined by the context of that situation, not by the existence of a hierarchy of research evidence (Upshur & Colak, 2003, p. 295).

Conclusion: So What Counts as Credible Evidence?

Arguing about whether qualitative or quantitative methods produce more credible evidence in and for evaluation is not a productive task. An adequate evidence base for decision making in evaluation is best thought of in terms of a fallibilistic epistemology and practical argument. Careful thinking about the credibility, relevance, and probative value of evidence in evaluation is not particularly advanced by arguing about hierarchies of evidence as a basis for deciding which evidence to collect. Perhaps the field of evaluation would be better served by working more diligently on a theory of evidence that took up matters of the nature of evidence as well as the context and ethics of its use in decision making.

Three important considerations ought to guide our discussion of what constitutes credible evidence in evaluation practice:

First, deciding the question of what constitutes credible evidence is not the same as deciding the question of what constitutes credible evaluation. In an evaluation, a number of different kinds of claims are put forth in arguing the case for the value (merit, worth, or significance) of a program, project, policy, and so on. Some of these claims are factual; others express value judgments, state definitions or principles, provide causal explanations, and recommend courses of action. Marshalling credible evidence in support of factual claims as well as causal explanations is, of course, an important part of what an evaluation entails. Yet, what constitutes a *credible evaluation* will depend, in part, on how each of the different claims is explained and defended (and how they are collectively assembled into an argument). However necessary, developing credible evidence in evaluation is not sufficient for establishing the credibility of an evaluation.

Second, what constitutes credible, trustworthy, believable, or convincing evidence cannot be decided by method choice alone. This is so for several reasons, such as the following: (a) Evidence is always put together in defense of some *particular* claim. Thus, we cannot discuss the matter of evidence in the abstract—that is, absent a thorough understanding of "evidence for what?" So, for example, if the claim in question is "X is important in understanding Y," or "We are doing the best we can to achieve Y given the resources at our disposal," or "This community ought to do Y," the kind of evidence we assemble in defense of these claims and the methods by which we assemble it are likely to be different from the kind we would gather if the claim is "Compared to A, B is a superior treatment for reducing the incidence of Y." (b) Appraising the credibility of evidence is never simply a matter of asking about the method used to generate it. Other relevant considerations include the credibility of the source/person (e.g., whether the person employing the method has the relevant expertise, a vested interest or bias, etc.); whether the claim itself is considered plausible and relatively in keeping with what we already know, or very unlikely, novel, and so forth; whether the evidence is derived in a more or less straightforward way from observation or involves a significant amount of inference; how the claim in question fits with other beliefs one holds; and whether there is corroborative evidence from other sources. (c) The circumstances and particular practice in which evidence is being argued influence appraisals of the probative (inferential) force of that evidence. Thus, for example, the same evidence generated with the same method is judged differently in a criminal court from how it is judged in a civil court.

Third, there is likely to be considerable payoff for the conduct of evaluation if we frame the account of evidence and its properties (e.g., credibility) in a practical-theoretical way rather an abstract/general-theoretical way. The latter is an attempt to develop a general theoretical account of what evidence is that originates in discussions of what constitutes correct beliefs about knowledge and its justification, the world, and methodology. It seeks to settle things, so to speak, by providing sure guidelines for testing the correctness of our beliefs or principles about evidence. The former, in contrast, is more or less a map of the kinds of practices and decisions within those practices in which we have come to regard evidence as something that matters. A practical theory guides us through those reason-giving practices, drawing our attention to the ways we construct the relationship between knowing and acting in particular situations. Put somewhat differently, concerns about the character of evidence, the ethics of evidence, the contexts in which evidence is used, and the kinds of arguments we make in which evidence plays an import role signify problems of action. Such concerns invite us to answer questions of how we act together meaningfully.

References

Banta, H. D. (2003). Considerations in defining evidence for public health. *International Journal of Technology Assessment in Health Care, 19*(3), 559–572.

Cartwright, N. (1989). *Nature's capacities and their measurement.* Oxford, UK: Clarendon Press.

Chelimsky, E. (2007). Factors influencing the choice of methods in federal evaluation practice. In G. Julnes & D. Rog (Eds.), *Informing federal policies on evaluation methodology* (pp. 13–33). (Vol. 113 of *New Directions for Evaluation* series). San Francisco: Jossey-Bass.

Cousins, B. (2004). Commentary: Minimizing evaluation misuse as principled practice. *American Journal of Evaluation, 25*(3), 391–397.

Fischer, F. (2003). *Reframing public policy: Discursive politics and deliberative practices.* Oxford, UK: Oxford University Press.

Fredrickson, G. M. (2006, May 25). They'll take their stand. *New York Review of Books, 53*(9), 34–36.

Grossman, J., & MacKenzie, F. J. (2005). The randomized controlled trial: Gold standard, or merely standard? *Perspectives in Biology and Medicine, 48*(4), 516–534.

Haack, S. (2003). *Defending science—within reason: Between scientism and cynicism.* Amherst, NY: Prometheus.

Hadorn, D. C., Baker, D., Hodges, J. S., & Hicks, N. (1996). Rating the quality of evidence for clinical practice guidelines. *Journal of Clinical Epidemiology, 49,* 749–754.

Hammersley, M. (2000). *Taking sides in social research: Essays on partisanship and bias.* London: Routledge.

House, E. R., & Howe, K. R. (1999). *Values in evaluation and social research.* Thousand Oaks, CA: Sage Publications.

Kravitz, R. L., Duan, N., & Braslow, J. (2004). Evidence-based medicine, heterogeneity of treatment effects, and the trouble with averages. *The Milbank Quarterly, 82*(94), 661–687.

Mirksy, J. (2006, May 11). China: The shame of the villagers. *New York Review of Books, 53*(8), 37–39.

Pellegrino, E. D. (1999). The ethical use of evidence in biomedicine. *Evaluation and the Health Professions, 22*(1), 33–43.

Petticrew, M., & Roberts, H. (2003). Evidence, hierarchies, and typologies: Horses for courses. *Journal of Epidemiology and Community Health, 57,* 527–529.

Rodwin, M. A. (2001). Commentary: The politics of evidence-based medicine. *Journal of Health Politics, 26*(2), 439–446.

Sackett, D. L., Strauss, S. E., Richardson, W. S., et al. (2000). *Evidence-based medicine: How to practice and teach EBM.* Philadelphia: Churchill-Livingstone.

Sackett, D. L., & Wennberg, J. E. (1997). Editorial: Choosing the best research design for each question. *British Medical Journal, 315,* 1636.

Thornton, T. (2006). Tacit knowledge as the unifying factor in evidence-based medicine and clinical judgment. *Philosophy, Ethics, and Humanities in Medicine, 1*(2). Available online at http://www.peh-med.com/content/1/1/2.

Trow, M. G. (1970). Comment on "Participant observation and interviewing: A comparison." In W. J. Filstead (Ed.), *Qualitative methodology.* Chicago: Markham.

Twining, W. (2005). *Evidence as a multi-disciplinary subject.* Paper prepared for the University College London research program, Evidence, Inference and Enquiry: Towards an Integrated Science of Evidence. Retrieved July 20, 2006, from http://www.evidencescience.org/projects/integrated/index.asp.

Upshur, R. E. G. (2000). Seven characteristics of medical evidence. *Journal of Evaluation in Clinical Practice, 6*(2), 93–97.

Upshur, R. E. G. (2001). The ethics of alpha: Reflections on statistics, evidence and values in medicine. *Theoretical Medicine, 22,* 565–576.

Upshur, R. E. G. (2002). If not evidence, then what? Or does medicine really need an evidence base? *Journal of Evaluation in Clinical Practice, 8*(2), 113–119.

Upshur, R. E. G., & Colak, E. (2003). Argumentation and evidence. *Theoretical Medicine, 24,* 283–299.

Upshur, R. E. G., VanDenKerkhof, E. G., & Goel, V. (2001). Meaning and measurement: An inclusive model of evidence in health care. *Journal of Evaluation in Clinical Practice, 7*(2), 91–96.

Urquhart, B. (2006, May 11). The Outlaw World. *New York Review of Books, 53*(8), 25–28.

Walton, D. (1998). *The new dialectic: Conversational contexts of argument.* Toronto, ON, Canada: University of Toronto Press.

Worrall, J. (2002). *What* evidence in evidence-based medicine? *Philosophy of Science, 69,* S316–S330.

PART IV

Conclusions

12

Credible Evidence

Changing the Terms of the Debate

Melvin M. Mark

Applied social research is typically undertaken with the hope that it will have positive consequences. Certainly this is true of policy and program evaluations that use social research methods. Evaluators widely hope that their work contributes to the world in some way or another (Mark & Henry, 2004). One contribution that might be desired involves improving the selection and retention of relatively effective programs. For example, an evaluator may hope that information about program effectiveness will influence policy makers' decisions about whether to adopt nationally a program that had been implemented in a few states. Alternatively, the evaluation might contribute by facilitating routine program modifications. For instance, program staff might use evaluation findings to guide their attempts to improve program operations and reduce barriers to participation. Alternatively, the evaluation might contribute by heightening people's understandings of social problems and their potential solutions, or by increasing the capacity of organizations, or by facilitating practitioners' judgments in context.

When we think about *how* evaluation or other applied social research can make a difference in the world, the concept of credibility readily comes to mind. Many evaluators and applied social researchers assume that, if an evaluation is not seen as credible, it will be far less likely to make a difference, to be used, to have consequences. If evaluation and applied social research are to make a difference, by any of several potential pathways (Mark & Henry, 2004), then one or more audiences, whether policy makers, program staff, or other stakeholders, will need to believe (or assume) that the study methods and findings are credible.

However, as the chapters in this volume demonstrate, the topic of "credible evidence" is not one where consensus exists. To the contrary, the chapter authors have offered a range of perspectives. On a very broad point or two, there may be agreement or something close to it. But in general, quite different perspectives exist, as the previous chapters clearly demonstrate. One overarching question for all the rest of us is, What are we to make of the divergent opinions? Should we simply take one side or the other? Should we instead try to find a principled location in the middle? Or should we somewhat cynically conclude that this is another debate in which some people have the time, energy, and proclivity to engage, while most of us need to get on with the everyday work of evaluating programs and conducting applied research?

In this chapter, I suggest that instead we should consider the possibility that closer examination of the disagreement about credible evidence may illuminate more fundamental points from which the disagreement arises. I further suggest that examination of the arguments that have been made can provide much of the groundwork for more productive future discussion and argument about credible evidence. And, because evaluation and applied social research must go on, even before the future discussion moves forward, I offer some suggestions for practice based on the examination of the different arguments that have been offered about credible evidence.

In short, in this chapter I suggest that a few underlying factors account for much if not most of the diversity in the views offered in this volume and elsewhere. That is, disparate views about what constitutes credible evidence are predicated on divergent, often implicit, assumptions. To elaborate briefly and preview the ideas that follow, I argue that divergent conceptions of credible evidence depend in part, first, upon beliefs about the typical or more desirable purpose of applied social research and evaluation. Some evaluators assume that evaluations commonly should focus on estimating the average effects of a program, with others seeing that as a rare, small, or even inappropriate focus. Second, the divergent views of credible evidence also arise from quite different assumptions about the relative ease or difficulty of getting actionable research findings about program effects. Some evaluators assume, for example, that randomized trials (or some approximation) are needed to obtain actionable evidence about program effects, while others assume that different methods will suffice for that purpose, and still others believe that the question of overall program effects is too complex to answer in a world in which context greatly matters.

If we could change the terms of the debate, so that future discussion focuses more on these and other factors that underlie opinions about credible evidence, then it might be possible to have more productive discussion in the future. For example, we might explicitly discuss the claim that evaluations should (or should not) often focus on getting the best possible estimate of a program's average effect on a set of outcomes identified prior to (that stage of) the evaluation. If we can change the terms of the debate, then future discussion might reduce some disagreements; clarify the rationale that underlies other disagreements; and perhaps even facilitate the injection of credible evidence into the debate itself, to support one rationale over another.

In addition to suggesting new terms of the debate, I highlight key aspects of several of the chapters, both critiquing and endorsing. This critical commentary on other chapters in this volume is necessarily quite selective and incomplete; contributors to this volume have made many important points that deserve a level of attention they do not receive here. I also suggest that one form of argument, seen in some of the chapters in this volume (and even more so in the symposium presentations on which most of the chapters were based), is neither so potent nor so interesting as its proponents have assumed.

Which Debate?

Before we think about how to change the terms of the debate, it is necessary to identify what the current debate is actually about. Looking across the chapters, I believe that two different debates can actually be identified. One debate is about the nature of credible evidence in general. This discussion is less contentious, perhaps, but also is given less attention by most of the contributors. The second debate is about the role of randomized experiments (and, sometimes, their closest quasi-experimental approximations) in applied social research, especially program and policy evaluation. These two debates are not completely independent, of course. One's views about the nature of credible evidence in general should have implications for how one thinks about randomized experiments. Nevertheless, it is useful, in trying to look at the factors underlying the current differences in views about credible evidence, to distinguish between the more general debate about credible evidence, on the one hand, and the more particular debate about randomized experiments, on the other. Because the debate about randomized experiments has received considerably more attention, I turn to it first.

The Debate About Randomized Experiments

Today's debate about randomized experiments arises in a historical context that has generated a great deal of interest in the topic. The U.S. Department of Education, through its Institute for Education Sciences (IES), established a priority for randomized trials for selected funding programs. In essence, this priority, when applied to a funding program, gives extra points to proposals that use randomized experiments when review panels discuss and score the proposals. Randomized experiments also receive special consideration in the review process at the What Works Clearinghouse (WWC), which is designed to identify educational interventions that have demonstrated effectiveness based on credible evidence (see Gersten & Hitchcock, Chapter 5 in this volume, for more detail). In education, this relatively new-found emphasis on randomized experiments arose in a context that led some observers to argue that the field of educational research had been underusing randomized trials, relative to their potential benefits (e.g., Cook, 2003). Of course, other observers, perhaps especially those who had been doing educational research and evaluation with methods other than randomized experiments, disagreed.

The IES priority and the WWC scoring preference for randomized experiments both created considerable controversy, as documented briefly by some of the chapter authors. Moreover, as contributors also noted, the preference for randomized trials (and close quasi-experimental approximations) is not limited to education. This preference has existed for some time in medicine, where the term *RCT*, for *randomized clinical trial*, was popularized (users of the term outside of medicine often refer to "controlled" rather than "clinical" trials). In other areas of practice, such as "development" evaluation, that is, the evaluation of international aid in developing countries, there are also moves afoot to give priority to RCTs as a method. Greene (this volume) and others see connections between support for RCTs and the more general evidence-based practice movement and to trends in public management.

Let me make an observation about a portion of the controversy that has been going on. From my perspective, thoughtful advocates of RCTs, many of whom had themselves articulated the conditions under which experiments do (and do not) make sense, too easily tended to argue for the IES priority without specifying the preconditions for using such methods. Critics of the IES priority too easily critiqued RCTs without the same level of critique of alternative methods, and did not adequately acknowledge the potential benefits and role of randomized experiments. Nor did partisans on either side seem to recognize that saints and sinners can come to the same position for different reasons. Each side seemed to point to the sinner's rationale on the other side, ignoring the statements and possible motives of the less noble allies standing with them. This personal observation may seem extreme to readers who are familiar with the debate only from this volume, which contains statements from a selected set of relatively thoughtful commentators. However, even in the carefully written and relatively civil presentations in this volume, some of the less desirable rhetorical features of the controversy remain.

With this brief historical review as background, I turn now to factors that appear to underlie the divergent perspectives about the credibility (and appropriateness) of RCTs in evaluation and other applied social research.

Disagreement About What the Right Research Question Is

Much of the disagreement about RCTs arises, I believe, because of different assumptions about what the key questions are that evaluation should generally, or at least frequently, undertake. On the one hand, advocates of RCTs and their quasi-experimental approximations presume that it is often, if not usually, valuable to assess the average effects of educational interventions. On the other hand, some of the critics of RCTs strongly prefer that evaluation emphasize a different research question most, if not all, of the time.

Sharon Rallis (Chapter 9) and Jennifer Greene (Chapter 8) most explicitly express the view that evaluation should generally address questions other than the average effectiveness of programs or policies. Rallis, in lauding evaluators who follow what she calls nonconsequentialist ethics, states that "These evaluators attend to the means and context more than to the outcome of a program. They ask, What does the experience mean to the individual?" Rallis, again referring to the nonconsequentialist perspective, continues, "As the evaluators, we want to understand the interactions and the relationships themselves, the interdependencies: how does one person's meaning-making interact with and influence another's?" Moreover, Rallis explicitly acknowledges that her perspective on what is the right research question determines her method preferences: "My evaluation approach is grounded in nonconsequentialist theories. These shape research ethics that turn away from the experimental type of studies that seek to know outcomes and turn toward the qualitative approaches that inform process and meanings." For Rallis, and I believe more generally, underlying assumptions about what the right research question is shape perceptions of what is credible, as well as desirable, evidence.

Greene also explicitly advocates research and evaluation questions other than the question of average program effectiveness. While she acknowledges that the question of the average program effect can be worthwhile, she clearly gives priority to research and evaluation that emphasizes other questions and concerns. She argues "primarily . . . for the importance of understanding the inherent *complexity* of human phenomena in contrast with evidence that both denies and simplifies the wondrous and diverse panorama of the human species." She returns frequently to the theme of human complexity. For example, she indicates that "a research or evaluation practice that envisions and endeavors to understand the full complexity of human action—in all of its contextual diversity—is a practice that legitimizes the multiple perspectives and experiences of all the people being studied. It is a practice that gives voice to these myriad perspectives and experiences." Greene discusses two examples of programs to be evaluated, and for each, provides a number of questions other than the average program effects question. Similar to Rallis, for Greene the prioritization of other questions affects perceived credibility. In Greene's case, priority is given especially to questions related to human complexity, and as a result she sees RCTs as both less desirable and less credible because they are designed to address a different question.

Advocates of RCTs, in contrast, hold in high regard the question of average program effects. They often offer support for this question by noting the kind of use that is facilitated by good answers to the question. Specifically, advocates of RCTs typically hold that a valuable form of use (if not the *most* valuable form) occurs when decision makers draw upon evidence of an intervention's average effects as they make choices about program or policy initiation, expansion, maintenance, or cessation. For example, Bickman and Reich (Chapter 4) make this point when talking about "the cost of making a wrong decision about causality." They state that

> We know that there are costs in making the wrong decision. To call a program effective when it is not means that valuable resources may be wasted and the search for other means to solve the problem will be hindered. Some programs may not only be ineffective but also harmful. In such cases, the costs of a wrong decision would be higher. On the other hand, falsely labeling the program as ineffective would mean that clients who would have benefited from the intervention will not have that benefit.

Ideas about what kind of use is valuable, and therefore what research question is important, again influence method choices and the perception of credibility. In Bickman and Reich's case, the use, program selection, calls for good evidence about program effectiveness, leading them to endorse RCTs (though with explicit awareness of the method's limits).

Similarly, Gersten and Hitchcock (Chapter 5) refer to the need "to dramatically increase the number of rigorous RCTs in education . . . so that professional educators would have an evidence base for making decisions about selecting curricula, intervention programs for students with learning problems, selecting professional development approaches, and determining effective structures for establishing tutoring programs." They also note that school administrators told the IES director that they "wanted clear guidance" for questions such as the selection of mathematics curricula.

Henry (Chapter 3) expands this kind of argument by explicitly locating it in the context of democratic decision making within representative democracies. The choice of better programs and policies, Henry argues, and especially the debunking of bad ideas are key needs within representative democracies. "Public policies and programs," Henry states,

> are intentional acts undertaken with the coercive force of government behind them. Authoritative bodies, such as legislatures, make public policy and program choices in most cases. The choices of these bodies are binding on the governed and therefore, to inform citizens' attitudes about which public programs are good or bad and potentially to influence voting decisions, democracies require that the consequences, both intended and unintended, of programs and policies are determined.

Henry goes on to say that, to achieve findings about program consequences that are "as conclusive as possible . . . [t]he most conclusive and widely regarded . . . means for producing findings that have these attributes are random assignment experiments."

In contrast, and perhaps not surprisingly, opposition to RCTs can arise in part because the same form of use is viewed quite differently, as inappropriate or as of lesser interest than other uses. Greene (Chapter 8) explicitly states this viewpoint, making what she calls a critical point: "questions about the causal effects of social interventions are characteristically those of policy and decision makers, while other stakeholders have other legitimate and important questions (Chelimsky, 2007). This privileging of the interests of the elite in evaluation and research is radically undemocratic." Again, it appears that one's underlying beliefs about the type of use that should occur have an influence on method preferences and, with that, on the perception of what constitutes credible evidence. In Greene's case, she generally has lower regard for evaluation that facilitates policy makers' decisions, relative to other forms of use. Henry, in contrast, presumes that choices, such as the selection of a math curriculum or the decision about whether to fund universal pre-K, will be made in representative democracy and, further, that evaluation does a notable service by providing the best possible evidence about the effects of such programs and policies.

Greene does explicitly acknowledge that the results of RCTs can sometimes be valuable. At the same time, in discussing two examples, she characterizes the question, "Does the program work?" as "one small question."

In contrast, advocates of RCTs view this question as a relatively big one, and see the potential policy-making and other uses of studies that address the question as truly important. For some advocates of RCTs, this position is implicit (and for the least thoughtful advocates of RCTs out there, perhaps not even recognized). For others, exemplified by Henry in this volume, the linkage between desired use and method preference is quite explicit.

Interestingly, both Greene and Henry cite democratic values in supporting their rather different positions. Henry refers to contemporary theory about representative democracy, and to the contribution that occurs when convincing information about program effects is available for democratically elected and appointed officials and voters. Greene, in contrast, emphasizes that stakeholders other than policy makers "have other legitimate and important questions" and that the "privileging of the interests of the elite in evaluation and research is radically undemocratic." The different perspectives on RCTs appear to arise in part from different visions of how evaluation and applied social research should contribute to democracy.

Let me restate the key premise of this section: Underlying assumptions about what the right research question (and the right evaluation use) is, shape perceptions of what constitutes credible, as well as desirable, evidence. Almost every contributor bows at the altar of contextualism, speaking of the multiple questions that evaluation can and should address and of the benefits of multiple methods. And it is a good thing to have general agreement that the selection of methods, and the assessment of credibility, should depend on the particulars of the situation.

Nevertheless, some authors clearly have very different priorities on average regarding research questions, and these priorities then determine judged credibility. Some of the authors are thinking predominantly about one target that research/evaluation might have (e.g., understanding the experience of the program participant), while others are generally assuming another target (e.g., estimating the average effect of the program). Which target the beholder is looking at—that is, which research question the beholder presumes that evaluation should typically (or at least commonly) address—affects what kind of evidence he or she sees as credible.

Here is one major place, then, where the desire to change the terms of the debate comes in. Rather than debating the credibility of RCTs in a general sense, with proponents and opponents drawing upon different rationales and often speaking past each other, perhaps we should focus in part on this key, underlying rationale for the disparate views. Consider the following questions for debate: How valuable is it for evaluation and applied social research to address the question that RCTs emphasize, that is, the question of the effectiveness of a particular "treatment"? How should this question rank, relative to other questions such as ones about clients' experience or giving voice to diverse perspectives and values? Under what conditions should the average effect question be given more priority, and under which conditions less? Who should decide, and how?

The reframed debate might also include a set of related, but somewhat more specific questions. If the RCT-focused research question, regarding the program's average effects, is appropriate, then what other procedures are needed in conjunction or previously (e.g., methods to allow input from various stakeholders about key aspects of the study, such as the selection of outcome measures)? Can evaluators be principled in serving the interests of elected and appointed officials, as in Henry's view of representative democracy, or need they focus on giving voice to the concerns to others, as in Greene's view, which appears to be related to views of direct, participatory democracy? What is the role of the evaluator in pushing for an evaluation purpose (such as representing diversity), relative to the input of (which) stakeholders?

To be explicit, I recognize that reframing the terms of the debate in the manner suggested here is not a magic bullet. In addition, my claim that beliefs about the research question affect perceptions of credibility is subject to criticism. In particular, what causes what? Do beliefs about the importance of a research question lead to method preferences and perceptions of credibility? Or are beliefs about the importance of a research question instead simply post hoc rationalizations for methods preferences which themselves derive from other sources, such as the way the researcher was socialized? Even if claims about the importance of assessing program effects are post hoc rationalizations, they are an important part of the rationale of arguments both for and against RCTs. Moreover, explicitly discussing this rationale seems more likely to lead to enlightenment, relative to further general and generic discussion about RCTs. Indeed, one could even imagine trying to generate credible evidence about the rationale itself. In particular, is the program effects question actually of interest to policy makers but not so interesting to other stakeholders? Or might, say, parents of school children sometimes be intensely interested in whether the educational programs, which supposedly benefit their children, are actually delivering?

Disagreement About the Feasibility of Actionable Answers About Program Effects

Another factor appears to underlie divergent views about the credibility and desirability of RCTs. This factor comes into play when the question of average program effects is taken as being of at least some degree of interest. Specifically, this basis of disagreement involves the judged feasibility that RCTs (perhaps relative to other methods) will provide valid and useful information.

There are (at least) two quite different arguments involving the feasibility of actionable answers from RCTs. The first, emphasized by Michael Scriven (Chapter 7 in this volume), suggests that other methods exist which are equally and sometimes better suited for estimating program effects. The second argument, suggested by Greene and others, instead contends that it is a fool's errand to expect actionable results from an RCT amidst the myriad complexities that exist within most program and policy contexts. Although these two variants draw on very different premises, each of these underlying assumptions would lead someone who held it to be skeptical of the relative value of RCTs and thus to doubt their credibility.

Version 1: RCTs Are Not Generally Better Than Other Cause-Probing Methods. Scriven argues forcefully against giving a general priority to RCTs. Note that I go into Scriven's argument in relative (and perhaps not always reader-friendly) detail here, because it is a potentially quite important and influential position, and deserves serious consideration. Scriven states, for example, "One of the main attractions of the RCT approach is that it appears to provide a greater degree of certainty than alternatives. There are circumstances in which this is true, but it is not true across the board for several reasons." Scriven acknowledges that randomized trials have a limited kind of "theoretical advantage," in terms of their ability to estimate the counterfactual while making selection bias implausible. But he suggests,

> We need to look at half a dozen of the alternative approaches rather carefully, to see whether they are in fact inferior in terms of their ability to substantiate causal claims *and* the respects in which they will sometimes have significant advantages over RCTs (e.g., completion speed, resulting confidence level, cost, burden on subjects, generalizability, ethicality, level of expertise required for implementation, and side effects, if any). It will be shown that the usual claimed intrinsic advantage of the RCT design is only a theoretical advantage, and its actual achievements are easily matched in practice by many other designs; that even such a theoretical advantage is not present in the RCT designs currently being advocated because they are not in fact true RCT designs; and that, nevertheless, there are real advantages for a near-RCT approach in some circumstances, although they can only be determined by weighing its comparative merits on (at least) the eight listed considerations (see Sundry Notes section, later in this chapter) that bear on the merit of a research design. The bottom line here is that the advantage of RCTs is by no means general and must be established in the particular case, a nontrivial task.

One way that Scriven makes his case is by pointing out, quite rightly, that in social and educational evaluations (unlike good drug trials), blindness to conditions is rare (i.e., participants and researchers typically know which condition they are in). As a result, the Hawthorne effect (and other expectancy-based effects) can occur. But presumably one should also consider the plausibility of Hawthorne effects as a *general* criticism of RCTs. One response from advocates of RCTs is to question the frequency or strength of Hawthorne effects. If these effects were so powerful, RCT advocates suggest, then almost surely they would have been used to create powerful interventions (and thus many treatments previously studied would not have been found to be ineffective).

Scriven also supports his arguments that RCTs do not have a general advantage by giving a hypothetical example. The treatment in the example is a new instructional method, studied with nonequivalent groups, pretest-posttest quasi-experimental design, using morning and afternoon college class sections as the nonequivalent groups. The one-semester study is replicated across two semesters, with the morning class assigned to the treatment in the first semester, while the afternoon class receives the treatment for the second semester. The same instructor teaches both sections, observers look for differences other than the intended ones (and do not find them), pretest scores are similar across groups, and in both semesters the treatment group students show about two standard deviations more improvement than the comparison group.

I agree with Scriven that the study, as described, is reasonably compelling in terms of demonstrating the effectiveness of the new instructional procedure. Certainly, I would want my daughter to be taught with the new instructional protocol rather than the old one (assuming no major negative side effects). More generally, Scriven is certainly correct that, at least under certain conditions, RCTs are not required for causal inference. As Scriven points out, children's learning about the world demonstrates that actionable causal inferences can be drawn without randomized trials. The question, however, is what if any implications this observation should have for the debate about RCTs. Do critics of the IES priority win the debate if they can point to a hypothetical or actual case in which some other method gives a compelling causal conclusion? I think not, and to demonstrate why helps clarify what I think would constitute improved terms of the debate. I believe Scriven's argument falls short in at least three interrelated ways, when viewed in relation to the IES priority for randomized experiments.

First, Scriven's treatment of RCTs and their alternatives is asymmetrical. That is, he allows assumptions in benefit of the alternative procedures that he does not allow for RCTs. In particular, he discounts the desirability of

RCTs and educational and social evaluation because, absent blinding to conditions, Hawthorne effects and the like are possible. But this same shortcoming does not lead him to discount the hypothetical study using the pretest-posttest nonequivalent design, which would seem to be equally susceptible to expectancy effects. He also builds into the hypothetical study design features such as the use of independent observers who assess implementation of the intervention and do not find other differences. However, a more symmetrical comparison would build the same design ancillaries, such as quality implementation assessment, into both RCTs and the alternatives with which they are being compared. Scriven also builds into the example a set of characteristics that contribute greatly to the strength of causal inference that the quasi-experimental design allows in this case: pretest equivalence, multiple replications, no apparent confounds in implementation, a huge treatment effect, and no other apparent validity threats. What are the odds that all of these will occur in practice? Wouldn't a fair comparison across method types endow RCTs with equally ideal circumstances (or at least circumstances that are equally likely to arise in practice)?

Moreover, the critic could suggest potential threats to the quasi-experimental design Scriven presents. These would include the possibility of an experimenter or instructor expectancy effect that the observers did not see, or initial differences that were not identified by the pretest because of its low reliability with students who are new to the course content, or selection effects that arise because of relevant factors other than those captured by the pretest (i.e., factors other than initial course-related content knowledge). For example, selection bias might arise because of the differential scheduling, across semesters, of another course that must be taken by some but not all of the students in this class, specifically those in a harder major. In practice, one would of course try to assess the plausibility of each threat (e.g., by looking for equivalence not only on pretest scores, but also on other factors such as student's major), and then consider any plausible threat's ability to account for the observed treatment effect. But in Scriven's argument, he uses the theoretical possibility of Hawthorne effects as a criticism of RCTs, but does not (I believe) comparably apply the theoretical possibility of selection biases due to factors other than pretest scores in his example. In short, for these reasons, I believe that Scriven's comparison between RCTs and their alternatives is asymmetrical. The argument is designed to show that alternatives *can* at least at times be equal or better, not that they *generally* are.

Second, then, the demonstration of at-least-occasional superiority of alternatives to RCTs is of questionable relevance to the controversies about RCTs, particularly for the IES priority. In this regard, the relevant considerations are somewhat different for the IES-type issue of *funding proposed research and evaluation,* compared to the WWC-type issue of *screening studies after the fact.* For IES-type funding decisions, the question must be about the *a priori* expectation of valid findings for the different kinds of designs under consideration, in the sort of contexts covered by the funding program. For instance, before Scriven's hypothetical study was conducted, it would not be possible to know with confidence that the treatment and comparison groups would be equivalent at the pretest, or that the treatment effect would be huge (relative to any likely selection effects or other validity threats). For funding decisions, it may be possible to know some general, likely characteristics of the research context (more on this momentarily), but one will not know the details of important things like pretest equivalence in the absence of random assignment. Instead, for funding decisions, the relevant task is to assess the *expected* validity of inferences in light of certain assumptions about the causal context in which the study will occur. One makes one's bets on expectations. Thus, Scriven's argument, at least the portion I have reviewed to this point, seems more applicable to the kind of after-the-fact screening done by the WWC, where in a particular review a nonrandom quasi-experiment could be rated more favorably than a (flawed) RCT. As Gersten and Hitchcock (Chapter 5) describe, the WWC rating procedure can downgrade an RCT—for example, if there are unaddressed attrition problems. (One wonders, however, whether the review protocol that has been used by the WWC captures well all the relevant factors for making such judgments in the context of individual studies.)

Third, and most importantly, Scriven's presuppositions about the causal field differ from those that I believe are assumed by thoughtful supporters of RCTs in educational and social evaluation (and that I personally take to be the case for most social and educational evaluation). As already noted, Scriven presumes relatively large effects of the treatment in his hypothetical example. Moreover, in his discussion of everyday causal inference and direct observation of causation, his examples typically involve a relatively stable causal field. For example, the child's shaking of a rattle leads to a noise, but the rattle does not become noisier over time as it matures with age. Moreover, there are not countless forces in the world other than its being shaken that might lead the rattle to make noise.

In contrast, advocates of RCTs appear to presume a very different kind of causal background. They assume, for example, that children commonly will do better over time, and so the study of the effects of educational interventions requires comparison groups. They further assume that individual differences exist, and that these often are related to the amount of improvement over time, and still further that nonrandom groupings into conditions will often be confounded with individual differences. Put somewhat differently, selection bias will often occur. The belief that selection biases are common drives the preference for random assignment in general. Advocates of RCTs also generally assume that a wide variety of forces (captured in a generic sense in the list of threats to internal validity popularized by Campbell and his colleagues [Campbell & Stanley, 1963; Shadish, Campbell, & Cook, 2002]) exist that can cause changes in the outcome variable of interest. In addition, most advocates of RCTs presume that it is worthwhile to identify much smaller effects than those assumed by Scriven in his hypothetical example. This presumption is important, for it reduces considerably the likelihood that other designs will allow confident judgment about whether or not a treatment effect occurred.

Scriven addresses the idea of the expected or worthwhile effect size, while presenting his hypothetical quasi-experiment. Scriven says, "Clearly the size of the difference [between the treatment and comparison group] is crucial here, as is often the case." He asks the reader to reflect "on the fact that you are not very interested in small differences because they have a track record of never showing up on the replications at distant sites." He also indicates that the pretest-posttest, nonequivalent groups design should be preferred "knowing that it's a net that will catch only big fish, but you don't want little fish." In contrast, I believe that many educational evaluators, looking at the track record of educational interventions (like other evaluators informed by meta-analyses in various program domains), presume that the typical fish is not a huge one. Moreover, many of these evaluators implicitly or explicitly assume that moderate effects, and perhaps even small ones, can make worthwhile contributions.

All this leads, I believe, to very different ideas about what the debate should be about. It should not be about the superiority of RCTs for every single possible circumstance, nor about the possibility of identifying particular cases in which other designs lead to at least equally confident causal inferences. Instead, the debate, at least for the IES-type issue of relative preference for funding RCTs versus other kinds of studies, should be about the expected quality of causal inference, for the specific kinds of circumstances expected in the kind of study being funded. In the case of educational interventions, one version of the debate question would be as follows: What is the a priori preferability of RCTs, relative to alternatives, when the research question involves estimating the effects of a given treatment (such as an educational intervention), when small-to-moderate effects are of interest, and when the causal field is such that the key outcome variables are likely to be affected by a range of other forces, such as maturation, history, and selection?

Admittedly, the preceding question frames the debate in terms of the view of the causal field presumed by advocates of RCTs and their closest quasi-experimentalist approximations. Thus, an alternative, perhaps prior question for debate is, To what extent is the preceding framing of the debate the proper one? For example, is Scriven correct that the relevant method choices need only to presume "big fish," that is, very large effect sizes, or is it important to choose methods that have the potential for identifying moderate or small effects? Again, credible evidence might be infused into the debate. What does the history of educational evaluation tell us about how big the fish usually are? In addition, more detailed arguments—rather than explicit claims or implicit assumptions—can be made about the relative value of small or moderate effects. Ideally, these would be made from the perspective of different stakeholder groups.

To be fair, there are reasons that Scriven tried to demonstrate that RCTs did not have a general advantage, and that alternatives can give equally compelling causal inference at times. His focus appears to be a response to the unfortunate language that has been used in promulgating the IES priority and the WWC review process. At times, that language has seemed to equate "scientific research" with randomized trials. Thus, critics of the IES priority and the WWC sometimes appear to think the debate is won simply by demonstrating that scientific procedures do not always involve random assignment (hence, for example, Scriven's reference to plate tectonics). Outcroppings of this unfortunate rhetorical stance are seen in the Gersten and Hitchcock chapter in the current volume. It would have been preferable, from my perspective, if advocates of RCTs themselves critiqued language that appears to equate science with random assignment studies. In addition, it would have been beneficial for the debate if critics of the IES priority had recognized that, in demonstrating the inaccuracy of such statements, while one can be value expressive and gain debating style points among those who share one's view, arguments that scientific method includes more than RCTs do not persuade those on the other side. Moreover, such arguments do not address what I suggest should be the more central question for debate (the issue of design strength for estimating small or moderate program effects amidst many factors in a complex causal field).

Scriven's emphasis on demonstrating that alternative designs can provide as confident a causal inference as RCTs may have also stemmed in part from a second source. That is, the IES priority gives extra points to grant proposals for *all* the proposals that include random assignment to conditions. The applicant does not have to demonstrate that RCTs are preferable in the particular case, or that alternatives would not be equally or more effective. In other words, the priority appears to assume the preferability of RCTs across the board. Thus, one might ask, wouldn't the logic of the priority be undercut if one demonstrates that RCTs do not have superiority across the board?

Again, my view is that the more appropriate question has to do with the expected strength of inferences that will arise, in the expected causal context, if the question of a program's effect is of interest. In the particular case of the IES priority, one could ask, Do the circumstances that most call for an RCT actually hold in the kind of places where Department of Education–funded research takes place, or is it more like the circumstances Scriven posits?

A Brief Aside: Arguments for Diverse Methods. Two chapters in the volume appear to have been predicated largely on the assumption that the debate about credible evidence is furthered by demonstrating the merit of methods that differ substantially from those of the RCT. Rallis (Chapter 9) argues for the value and credibility of qualitative data consisting of verbal reports from program participants. Her closing words demonstrate that she presented her argument in order to demonstrate that such verbal reports fall within the scope of scientific research: "The reported voices are the product of rigorous reasoning, and they embody probity. This credible form of evidence offers insights that can help us improve policy and programming and better serve the people involved. I argue that this is the real basis of scientific inquiry." Mathison (Chapter 10) argues for the value and credibility of images as data and as a representation of knowledge. She contends that "Images, in fact, are no more suspect than other sorts of data, such as numbers or text." These arguments are relevant to the debate, *if* the debate consists of a dispute about the global scientific standing of RCTs versus all other forms of inquiry (as it largely has to date). Moving into the future, I hope that we will have more nuanced terms of debate.

Version 2: RCTs and Related Cause-Probing Methods Lack Value, in Light of the Context, Contingencies, and Particularities Involved. As noted above, Scriven (Chapter 7) argues against giving a general priority to RCTs, because he holds that other methods can have comparable validity. His discussion of direct perception of cause and of large effects reveals his assumption that many program effects of interest will be reasonably easy to detect. Another argument reaches a similar conclusion—that RCTs will not provide more valid and useful information about program effects than will alternative methods—but is based on very different premises from Scriven's. The second argument, advanced most forcefully by Greene (Chapter 8) but alluded to by others, suggests that program effects are so situationally specific that the RCT, with its focus on average effect size, will not provide actionable information.

Citing Berliner (2002), Greene points to the power of contexts, and to the numerous interactions that may exist in educational settings. For example, in the classroom, teacher behavior may depend upon student characteristics, student learning may depend upon teacher behavior, all of these may be conditional upon background characteristics of the community or the curriculum, etc., etc. Moreover, the relevant processes may be different at one point in history from another. Greene emphasizes both differences across context and diversity within a given context. Again citing Berliner, she notes that "it is because of the need to understand the particularities of each local context that 'qualitative inquiry has become so important in educational research' (p. 19)." While Greene does not explicitly critique RCTs in terms of the presumed potency of context and interactions, her advocacy of qualitative methods and her raising of multiple other research questions constitute an implicit critique on this basis. As I see it, the context/interaction/complexity argument against RCTs is that they are not up to the challenge of providing actionable evidence about programs, because they are likely to miss the real action, the particularity, and the many interactions with context.

In a relatively detailed and thoughtful discussion of the limits of RCTs, Bickman and Reich (Chapter 4) point out that "the most often-cited criticism of this design is its reduced external validity," that is, the possibility that one may not be able to generalize from the perhaps artificial circumstances that allow random assignment to other circumstances about which decisions are to be made. Bickman and Reich quote Berk (2005): "'[I]t cannot be overemphasized that unless an experiment can be generalized at least a bit, time and resources have been wasted. One does not really care about the results of a study unless its conclusions can be used to guide future decisions' . . . (p. 428)." Bickman and Reich do not emphasize the power of context and the prevalence of interactions to the same extent as Greene. And, unlike Greene, they conclude that, for estimating program effects, "the randomized design is the worst form of design except all the others that have been tried." Still, even as (relative) advocates of RCTs, they recognize that results from these studies may not generalize.

This suggests a profitable question for future debate: To what extent do the findings of RCTs suffice to guide understandings and actions across varied settings? In part, this question is one about the robustness of study conclusions across different contexts, and across different settings, persons, and times. However, following the lead of Bickman and Reich, the question should be construed as a comparative one, that is, a question of the capacity for RCTs to guide understandings and actions, relative to the capacity provided by alternative methods. Do RCTs provide better or worse evidence than a set of smaller qualitative studies, each examining particularities, as would appear to be Greene's preference. As Bickman and Reich note, increased discussion about the consequences of context/interactions/generalizability for different kinds of evaluation designs would reignite a classic debate between

Campbell and Cronbach (see, e.g., Cronbach, 1982). However, it can include questions not present at the time of that classic debate. For example, are RCTs with theory-driven tests of moderation, value-driven tests of moderation (e.g., testing whether the program is as effective for the least well off as for others), and tests of mediation as good at dealing with contextual effects as alternative approaches?

A new debate of this kind will not be simple. One might guess, for example, that the effects of certain (kinds of) educational interventions will be relatively robust across contexts, while the effects of other interventions will be fairly context specific. Credible research evidence on the size of interactions, relative to overall (main) effects of programs, will be of great interest, even if difficult to obtain in a convincing fashion (because the most important interactions might not have been tested). Concerns will be raised about the relative merits of implementation that is faithful to a prescribed protocol versus implementation that emphasizes adaptation to the local context. The debate may soon highlight that, despite the volume of words spoken and printed on the importance of context, we are (at least in most areas with which I am familiar) lacking good theories of context. That is, there is a paucity of good theory about which of the nearly infinite contextual variables will be relevant in a particular circumstance, how, and why. Having such theory would be quite valuable, because one of the time-honored ways of assessing the robustness of a program effect is by testing it across settings that vary. Without knowing which contextual variables are likely to matter, and when, this approach to assessing generalizability is more limited than one would like. The debate about interactions and the complexity of context may well be complicated in these and other ways, but perhaps this is fitting. And, I would argue, the possibility of moving forward is greater than would occur with continued, general debate about relative credibility of various designs.

When Greene (Chapter 8) writes about the methodological implications of the presumed power of context, she also touches upon the debate about proper use of evaluation, discussed above. Greene cites with approval the position of qualitative scholars (Erickson & Gutierrez, 2002) who argue that it is essential to study causal mechanisms "'within the local situation of complexity and contingency' (p. 23)." She also cites Helen Simons (2004) as "arguing in particular for the vital importance of narratives of lived experience for inquiry intending to enhance professional practice." Implicit in this statement is the idea that evaluation and applied social research can provide answers that fit well within particular, local contexts of professional practice. In contrast, Henry (Chapter 3) focuses on the idea that governments commonly take actions that apply across a wider scope of persons, settings, and times. A math curriculum is selected for an entire school district, not for the specific interactions that may influence a given child in a specific classroom with a particular teacher. Classroom size laws may be implemented at the state level, again cutting across a wide range of contexts. Once again, changes to the terms of the debate seem useful. Imagine debates about the proper uses of evaluation, about whether and when use can be more contextual versus when it must be nonindividuating, and about the corresponding preference for some methods over others. This might be a far more fruitful debate in the future than continued general debate about the credibility of RCTs versus other methods.

The Debate About Credible Evidence and the Logic of Method Choice

As noted previously, the contributions to this volume address two different, albeit interrelated debates. This chapter has given considerable attention to one of them, the more specific debate about the relative credibility and appropriateness of RCTs, especially in contemporary educational evaluation and applied research. The second, more general debate, involves the more general nature of credibility (and other criteria for judging research) and the logic of method choice in light of judged credibility and other considerations. This second debate receives less attention in the present chapter than it deserves, except in one important sense. Many of the preceding suggestions about changing the terms of the debate about RCTs represent an effort to shift from a particular, historically located controversy about RCTs, and instead to elevate the discussion into questions that better fit with a more general debate about credibility and method choice.

Of the chapters in this volume, Schwandt's (Chapter 11) is most explicit in striving to rise above the particular debate about RCTs and to move us toward a more general theory of evidence. In addition, Julnes and Rog (Chapter 6), while shifting at times from the more specific to the more general debate, give a relatively substantial amount of attention to the general debate. In addition, several other authors, notably Scriven (Chapter 7) and Henry (Chapter 3), contribute in notable ways to the general discussion about evidence, even while giving most of their attention to the more specific debate about RCTs.

Schwandt contends that "the present iteration of the debate is misguided because, once again, it centers on questions of the method while ignoring more primary matters concerning what constitutes evidence and its responsible use." He examines "the character of evidence, the ethics of evidence, the contexts of the application of evidence, and the nature of rationality and argumentation." With regard to the character of evidence, Schwandt points out that credibility is but one criterion (a point briefly made in several of the chapters). Schwandt suggests that three properties of evidence should be assessed: "*Relevance*—Does the information bear directly on the hypothesis or claim in question? *Credibility*—Can we believe the information? *Probative (inferential) force*—How strongly does the information point toward the claim or hypothesis being considered?"

Several of the suggestions in the preceding section, about reframing the terms of the debate, could be interpreted in terms of these three characteristics. However, many of my previous suggestions have to do with the specification of what the "hypothesis or claim in question" *should be*. This issue, of whether the question of program effects should be given priority or avoided (or something in between) relates to Schwandt's third property, the context of the application of evidence. Schwandt indicates that "This third requirement of a theory of evidence for evaluation invites us to consider types of evidence and how they are brought to bear in making decisions about the value of an evaluand." Shifting from the more general debate about evidence to the more specific debate about RCTs, Schwandt indicates that, "In evaluation, *useful* knowledge is that which bears on the question of the *value* of a given evaluand: (a) Value is not solely determined by causal efficacy; and (b) useful knowledge takes both numerical and non-numerical forms." While I find it hard to disagree with this statement in general, if we shift to the more specific debate about RCTs, then supporters of this method could make a counterargument. In many contexts, they might argue, the most important and contentious question relevant to the relative valuing of a set of alternative evaluands is the question of their causal effects. For instance, in judging the precalculus math curricula developed by most textbook publishers, I expect many stakeholders would agree that relative effectiveness of the curricula in helping students to learn the relevant math concepts and skills is by far the most important concern for assessing relative value.

Julnes and Rog (Chapter 6), while commenting in several interesting ways on the specific debate about RCTs, largely emphasize the more general debate about the nature of credibility. They especially address the linking of method choice to general considerations. For example, they discuss a set of contextual factors, which they see as determining the nature of the evidence that is required in order to support an actionable causal conclusion. These include the nature of the phenomenon studied, such as whether the relevant causal question is complex in terms of its underlying mechanism or system-context dynamics, the degree of existing knowledge about the causal relationship in question, and the degree of confidence that is needed for the causal inference in question. Future attempts to integrate Schwandt's and Julnes and Rog's analyses could be quite interesting.

Scriven and Henry, in different ways, raise a very important consideration for a more general theory of credibility and value of evaluation and applied research. Scriven (Chapter 7) thoughtfully and explicitly raises the question of funding priorities, not for individual studies, but rather for broader portfolios of studies. He suggests that, even if RCTs are preferable in general, one would likely be better off not putting all investment eggs in the basket of RCTs. This is a relatively compelling point, especially in light of the kind of external validity and other validity limits noted by Bickman and Reich. For example, RCTs might give the most internally valid, unbiased estimates of the effects of a program; nevertheless, because of the limited circumstances in which random assignment is feasible, RCTs might result in serious reservations about external validity. If true, funding a second RCT with the same external validity limits might purchase less of an increment in confidence, relative to funding a strong quasi-experiment. Although the latter would allow less study-specific confidence about the program's effects, it could better facilitate generalization to policy-relevant settings. Recognition that the considerations that guide method choices for one study might be quite different from the considerations that guide method choices for a second, third, or subsequent study is quite consistent with the literature on critical multiplism (e.g., Cook, 1985), but this point has not been adequately recognized in contemporary debates about method preferences and credibility, such as the debate about RCTs in education.

Henry (Chapter 3) reminds us that any single funding stream is part of a broader portfolio. He states that

> we need to begin to consider whether there is a point at which a careful, rigorous assessment of the consequences of public policies and programs must be undertaken. It is possible for administrators who also control evaluation funds to focus evaluations on questions of program coverage, studies of variation in implementation, single case studies of a program or organization, descriptive studies of program participants, or subjective assessments of satisfaction. At a given time and in a specific situation, any of these could be the best choice for evaluation funding. But continually and indefinitely postponing addressing the public program effectiveness question cannot be in the interest of society. . . .
>
> It may be that alternative institutions are needed to provide funding priorities for evaluations to assess program effectiveness. It may be that the role of agencies such as IES, the National Institute of Justice, and the National Institutes of Health is in part to rebalance existing institutional priorities. While evaluations sponsored and conducted by the agencies administering the programs are likely to be biased toward questions that do not include an assessment of the program's consequences, these quasi-independent institutes can help to ensure that methodologically sound evaluations of the consequences of public policies and programs receive a portion of the funding for evaluation.

Expanding on this point, we can raise a question, for the more specific debate, about what the conceptual boundary is of the "portfolio." Is it the particular funding program that uses the IES priority for random assignment? Or is it the broader array of Department of Education funding programs, some of which rarely if ever fund RCTs? Or is it the still broader set of educational research and evaluation, with numerous funding sources?

Selected Suggestions for Practice

For the most part in this chapter, I have suggested ways that comparative analysis of the divergent views in this volume (and elsewhere) can lead to improved terms for future debate. This, I hope, is not a purely scholarly or theoretical exercise. More fruitful future debate should lead to better guidance for future practice. But what about the applied research and evaluation practice that needs to be done before the more specific future debate that I hope will further advance our thinking and practice? Let me offer a few suggestions, drawing on (and reiterating) several major themes of this chapter.

First, when planning an upcoming evaluation or other applied study, you should *ask whether the study's focus should be on a causal question*. More specifically, consider whether a key research question is, What are the effects of some identifiable treatment? An example would be, "Stakeholders want to know whether the new pre-algebra math curriculum actually leads to improved student performance and interest in math." *If* the upcoming research ought to estimate the effect of a specific intervention (e.g., the new math curriculum) on already identified outcomes (e.g., math performance and interest), then experiments, quasi-experiments, and other cause-probing techniques are relevant. In contrast, if the key question instead is, "What is the lived experience of program participants?" then experiments and their approximations are not even relevant—and their irrelevance would undercut their credibility.

Second, think about how you come to the answer of the first question. That is, *what is the basis for deciding whether the causal question is relevant or irrelevant?* One possible factor was reviewed in detail in this chapter: Might information about a program's average effects usefully inform decisions about the adoption, expansion, revision, or cessation of the program? Or would this kind of use be inappropriate, or at least less valuable than other forms of use that could be enhanced by other methods? As we have seen through contributors to this volume, some researchers and evaluators emphasize representative democracy (and, typically, providing information for elected and appointed officials), while others prefer to give voice to the least powerful (perhaps by studying lived experience). Sometimes, of course, the individual researcher comes to the scene after the answers to these two questions have been provided (e.g., by the funding agency). In other cases, the researcher or evaluator has some latitude to set or at least influence the answers.

Preference for different forms of use is only one of several factors that drive the decision about whether treatment effects are of interest, and the more general question of credibility. Researchers' preferences are likely to be driven in part by epistemological stances and training traditions, as noted in Chapter 2. Stakeholders, too, have existing perspectives that may influence credibility. For example, it has been argued that qualitative methods may be better received by key stakeholder groups when arts programs or storytelling programs are evaluated. As the old saying goes, "credibility is in the eye of the beholder." But the practitioner should consider what initial assumptions of credibility an audience will have, in contrast to the judgments of credibility the audience might have after the researcher or evaluator has undertaken an educative function with the stakeholders. Limits exist on one's powers of persuasion, of course, but stakeholders' initial judgments of credibility sometimes will change (e.g., with information about validity threats).

A final consideration on this general point is, can you provide a reasoned justification for the choice of one research question (or set of questions) over others? To take one example, many evaluation reports describe the key evaluation questions, but offer no explanation about where they came from. Sometimes it seems like the evaluator's preferences may be the driving force. In other cases, reference is made to consultation with stakeholders, but without details of how stakeholders were chosen for consultation, how they were consulted, what they said, and how that translated into the key evaluation questions and other choices. In short, be concerned about the credibility of judgments about what the key research questions are.

Third, *given that one research question (or more) is at issue, what methods are needed to provide an answer with the needed level of confidence?* Strategies for addressing this question are the stuff of methods texts and research methods courses (although traditional methods training often leaves out the question of what level of confidence is needed in a particular case). *If the question of program effect is at issue in a study, then you should consider whether the particular context for causal inference is more akin to that implied by Scriven, or to that suggested by Bickman and Reich, or to that alluded to by Greene. What is the relative ease, challenge, or feasibility of obtaining useful conclusions about average program effects? Are only "big fish" of interest? In addition, Julnes and Rog offer a set of factors to consider.

Fourth, *think about the next study in context of a portfolio of studies, if more than one study has been or will be done.* Much of the past debate implies that one size fits all, and that the fifth study should aspire to the same "gold standard" as the first four. This is undesirable. For example, the fifth highly credible study about a program's average treatment effect may provide less value-added, relative to the first study that examines another important question. As another example, a fifth study that is less credible in terms of internal validity could add great value by extending external validity by examining clients and settings not included in the previous four studies.

Fifth, *think more generally about external validity as an aspect of credibility.* Bickman and Reich suggest a comparative perspective on this issue. That is, one should not critique a single method in terms of external validity; rather, the emphasis should be on comparing the ability of various methods, including RCTs, to deal with challenges of generalizing to different subgroups and contexts. Often in practice, this will call for consideration of the kinds of persons and settings potential users of the study most need to know about. This reminds us that credibility is not a uniform characteristic. It does not apply equally to all observers and all potential uses. For example, a study might be highly credible for one context and less credible for others. In thinking about ways to increase external validity, and thus increase credibility of application across contexts, theory-based tests of moderation and mediation may be as valuable as is the sampling of different contexts and subgroups.

Sixth, *keep in mind that credibility is not all that matters.* For example, Schwandt identifies credibility as one property of evidence, the others being relevance and probative (inferential) force. In addition, studies take place in real-world settings where resources are limited, certain time lines may have to be met or the findings won't be available until after the decision at hand has been made, participants may act in ways that degrade the theoretical quality of a study design, and so on. In short, reality commonly calls for trade-offs. The thoughtful researcher keeps in mind the costs of various trade-offs, and attempts to make the choices that maintain credibility in light of the specific constraints faced. The best researcher will be able to explain why a choice was made in the face of a given trade-off. This is quite useful when others critique a study or conduct a meta-evaluation.

Conclusion: So What Counts as Credible Evidence?

Extensive and continued discussion of the relative merits and credibility of RCTs versus other methods would have limited capacity to move forward our understanding and our practice. It could duplicate the earlier quantitative–qualitative debate, consuming large amounts of human capital, with less payoff than cost. However, by changing the terms of the debate, we may be able to improve understandings of deeply entrenched disagreements; move toward a common ground where such can be found; better understand the disagreements that remain; allow, at least in select places, credible evidence as part of the conversation; and enhance the capacity of stakeholders to make sensible decisions rather than be bewildered by our disagreement or draw allegiances based on superficial considerations. May the discussion, with revised terms of the debate, continue.

References

Berk, R. A. (2005). Randomized experiments as the bronze standard. *Journal of Experimental Criminology, 1,* 417–433.

Berliner, D. C. (2002). Educational research: The hardest science of them all. *Educational Researcher, 31,* 18–20.

Campbell, D. T., & Stanley, J. C. (1963). *Experimental and quasi-experimental designs for research.* Boston: Houghton Mifflin.

Chelimsky, E. (2007). Factors influencing the choice of methods in federal evaluation practice. In G. Julnes & D. Rog (Eds.), *Informing federal policies on evaluation methodology* (pp. 13–33). (Vol. 113 of *New Directions for Evaluation* series). San Francisco: Jossey-Bass.

Cook, T. D. (1985). Post-positivist critical multiplism. In R. L. Shotland & M. M. Mark (Eds.), *Social science and social policy* (pp. 21–62). Beverly Hills, CA: Sage Publications.

Cook, T. D. (2003). Why have educational evaluators chosen not to do randomized experiments? *Annals of American Academy of Political and Social Science, 589,* 114–149.

Cronbach, L. J. (1982). *Designing evaluations of educational and social programs.* San Francisco: Jossey-Bass.

Erickson, F., & Gutierrez, K. (2002). Culture, rigor, and science in educational research. *Educational Researcher, 31*(8), 21–24.

Mark, M. M., & Henry, G. T. (2004). The mechanisms and outcomes of evaluation influence. *Evaluation, 10,* 35–57.

Shadish, W. R., Campbell, D. T., & Cook, T. D. (2002). *Experimental and quasi-experimental designs for generalized causal inference.* Boston: Houghton Mifflin.

Simons, H. (2004). Utilizing evidence to enhance professional practice. *Evaluation, 10,* 410–429.

Epilogue

A Practitioner's Guide for Gathering Credible Evidence in the Evidence-Based Global Society

Stewart I. Donaldson

What do the discussions and debates about credible evidence offer practitioners? I will attempt to answer this question for you by briefly providing some observations about the diversity and changing nature of the enterprise, by offering some lessons from my own applied research and evaluation practice, and by discussing how practitioners might address some of the key issues and challenges of collecting credible evidence raised throughout the chapters in this volume.

Understanding Practice Today

In Chapter 1, I discussed indicators that suggest the demand for credible evidence is at an all-time high across the globe, and that applied research and evaluation practice is booming. The recent surge of activity has expanded well beyond the evaluation of traditional, large-scale, government programs. Evaluation and applied research are being conducted on a much wider range of problems, programs, policies, practices, products, personnel, organizations, proposals, and the like across a diverse range of community, organizational, government, and global settings. Practitioners today are confronted with a shifting landscape of applied research and evaluation practice.

I have suggested that this changing landscape has set the stage for a similar but broader perspective on evidence than D. T. Campbell's (1991) earlier vision of an "experimenting society." This new vision of an "evidence-based global society" promotes the search for and thoughtful reflection about evidence collected from a wide range of designs and methods to answer key applied research and evaluation questions. While the gold standard in the evidence-based society might be thought of as "methodological appropriateness" (Mark, Chapter 12; Schwandt, Chapter 11), it is important to underscore that RCTs will play a very important role and will be considered the gold standard for answering some questions under specific circumstances, as will other research and evaluation approaches, designs, and methods when the conditions are optimal for their use.

It is most likely a healthy sign for the intellectual development of the field if the debates rage on about credible evidence, gold standards, and optimal research and evaluation paradigms and designs. Our hope should be that these discussions in the scholarly literature, perhaps reframed as Mark suggests (Chapter 12), will inspire research and inquiries that someday provide practitioners with more evidence-based guidance about how best to practice applied research and evaluation. But in the meantime, there is critically important work to be done and this natural uncertainty in a young field should not slow us down in our pursuit to help solve the important problems of the day. As we practice applied research and evaluation, let me suggest that we as practitioners draw on the body of knowledge about practice we have now accumulated. Below, I briefly review the value of our knowledge base with respect to evaluation theory, design and methods, the profession, and research on evaluation.

Evaluation Theory

Practitioners working in the new "evidence-based global society" can benefit greatly from understanding how to use theory to enhance their practice. Donaldson and Lipsey (2006) have spelled out in some detail the different roles that different types of theory can play to improve contemporary applied research and evaluation practice. One of these theory forms is evaluation theory, which is largely prescriptive theory that "offers a set of rules, prescriptions, prohibitions, and guiding frameworks that specify what a good or proper evaluation is and how evaluation should be done" (Alkin, 2004). Evaluation theories are thus theories of evaluation practice that address such enduring themes as how to understand the nature of what we evaluate, how to assign value to programs and their performance, how to construct knowledge, and how to use the knowledge generated by evaluation (e.g., Alkin, 2004; Donaldson & Scriven, 2003; Shadish, Cook, & Leviton, 1991).

In 1997, the president of the American Evaluation Association, William Shadish, emphasized the vast importance of teaching practitioners how to benefit from and use evaluation theory to improve practice. His presidential address was entitled "Evaluation Theory Is Who We Are," and emphasized the following:

> All evaluators should know evaluation theory because it is central to our professional identity. It is what we talk about more than anything else, it seems to give rise to our most trenchant debates, it gives us the language we use for talking to ourselves and others, and perhaps most important, it is what makes us different from other professions. Especially in the latter regards, it is in our own self-interest to be explicit about this message, and to make evaluation theory the very core of our identity. Every profession needs a unique knowledge base. For us, evaluation theory is that knowledge base. (Shadish, 1998, p. 1)

Evaluation theories can also help us understand our quest as practitioners to gather credible evidence. They often take a stand on what counts as credible evidence in practice. However, evaluation theories today are rather diverse and some are at odds with one another (see Donaldson & Scriven, 2003). Understanding these differences between theories of practice can help us understand disagreements about what counts as credible evidence.

In professional practice, it is vitally important that we are clear about our assumptions and purposes for conducting applied research and evaluation. Evaluation theory can help us make those decisions, and help us understand why other applied researchers and evaluators might make different decisions in practice, or criticize the decisions we have made about gathering credible evidence. In summary, being well-versed in contemporary theories of evaluation practice can enhance our ability to make sound choices about gathering evidence to answer the key applied research and evaluation questions we are being paid to address.

Design and Methods

The decisions made in practice about research and evaluation design and methods can often be traced back to evaluation theory, or at least a practitioner's assumptions and views about what constitutes good evaluation practice. Christie and Fleischer (Chapter 2) discussed how assumptions about social inquiry and scientific paradigms seem to color views about which designs and methods provide the most credible evidence. What should be clear from the chapters in this volume is that contemporary practitioners now have a wide range of designs and methods to choose from when they are charged to gather credible evidence. The discussions throughout the previous chapters take us to a new level of understanding about the strengths and limitations of these various designs and methods. I will discuss in more detail later the ways that a practitioner can use this knowledge to make decisions about which designs and methods to employ in practice.

The Profession

The profession of applied research and evaluation is maturing. As was discussed in Chapter 1, more practitioners than ever before are participating in annual professional meetings, going to professional development activities, and collaborating with one another in an effort to learn about best practices. The number of professional associations has grown dramatically throughout the world in the past 15 years, and the size of the more established associations has increased substantially. These organizations now offer us as practitioners a wide range of resources for improving our practice such as the latest books and journals, regular convenings, a range of professional development opportunities, guiding principles, and evaluation standards. Donaldson and Christie (2006) describe the emerging transdiscipline and profession in some detail, and provide examples of the broad array of career opportunities that now exist in applied research and evaluation. The resources now available from the profession can greatly enhance a practitioner's ability to gather credible evidence and to provide accurate and useful applied research and evaluations.

Research on Evaluation

Theories of evaluation practice tend to be based more on philosophy and experience than on systematic evidence of their effectiveness. That is, unlike social science theories used to help program and policy design, evaluation theories remain largely prescriptive and unverified. There has been a recent surge of interest in developing an evidence base to complement theory for guiding how best to practice applied research and evaluation (Donaldson, 2007; Henry & Mark, 2003; Mark, 2003, 2007).

Although research on evaluation is an emerging area and a limited source of help for practitioners at the present time, there are now important works we can point to as exemplars for how research can improve the way we practice in the future. For example, there is a long tradition of research illuminating how to conduct evaluations so they are useful and have influence (Cousins, 2007). Other recent studies examine the links between evaluation theory and practice (Alkin & Christie, 2005; Christie, 2003; Fitzpatrick, 2004), the development of evaluation practice competencies (Ghere, King, Stevahn, & Minnema, 2006), strategies for managing evaluation anxiety (Donaldson, Gooler, & Scriven, 2002), improving the relationships between evaluators and stakeholders (Donaldson, 2001; B. Campbell & Mark, 2006), and the like. Along these same lines, Schwandt (Chapter 11, this volume) proposes an agenda of inquiry that might lead to the development of a practical theory of how to gather credible evidence in applied research and evaluation. Furthermore, the American Evaluation Association has recently supported the development of a new Topic Interest Group charged with expanding the evidence base for practice by promoting much more research on evaluation. All of these examples underscore the point that research on evaluation holds great promise for advancing our understanding of how best to practice in contemporary times in general, and more specifically how best to gather credible evidence.

Program Theory–Driven Evaluation Science

I have recently provided a framework and detailed examples of how to gather credible evidence in contemporary, practical program evaluations (Donaldson, 2007). This framework attempts to incorporate many of the hard-won lessons in applied research and evaluation practice over the past 30 years, and to provide an evolving, integrative, and contingency-based theory of practice. *Program theory–driven evaluation science* offers practitioners the following concise, three-step approach to practice:

1. Developing program impact theory

2. Formulating and prioritizing evaluation questions

3. Answering evaluation questions

Simply stated, evaluators work with stakeholders to develop a common understanding of how a program is presumed to solve the problem(s) of interest; to formulate and prioritize key evaluation questions; and then to decide how best to gather credible evidence to answer those questions within practical, time, and resource constraints.

This practical program evaluation approach is essentially method neutral within the broad domain of social science methodology. The focus on the development of program theory and evaluation questions frees evaluators initially from having to presuppose use of one evaluation design or another.

The choice of the evaluation design and methods used to gather credible evidence is made in collaboration with the relevant stakeholders, and is not solely decided by the evaluation team. The decisions about how best to go about collecting credible evidence to answer the key evaluation questions are typically thought to be contingent on the nature of the questions to be answered and the context of the setting. Stakeholders are provided with a wide range of choices for gathering credible evidence, which reinforces the idea that neither quantitative, qualitative, nor mixed method designs are necessarily superior or applicable in every applied research and evaluation context (e.g., Chen, 1997). Whether an evaluator uses case studies, observational methods, structured or unstructured interviews, online or telephone survey research, a quasi-experiment, or an RCT to answer the key evaluation questions is dependent on discussions with relevant stakeholders about what would constitute credible evidence in this context, and what is feasible given the practical, time, and financial constraints (Donaldson, 2007; Donaldson & Lipsey, 2006).

This practical approach for gathering credible evidence is highly consistent with the profession's guiding principles, evaluation standards, and other mainstream approaches to practical program evaluation (Chen, 2005; Rossi, Lipsey, & Freeman, 2004; Weiss, 1998). One of the best examples to date of program theory–driven evaluation science in action is embodied in the Centers for Disease Control and Prevention's (1999) six-step Program Evaluation Framework. This framework is not only conceptually well developed and instructive for evaluation practitioners, it also has been widely adopted for evaluating federally funded public health programs throughout the United States. One of the six key steps in this framework is Step 4: Gather Credible Evidence. Step 4 is defined in the following way:

> Compiling information that stakeholders perceive as trustworthy and relevant for answering their questions. Such evidence can be experimental or observational, qualitative or quantitative, or it can include a mixture of methods. Adequate data might be available and easily accessed, or it might need to be defined and new data collected. Whether a body of evidence is credible to stakeholders might depend on such factors as how the questions were posed, sources of information, conditions of data collection, reliability of measurement, validity of interpretations, and quality control procedures.

Program theory–driven evaluation science is just one of many forms of evaluation theory available today to help guide evaluation practice (see Donaldson & Scriven, 2003). It is summarized here to illustrate how evaluation theories do offer guidance in terms of how to gather credible evidence in contemporary practice. This particular perspective remains open to the wide range of experimental and nonexperimental views about what counts as credible evidence that have been expressed throughout this volume.

However, it clearly specifies that there is not a universal answer to the question of what counts as credible evidence. Rather, the answer to this question in any particular evaluation context is contingent on the evaluation questions, and choices made by the relevant stakeholders in the light of practical, time, and resource constraints.

Some Final Thoughts About the Debates on Credible Evidence

The chapter authors in Section II presented us with some very compelling arguments about the strengths of RCTs and experimental approaches as the route to credible evidence, particularly when the stakes are high for determining "what works." It is laudable that these chapters also explored the limitations and boundary conditions of the experimental approach to gathering credible evidence. The chapters in Section III do an excellent job of extending our understanding of the limitations of the experimental approach, and highlighting the problems of considering the RCT as a universal gold standard for gathering credible evidence. These chapters also provide us with a much deeper understanding of the increasing range of nonexperimental approaches to gathering credible evidence, and the broad array of evaluation questions that can be answered in applied research and evaluation, moving us way beyond the common question of "what works."

However, as Mark points out in Chapter 12, it should be underscored that the chapters in this volume demonstrate that the topic of "what counts as credible evidence" is not one where consensus exists at this time in our history. In fact, while the volume has been in production there has been a plethora of new disputes and debates about credible evidence across the emerging evidence-based global society. For example, the European Evaluation Society (EES, 2007) recently issued a statement in response to strong pressure from some interests advocating for "scientific" and "rigorous" impact of development aid, where this is defined as primarily involving RCTs: "EES deplores one perspective currently being strongly advocated: that the best or only rigorous and scientific way of doing so is through randomised controlled trials (RCTs). In contrast, the EES supports multimethod approaches to IE and does not consider any single method such as RCTs as first choice or as the 'gold standard'." This new statement briefly discusses the rationale for this perspective, and lists examples of publications that consider a number of alternative approaches for establishing impact.

Please note the similarities of the debate now going on in Europe and other parts of the world, with the North American version as expressed in the AEA Statement and Not AEA Statement displayed in Chapter 1.

EES Statement: The importance of a methodologically diverse approach to impact evaluation—specifically with respect to development aid and development interventions.

December 2007

The European Evaluation Society (EES), consistent with its mission to promote the "theory, practice and utilization of high quality evaluation," notes the current interest in improving impact evaluation and assessment (IE) with respect to development and development aid. EES however deplores one perspective currently being strongly advocated: that the best or only rigorous and scientific way of doing so is through randomised controlled trials (RCTs).

In contrast, the EES supports multi-method approaches to IE and does not consider any single method such as RCTs as first choice or as the "gold standard":

- The literature clearly documents how all methods and approaches have strengths and limitations and that there are a wide range of scientific, evidence-based, rigorous approaches to evaluation that have been used in varying contexts for assessing impact.
- IE is complex, particularly of multi-dimensional interventions such as many forms of development (e.g., capacity building, Global Budget Support, sectoral development) and consequently requires the use of a variety of different methods that can take into account rather than dismiss this inherent complexity.
- Evaluation standards and principles from across Europe and other parts of the world do not favor a specific approach or group of approaches—although they may require that the evaluator give reasons for selecting a particular evaluation design or combination.

RCTs represent one possible approach for establishing impact, that may be suitable in some situations, e.g.:

- With simple interventions where a linear relationship can be established between the intervention and an expected outcome that can be clearly defined;
- Where it is possible and where it makes sense to "control" for context and other intervening factors (e.g., where contexts are sufficiently comparable);
- When it can be anticipated that programmes under both experimental and control conditions can be expected to remain static (e.g., not attempt to make changes or improvements), often for a considerable period of time;

- Where it is possible and ethically appropriate to engage in randomization and to ensure the integrity of the differences between the experimental and control conditions.

Even in these circumstances, it would be "good practice" not to rely on one method but rather combine RCTs with other methods—and to triangulate the results obtained.

As with any other method, an RCT approach also has considerable limitations that may limit its applicability and ability to contribute to policy, e.g.:

- RCT designs are acknowledged even by many of its proponents to be weak in external validity (or generalisability), as well as in identifying the actual mechanisms that may be responsible for differences in outcomes between the experimental and control situations;
- "Scaling up," across-the-board implementation based upon the results of a limited and closely controlled pilot situation, can be appropriate for those interventions (e.g., drug trials) where the conditions of implementation would be the same as in the trial, but this is rarely the case for most socio-economic interventions where policy or program "fidelity" cannot be taken for granted;
- An RCT approach is rarely appropriate in complex situations where an outcome arises from interaction of multiple factors and interventions, and where it makes little sense to "control" for these other factors. In a development context, as for most complex policy interventions, outcomes are the result of multiple factors interacting simultaneously, rather than of a single "cause";
- RCTs are limited in their ability to deal with emergent and/or unintended and unanticipated outcomes as is increasingly recognized in complexity and systems research—many positive benefits of development interventions will often be related rather than identical to those anticipated at the policy/program design stage;
- RCTs generally are less suited than other approaches in identifying what works for whom and under what circumstances. Identifying what mechanisms lead to an identified change is particularly important given the varying contexts under which development typically takes place and is essential for making evidence-based improvements.

We also note that RCTs are based upon a successionist (sometimes referred to as "factual") model of causality that neglects the links between intervention and impact and ignores other well-understood scientific means of establishing causality, e.g.:

(Continued)

(Continued)

- Both the natural and social sciences (e.g., physics, astronomy, economics) recognize other forms of causality, such as generative (sometimes referred to as "physical") causality that involve identifying the underlying processes that lead to a change. An important variant of generative causality is known as the modus operandi that involves tracing the "signature," where one can trace an observable chain of events that links to the impact.
- Other forms of causality recognize simultaneous and/or alternative causal strands, e.g., acknowledging that some factors may be necessary but not sufficient to bring about a given result, or that an intervention could work through one or more causal paths. In non-linear relationships, sometimes a small additional effort can serve as a "tipping point" and have a disproportionately large effect.
- Some research literature questions whether simple "causality" (vs. "contribution" or "reasonable attribution") is always the right approach, given the complexity of factors that necessarily interact in contemporary policy—many of them in specific contexts.

EES also notes that in the context of the Paris Declaration, it is appropriate for the international evaluation community to work together in supporting the enhancement of development partner capacity to undertake IE. Mandating a specific approach could undermine the spirit of the Paris Declaration and as the literature on evaluation utilization has demonstrated, limit buy-in and support for evaluation and for subsequent action.

In conclusion, EES welcomes the increased attention and funding for improving IE, provided that this takes a multi-method approach drawing from the rich diversity of existing frameworks and one that engages both the developed and developing world. We would be pleased to join with others in participating in this endeavour. (European Evaluation Society, 2007)

Conclusion: So What Counts as Credible Evidence?

It depends! The chapters in this volume have shown us that the answer to this question depends on characteristics such as

- The question(s) of interest
- The context
- Assumptions made by the evaluators and stakeholders

- The evaluation theory used to guide practice
- Practical, time, and resource constraints

Let these subtle nuances help you answer that question clearly in the context of your own evaluation practice.

Stated another way, I think it is safe to say we are a long way from consensus and a universal answer to the question of what counts as credible evidence in contemporary applied research and evaluation. However, the very rich discussions throughout this volume and the debates across the globe are providing us with ideas for what might go into an early draft of a blueprint for the emerging "evidence-based global society." It now seems clear that disparate views about what constitutes credible evidence are predicated on divergent assumptions, often implicit (Mark, Chapter 12). Practitioners should be well advised to explore these assumptions in great depth with their stakeholders before embarking on their quest to gather credible evidence. A full exploration of the strengths and weaknesses for the range of designs and methods available for any given applied research and evaluation problem seems warranted. A goal to strive for is to fully inform the key stakeholders of the benefits and costs of the wide range of approaches available to answer their key applied research and evaluation questions before they embark with you on the journey of gathering credible evidence (Donaldson, 2007).

A potential unintended positive consequence of disagreements about how to best gather evidence is that of the interest being sparked to support more serious research and scholarship that focuses on advancing the understanding of how best to practice applied research and evaluation. Practitioners now have a wealth of resources to help guide their practice such as evaluation theory, a range of professional development opportunities, many more design and method options, and the promise of "research on evaluation" sorting out some of the more intractable problems preventing good practice. This volume has offered you a plethora of ideas and new directions to explore as you continue your pursuits of gathering credible evidence. It is my hope that this volume will inspire you to be much more reflective about your practice and the range of designs and methods that might be feasible to help you answer the pressing applied research and evaluation questions you encounter. In the end, great minds may disagree that there is a best road to travel to get to credible evidence, but they do seem to come together in consensus around the view that applied research and evaluation are critical activities for improving societies and the human condition as we venture into the unknowns of the 21st-century evidence-based global society.

References

Alkin, M. C. (Ed.). (2004). *Evaluation roots: Tracing theorists' views and influences.* Thousand Oaks, CA: Sage Publications.

Alkin, M. C., & Christie, C. A. (2005). Theorists' models in action [Entire issue]. *New Directions for Evaluation, 106.*

Campbell, B., & Mark, M. M. (2006). Toward more effective stakeholder dialogue: Applying theories of negotiation to policy and program evaluation. *Journal of Applied Social Psychology, 36*(12), 2834–2863.

Campbell, D. T. (1991). Methods for the experimenting society. *American Journal of Evaluation, 12*(3), 223–260.

Centers for Disease Control and Prevention. (1999). Framework for program evaluation in public health. *MMWR, 48* (No. RR-11). CDC Evaluation Working Group.

Chen, H. T. (1997). Applying mixed methods under the framework of theory-driven evaluations. In J. Greene & V. Caracelli (Eds.), *Advances in mixed methods evaluation: The challenge and benefits of integrating diverse paradigms* (pp. 61–72). (Vol. 74 of *New Directions for Evaluation* series). San Francisco: Jossey-Bass.

Chen, H. T. (2005). *Practical program evaluation: Assessing and improving planning, implementation, and effectiveness.* Thousand Oaks, CA: Sage Publications.

Christie, C. A. (2003). What guides evaluation? A study of how evaluation practice maps onto evaluation theory. In C. A. Christie (Ed.), *The practice–theory relationship in evaluation* (pp. 1–35). (Vol. 97 of *New Directions for Evaluation* series). San Francisco: Jossey-Bass.

Cousins, J. B. (Ed.). (2007). Process use in theory, research, and practice [Entire issue]. *New Directions for Evaluation, 116.*

Donaldson, S. I. (2001). Overcoming our negative reputation: Evaluation becomes known as a helping profession. *American Journal of Evaluation, 22*(3), 355–361.

Donaldson, S. I. (2005). Using program theory–driven evaluation science to crack the Da Vinci code. In M. Alkin & C. Christie (Eds.), *Theorists' models in action* (pp. 65–84). (Volume 106 of *New Directions for Evaluation* series). San Francisco: Jossey-Bass.

Donaldson, S. I. (2007). *Program theory–driven evaluation science: Strategies and applications.* Mahwah, NJ: Erlbaum.

Donaldson, S. I., & Christie, C. A. (2006). Emerging career opportunities in the transdiscipline of evaluation science. In S. I. Donaldson, D. E. Berger, & K. Pezdek (Eds.), *Applied psychology: New frontiers and rewarding careers* (pp. 243–260). Mahwah, NJ: Erlbaum.

Donaldson, S. I., Gooler, L. E., & Scriven, M. (2002). Strategies for managing evaluation anxiety: Toward a psychology of program evaluation. *American Journal of Evaluation, 23*(3), 261–273.

Donaldson, S. I., & Lipsey, M. W. (2006). Roles for theory in contemporary evaluation practice: Developing practice knowledge. In I. Shaw, J. C. Greene, & M. M. Mark (Eds.), *The handbook of evaluation: Policies, programs, and practices* (pp. 56–75). London: Sage Publications.

Donaldson, S. I., & Scriven, M. (Eds.). (2003). *Evaluating social programs and problems: Visions for the new millennium.* Mahwah, NJ: Erlbaum.

European Evaluation Society. (2007). *EES Statement: The importance of a methodologically diverse approach to impact evaluation—specifically with respect to development aid and development interventions.* Retrieved February 7, 2008, from http://www.europeanevaluation.org/download/?id=1969403.

Fitzpatrick, J. L. (2004). Exemplars as case studies: Reflections on the links between theory, practice, and context. *American Journal of Evaluation, 25*(4), 541–559.

Ghere, G., King, J. A., Stevahn, L., & Minnema, J. (2006). A professional development unit for reflecting on program evaluator competencies. *American Journal of Evaluation, 27*(1), 108–123.

Henry, G. T., & Mark, M. M. (2003). Toward an agenda for research on evaluation. In C. A. Christie (Ed.), *The practice–theory relationship in evaluation* (pp. 69–80). (Vol. 97 of *New Directions for Evaluation* series). San Francisco: Jossey-Bass.

Mark, M. M. (2003). Toward an integrated view of the theory and practice of program and policy evaluation. In S. I. Donaldson & M. Scriven (Eds.), *Evaluating social programs and problems: Visions for the new millennium* (pp. 183–204). Mahwah, NJ: Erlbaum.

Mark, M. M. (2007). Building a better evidence base for evaluation theory: Beyond general calls to a framework of types of research on evaluation. In N. L. Smith & P. R. Brandon (Eds.), *Fundamental issues in evaluation* (pp. 111–134). New York: Guilford Press.

Rossi, P. H., Lipsey, M. W., & Freeman, H. E. (2004). *Evaluation: A systematic approach* (7th ed.). Thousand Oaks, CA: Sage Publications.

Shadish, W. R. (1998). Evaluation theory is who we are. *American Journal of Evaluation, 19*(1), 1–19.

Shadish, W. R., Cook, T. D., & Leviton, L. C. (1991). *Foundations of program evaluation: Theories of practice.* Newbury Park, CA: Sage Publications.

Weiss, C. H. (1998). *Evaluation: Methods for studying programs and policies* (2nd ed.). Upper Saddle River, NJ: Prentice Hall.

Author Index

Subject Index